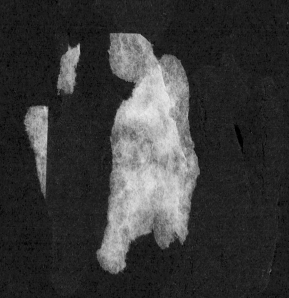

THE STATES AND THE NATION SERIES, of which this volume is a part, is designed to assist the American people in a serious look at the ideals they have espoused and the experiences they have undergone in the history of the nation. The content of every volume represents the scholarship, experience, and opinions of its author. The costs of writing and editing were met mainly by grants from the National Endowment for the Humanities, a federal agency. The project was administered by the American Association for State and Local History, a nonprofit learned society, working with an Editorial Board of distinguished editors, authors, and historians, whose names are listed below.

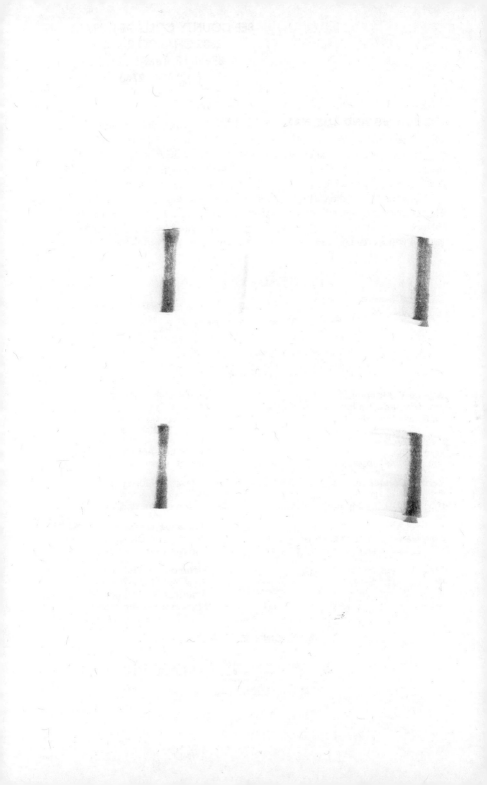

Montana

A Bicentennial History

Clark C. Spence

W. W. Norton & Company, Inc.
New York

American Association for State and Local History
Nashville

The author and publishers make grateful acknowledgement to

Brandt & Brandt for permission to quote from the poem "Lewis and Clark" by Rosemary and Stephen Vincent Benét, from *A Book of Americans*. Copyright 1933 by Rosemary and Stephen Vincent Benét. Copyright renewed © 1961 by Rosemary Carr Benét.

The New York Times Company for permission to quote from *The New York Times* magazine (November 19, 1916). Copyright 1916 by The New York Times Company.

The Dude Ranchers' Association for permission to quote lines from "Montana: A Land of Contrasts." © 1945 by *The Dude Rancher*.

Copyright © 1978
American Association for State and Local History
Nashville, Tennessee

Published and distributed by
W. W. Norton & Company, Inc.
500 Fifth Avenue
New York, New York   10036

Library of Congress Cataloging in Publication Data
Spence, Clark C
    Montana: a bicentennial history.

    (The States and the Nation series)
    Bibliography: p.
    Includes index.
    1. Montana—History. I. Title. II. Series.
F731.S62   1978   978.6   77–18829
ISBN 0–393–05679–1

Printed in the United States of America
1 2 3 4 5 6 7 8 9 0

For Ann,
who lost her first tooth
in the cabin on Alice Creek

Contents

Illustrations

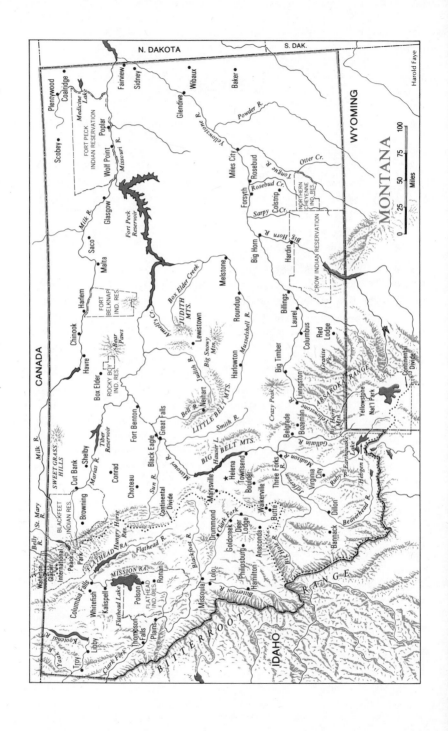

Invitation to the Reader

IN 1807, former President John Adams argued that a complete history of the American Revolution could not be written until the history of change in each state was known, because the principles of the Revolution were as various as the states that went through it. Two hundred years after the Declaration of Independence, the American nation has spread over a continent and beyond. The states have grown in number from thirteen to fifty. And democratic principles have been interpreted differently in every one of them.

We therefore invite you to consider that the history of your state may have more to do with the bicentennial review of the American Revolution than does the story of Bunker Hill or Valley Forge. The Revolution has continued as Americans extended liberty and democracy over a vast territory. John Adams was right: the states are part of that story, and the story is incomplete without an account of their diversity.

The Declaration of Independence stressed life, liberty, and the pursuit of happiness; accordingly, it shattered the notion of holding new territories in the subordinate status of colonies. The Northwest Ordinance of 1787 set forth a procedure for new states to enter the Union on an equal footing with the old. The Federal Constitution shortly confirmed this novel means of building a nation out of equal states. The step-by-step process through which territories have achieved self-government and national representation is among the most important of the Founding Fathers' legacies.

The method of state-making reconciled the ancient conflict between liberty and empire, resulting in what Thomas Jefferson called an empire for liberty. The system has worked and remains unaltered, despite enormous changes that have taken place in the nation. The country's extent and variety now surpass anything the patriots of '76 could likely have imagined. The United States has changed from an agrarian republic into a highly industrial and urban democracy, from a fledgling nation into a major world power. As Oliver Wendell Holmes remarked in 1920, the creators of the nation could not have seen completely how it and its constitution and its states would develop. Any meaningful review in the bicentennial era must consider what the country has become, as well as what it was.

The new nation of equal states took as its motto *E Pluribus Unum*—"out of many, one." But just as many peoples have become Americans without complete loss of ethnic and cultural identities, so have the states retained differences of character. Some have been superficial, expressed in stereotyped images—big, boastful Texas, "sophisticated" New York, "hillbilly" Arkansas. Other differences have been more real, sometimes instructively, sometimes amusingly; democracy has embraced Huey Long's Louisiana, bilingual New Mexico, unicameral Nebraska, and a Texas that once taxed fortunetellers and spawned politicians called "Woodpecker Republicans" and "Skunk Democrats." Some differences have been profound, as when South Carolina secessionists led other states out of the Union in opposition to abolitionists in Massachusetts and Ohio. The result was a bitter Civil War.

The Revolution's first shots may have sounded in Lexington and Concord; but fights over what democracy should mean and who should have independence have erupted from Pennsylvania's Gettysburg to the "Bleeding Kansas" of John Brown, from the Alamo in Texas to the Indian battles at Montana's Little Bighorn. Utah Mormons have known the strain of isolation; Hawaiians at Pearl Harbor, the terror of attack; Georgians during Sherman's march, the sadness of defeat and devastation. Each state's experience differs instructively; each adds understanding to the whole.

The purpose of this series of books is to make that kind of understanding accessible, in a way that will last in value far beyond the bicentennial fireworks. The series offers a volume on every state, plus the District of Columbia—fifty-one, in all.

Each book contains, besides the text, a view of the state through eyes other than the author's—a "photographer's essay," in which a skilled photographer presents his own personal perceptions of the state's contemporary flavor.

We have asked authors not for comprehensive chronicles, nor for research monographs or new data for scholars. Bibliographies and footnotes are minimal. We have asked each author for a summing up—interpretive, sensitive, thoughtful, individual, even personal—of what seems significant about his or her state's history. What distinguishes it? What has mattered about it, to its own people and to the rest of the nation? What has it come to now?

To interpret the states in all their variety, we have sought a variety of backgrounds in authors themselves and have encouraged variety in the approaches they take. They have in common only these things: historical knowledge, writing skill, and strong personal feelings about a particular state. Each has wide latitude for the use of the short space. And if each succeeds, it will be by offering you, in your capacity as a *citizen* of a state *and* of a nation, stimulating insights to test against your own.

James Morton Smith
General Editor

Montana

1

An Introduction

"A Great Splash of Grandeur"

*M*ONTANA is a big and brawny land "molded in the heroic style of terrestrial architecture," according to her imaginative early promoters.[1] Inhabitants once boasted that she was "bounded on the west by the Japan current, on the north by the aurora borealis, on the south by Price's Army, and on the east by the Day of Judgement." [2] Three times the size of Pennsylvania but with only one-sixteenth the population, Montana encompasses 147,138 square miles, more than East Germany and West Germany combined. On the same scale her largest county, Beaverhead, is more extensive than the entire state of Connecticut.

Like the Roman god Janus, Montana faces two ways. The eastern three-fifths is plains country—part of what Walter P. Webb calls "the burnt right flank of the desert." [3] This is high, rolling prairie land, grazing land rich in blue grama, bunch,

John Steinbeck, *Travels with Charley* (New York: Bantam Books, 1963), p. 158.

1. Robert E. Strahorn, *The Resources of Montana Territory and Attractions of Yellowstone National Park* (Helena: n.p., 1879), pp. 4, 5.

2. Quoted in William R. Allen, *The Chequemegon* (New York: William-Frederick Press, 1949), p. ix.

3. Walter P. Webb, "The West and the Desert," *Montana*, 8 (January 1958): 3.

bluestem, needle, or other grasses. It is punctuated by hills, unusual butte formations, wide river valleys, and sharply rising
isolated mountain ranges like the Bear Paws, at the base of
which Chief Joseph and his people gave up in 1877, or the
Judiths, to which cattlemen and Fort Maginnis came about the
same time in 1880.

Described by John Steinbeck as "a great splash of grandeur," [4] the western two-fifths of Montana is dominated by the
sprawling Rockies and the twenty-five or so kindred ranges that
make up the system. The nation's physical spine, the Continental Divide, meanders in a general north-south direction for a
time, when it chooses, forming part of the boundary between
Montana and her western neighbor. This is a region of rugged,
white-capped summits, dominated by 12,788-foot Granite Peak
in the Beartooths, north and east of Yellowstone National Park;
of spectacular glacial valleys, knifelike ridges, and sharp crags
of the Mission Range and of Glacier National Park to the north;
of carpeted mountain meadows set in splendid north-south
troughs; and of icy, fast-moving streams and sparkling blue
lakes like Flathead. This western portion is heavily forested:
roughly thirteen million acres of timber lie west of the Divide
and nine million east of it—some white pine, Douglas fir, larch,
lodgepole pine, western red cedar, and the official state tree, the
ponderosa pine.

The mountains, of course, control the drainage pattern, and
Montana is unique in that its watersheds drain into three different oceans. Rising in Glacier National Park and in Teton
County, streams flow, via the Belly, the St. Mary's, and the
Waterson, across Canada, ultimately into Hudson Bay and the
Arctic Ocean. From its source near Butte, the Clark Fork
gathers the waters of the Blackfoot, the Bitterroot, and the Flathead, among others, as it winds its way to the Pacific. And
making a huge, irregular northern arc from its beginning in
southwestern Montana before it begins its eastern journey to the
Gulf of Mexico, is the Missouri, the early highroad to the frontier, its navigable section at least sometimes referred to as the

4. Steinbeck, *Travels with Charley*, p. 158.

"Montana seacoast." [5] Crabby or calm by turn, its waters range in color from a muddy brown to that of a "particularly badly-made pea soup," according to a British viewer. [6] Although it sometimes changed its mind as it went, the Missouri gave a positive link with the entrepôt St. Louis, and more than by chance did Chouteau County and Fort Benton, its seat, take their names from prominent St. Louis families. Not only would the Missouri provide a commercial waterway to tap upriver resources and help shape the course of population and politics, ultimately its cottonwood or box-elder bottoms and those of tributaries like the Yellowstone would furnish rich farmlands and hydroelectric power sites.

Early promotional literature extolled Montana's "genial and salubrious clime," [7] noted that the mean annual temperature was "the same as that of Santa Fé," [8] and regretted that it was not possible to display the state's climate along with her other resources at the great 1893 world's fair in Chicago. Since Montana's northern boundary was on the same latitude as Paris, and Deer Lodge was on that of Venice, it followed by implication that Montana's healthful temperatures were mild. The severity of the cold was "ridiculously overrated"; [9] "occasional blizzards" were often followed by Chinook winds, "warm as the breath of spring," which changed seasons "as if by magic." [10]

Being what they are, promoters must be forgiven both their enthusiasm and their lack of realism. Climatically, the upthrust mountains cleave the state, but nowhere does the semitropical dominate. Where the average rainfall is 15.48 inches, western

5. Russell McKee, *The Last West* (New York: T. Y. Crowell, Co., 1974), p. 264.

6. Paul Fountain, *The Eleven Eaglets of the West* (New York: E. P. Dutton & Co., 1906), p. 170.

7. J. R. Boyce, *Facts about Montana Territory and the Way to Get There* (Helena: Rocky Mountain Gazette, 1872), p. 13.

8. Quoted in Ferdinand V. Hayden, *The Great West: Its Attractions and Resources* (Bloomington, Illinois: Charles R. Brodix, 1880), p. 211.

9. *Montana: Its Climate, Industries and Resources* (Helena: George Boos & Co., 1885), p. 7.

10. *Montana Exhibit at the Worlds Fair and a Description of the Various Resources of the State* (Butte: Butte Inter Mountain Print, 1893), pp. 10–11.

Montana gets 18 inches and the east only 13. Latitude to the contrary, winter can be cold and raw; summer hot and ungracious, at least in the plains. Seventy below zero was recorded at Roger's Pass, northwest of Helena, in January 1954; a high of 117 degrees at Glendive in 1893 and at Medicine Lake in 1937. Eastern Montana tends to be more extreme—harsh and open in winter and more sweltering in summer, while the mountainous west has more snow, greater protection from the winds, and benefit of the Chinook belt. On-the-spot observers believe that Billings or Great Falls or Butte has more in common with Minneapolis or Milwaukee than with Paris or Venice. Some claim that the wind in the Madison Valley blows four ways at once. A. B. Guthrie calls April "a harsh and fretful month," a time of "wayward winds and unpredicted snows. . . ." [11] Even May could be uncertain in the shadow of the Crazy Mountains, as a rancher indicated in 1927 when he wrote in his diary on May 7th: "Weather man still turning loose a lot of snow. You'd think the son of a bitch would run out of stock some time." A day later he added, "WOW! BASTARDLY BLIZZARD." [12]

If the land presented contrast and diversity, so also did the people who used it, whether the original Indian dwellers, the free-spirited men who followed the beaver, the hardy optimists who poured in in the sixties, half-blind with visions of gold shining in their eyes, the sodbusters who tried to turn rangeland into wheatfields, or the stockmen who knew what the lush prairie grass was for and yearned for the day when "the coyotes would get big enough to eat the damn farmers," as Charlie Russell is supposed to have said. [13] Add the latecomers who swelled Montana's population in the twentieth century to homestead, to labor in the mines at Butte or the smelters of Anaconda or Great Falls, to "mine with axes" in the forests of the western mountains, to man the SAC airbases and the missile sites, or to direct

11. A. B. Guthrie, Jr., *The Blue Hen's Chick* (New York: McGraw-Hill, 1965), p. 253.

12. Quoted in Montana Historical Society (hereafter referred to as MHS), *Not in Precious Metals Alone* (Helena: MHS, 1976), p. 227.

13. Quoted in Stanley Vestal, *The Missouri* (New York: Farrar & Rinehart, 1945), p. 166.

the giant machines ripping open the earth at the Colstrip coalfields.

But what of Montana's past was typical? Was it roistering,
swaggering Butte, as ugly as sin and steeped in it, described as
"a painted trollop—with a heart as big as a mountain"? [14] Was
it Butte, that ethnic melange, where mayors won election with
the slogan "The Chinese must go," and yet Chinese Jimmy
July could deliver the main Independence Day oration? Where
the Irish—"them Harps"—whooped it up on St. Patrick's Day
and the Cornish Cousin Jacks celebrated the Battle of the Boyne
every July 12th? Where rug dealer Mohammed Akara legally
changed his name to Mohammed Murphy "for business reasons"? Where Italian Joe Pinazza grunted "I getta" and
climbed into a gas-filled stope to rescue an unconscious Polish
miner? When he had accomplished his task, he repeated, "I
getta," and fell dead. [15]

Or were the other major cities more typical? What of Helena,
tucked against the mountains overlooking the flat Prickly Pear
Valley, mingling legislators and far more than its share of millionaires; or Great Falls, in the bend of the Missouri opposite
the mouth of the Sun, its fortunes tied at various times to wheat,
coal, electricity, smelting, and defense; or Billings, on the bank
of the Yellowstone, at the juncture of cattle ranching and dirt-
farming, sugar and oil refining; or possibly Fort Benton, the perennial bridesmaid, bustling river port where even ministers
painted sermon portraits of a city of splendor with magnificent
spired cathedrals that never materialized?

Since Montana until well into the twentieth century was rural,
perhaps the little places were more representative. Any
crossroads was labeled a city by early Montanans: Superior City
in 1881 consisted of a log house and a barn. Towns like Wibaux, Malta, and Roundup in their heyday knew bawling cattle
and driving dust and invariably regarded themselves as the

14. Quoted in Montana Writers' Project, *Copper Camp* (New York: Hastings House,
1943), p. 22.
15. Berton Braley, *Pegasus Pulls a Hack: Memoirs of a Modern Minstrel* (New York:
Minton, Balch & Co., 1934), pp. 86–87.

"biggest little towns" in the stockman's West. Or was the real Montana to be found in the prosaic little farm centers built around grain elevators spaced regularly like separated pearls along railroad lines, with neat little churches and an occasional incongruous sign over the local brothel, INDIAN TRADE NOT SOLICITED? Perhaps, too, there was something unique in the brash post-World War II boom towns "living solely on beer and hope" near the Hungry Horse Dam site, one of them planning its Pioneer Days celebration to honor its old-timers—to be held on its first birthday.[16]

Or maybe the essence of Montana was not in the towns at all, but in the country—on the isolated ranches like the DHS in the fringe of the Judith Mountains, where Granville Stuart's daughters roller-skated on the dining-room floor and entertained a steady stream of eligible swains. This only bore out what everyone knew—that with a shortage of suitable females, Montana has long been a "schoolmarm's paradise": one young woman, traveling by stagecoach from Utah to Helena to take a job as maid, had five offers of marriage—all from strangers—during the trip! Or might not the real spirit of the Montana past be found in scattered shacks of the 320-acre homesteads of the twentieth century, when thousands of dry-land farmers swarmed onto the more arid sections of the state.

No doubt the making of modern Montana was a blending of all these—and more; it is the product of the environment and of the sum of its people as they reacted to their surroundings. To an extent they molded the land, and to a greater extent the land shaped them and their way of thinking. Montana combines space, nature, and a rich storehouse of resources. From the fur-trade era down to World War II, Montanans and outsiders alike plundered the earth with too little concern for the environment itself or for future generations. Nature, they were convinced, was inexhaustible. At the same time, the vastness of the land and the process of subduing it persuaded those who had pioneered that there was something special about their experience and that it left an imprint on them and upon those who fol-

16. Quoted in MHS, *Precious Metals*, p. 269.

lowed. Old-time cowboys like Con Price were sure that no area produced the same brand of people. This is what James Fergus alluded to when he became the first president of the Society of Montana Pioneers in 1884 and said he would rather be that than President of the United States. This was what one of the early leaders of the woman-suffrage movement had in mind when she asserted that it was not the ballot, but an intangible "pioneer spirit" which was "the greatest heritage that has come or can come to the women of Montana." [17] Even in the mid-twentieth century, the legacy remained. John Steinbeck thought that the "calm of the mountains and the rolling grasslands had got into the inhabitants," [18] while a British visitor found "a nuclear something of the frontier spirit" retained in the state.[19]

17. Quoted in Mary L. Alderson, "A Half Century of Progress for Montana Women" (Helena: typescript. 1935), p. 85.
18. Steinbeck, *Travels with Charley*, p. 158.
19. Herbert Howarth, "Montana: The Frontier Went Thataway," *Harper's Monthly*, 216 (March 1958): 52.

2

Exploration and Fur Hunters

The First Touch of Spring Lay on the Land.

ᴇVEN before the United States had completed the greatest real estate bargain in history, the purchase of Louisiana—828,000 square miles at approximately three cents an acre—from France, President Jefferson had contemplated sending a military party to explore that vast region. In 1803 much of Louisiana was terra incognita—reason enough for its investigation. As Jefferson pointed out to Meriwether Lewis, his hand-picked co-leader of the expedition, he hoped to gain a mass of scientific information about the West, its flora, fauna, and native inhabitants. He hoped to survey a possible water route via the Missouri and Columbia rivers to the Pacific, a direct link with the maritime trade of the northwest coast. He sought to promote as much intertribal peace as possible, in preparation for American trade, which hopefully would replace that of the British Northwest Company. At the same time, Jefferson pursued the sources of rivers in order to clarify boundary lines, and no doubt he hoped to buttress American claims to the Oregon country going back to Captain Robert Gray's voyage of 1792.

It was in this context that the expedition headed by Lewis and William Clark first penetrated Montana, leaving St. Louis in May 1804, traveling laboriously up the Missouri to the Great

Falls ("the grandest sight I ever beheld," Lewis called it [1]), on to the Three Forks, then up the Jefferson and eventually into the Bitterroot Valley, via Lolo Pass over to the Clearwater, the Snake, and the Columbia, and finally to the Pacific Ocean. On the return, the group split at Traveler's Rest, a camp site in the Bitterroot Valley near the present village of Lolo. Lewis and a small party would move northeast to White Bear Islands, the portage camp, then swing more northerly and explore up the Marias, where, despite Lewis's effort to "avoid an interview" with the Blackfeet, there occurred the only bloody encounter of the entire trip, with two Indians left for dead and the whites fleeing for their lives. Meanwhile, under Clark, the main body crossed from the Bitterroot Valley over Gibbons Pass into the Big Hole River country, struck and followed the Jefferson to Three Forks, then cut overland to the Yellowstone and down that stream to a reunion with Lewis below its juncture with the Missouri itself.

In Montana history the Lewis and Clark expedition looms large. It spent more time and covered more miles in Montana than in any other area. In terms of description and of place names left behind, it had more of an impact here than elsewhere. For modern Montanans it left a proud, fierce spirit of kinship with the greatest of early explorers. Lewis and Clark belong to Montana in a way that they are claimed by no other state.

Traditionally, historians of Montana have focused on the leading figures and on the dangerous and more compelling aspects of the drama. Every Montana schoolchild knows about sunny-haired Meriwether Lewis, the serious, somewhat reserved, and decidedly bowlegged Virginian who shared command with the red-haired six-footer William Clark, the perennial bachelor with whom he had seen extensive frontier military service. Both were men of ingenuity and resourcefulness; both would go down as great geographers. Diplomat, scientist, commercial thinker, and original speller, Lewis would complement

---

1. Reuben Gold Thwaites, ed., *Original Journals of the Lewis and Clark Expedition, 1804–1806*, 8 vols. (New York: Dodd, Mead & Co., 1905), 2:148.

Clark, the engineer, craftsman, and boat manager. Every schoolgirl thrills to the name of Sacagawea, the Shoshone lass, a mere slip of a girl of seventeen who carried her infant son, Pomp, on her back to the Pacific and return, and who made real contributions, though often her role is unduly magnified.

But what of the more than two dozen other members, including Sacagawea's inept husband, Charbonneau, that "man of no particular merit" and "most timid waterman in the world"? [2] What of Scannon, Lewis's Newfoundland dog, much admired by the Indians along the way, who shared the discomforts of mosquitoes with his human companions and who more than paid his way by heckling countless bears and by alerting the sleeping camp when a bull buffalo stomped through in the dark? What of Clark's ebony-hued slave York, kinky-haired, large and muscular, a wit and a wag, whose dancing and strong-arm demonstrations delighted all, and whose romantic prowess pleased at least some of the Indians?

Or what of the lesser knowns: the bushy-bearded, barrel-chested Irishman Patrick Gass, superb woodsman and boat builder; the Field brothers, Joseph and Reuben, skilled in hunting and woodlore and able to repair practically anything; Alex Willard, a giant of a man and a remarkably good cook, given his kitchen facilities; Silas Goodrich, a wizard at fishing who once netted 528 fish in two hours, using a willow-and-brush seine? There was indispensable George Druillard, son of a Shawnee mother and a French father, fluent in sign language, who more than earned his twenty-five dollars a month as hunter, scout, and interpreter: he was to Lewis what Kit Carson would later be to Frémont. Or wiry Pete Cruzatte, the one-eyed ex-trader whose fiddle did much to lift morale and who once, mistaking Lewis for an elk, shot him in the thigh. Consider Hugh McNeal, who stood with one foot on each side of Pine Trail Creek, one of the sources of the Missouri, and thanked God he had lived to straddle that mighty river.

Schoolchildren know the expedition for its color and its dangers, less for its routine of daily human life. They know of numerous close calls with grizzlies and rattlesnakes, or the clash

2. Thwaites, *Original Journals*, 2:34.

with the Blackfeet up the Marias. They know of the profusion of game in Montana, of Lewis commenting on the "tremendious roaring" of buffalo bulls near Great Falls. "I sincerely beleif that there were not less than 10 thousand buffaloe within a circle of 2 miles . . . ," he wrote. But not much attention is paid to the everyday labor of hunting and the dressing of meat, often to be taken in new recipes, as when Lewis near the Smith River in July 1805, for the first time "ate of the small guts of the buffaloe cooked over a blazing fire in the Indian stile without any preparation of washing or other clensing and found them very good." [3] Nor do historians dwell upon the hard work and the skills necessary to process game: rendering out tallow or bear grease, curing hides and sewing them into leggings, moccasins, clothing, or bullboats. Taken for granted are run-of-the-mill jobs—repairing guns, packsaddles, or other equipment; felling trees or making dugout canoes. Illness and physical ailments are often minimized, although all members suffered, including Lewis and "Janey," as Clark called Sacagawea, from a variety of complaints, ranging from toothache, sore eyes, and painful boils to severe fever and chills.

The eighteen-mile portage of the Great Falls, even when spread over a month, was laborious and painful: trees had to be cut and from them wheels fashioned to haul the boats around over hard terrain and through prickly pears by brute human force. As Lewis noted in his journal:

> . . . at every halt these poor fellows tumble down and are so much fortiegues that many of them are asleep in an instant; in short their fatiegues are incredible; some are limping from the soreness of their feet, others faint and unable to stand for a few minutes, with heat and fatiegue, yet no one complains, all go with cheerfulness.

One of the more ingenious even hoisted a sail on one of the canoes being portaged, an approach Clark called "Saleing on Dry land in every sence of the word." As the group progressed toward the Three Forks, its diarist described other difficulties. "Our trio of pests still invade and obstruct us on all occasions," recorded Lewis, "these are the musquetoes eye knats and prickley pears, equal to any three curses that ever poor Egypt

3. Thwaites, *Original Journals,* 5:199, 2:234.

laiboured under, except the *Mahometant yoke.*" [4] It was to lighten such hardship and in celebration of the Fourth of July, 1805, that the party finished off the last of its ardent spirits, keeping a little in reserve for sickness, and all amused themselves until ten at night singing and dancing to Cruzatte's magic fiddle "in a Civil & jovil manner." [5]

Montana's most tangible heritage of Lewis and Clark is a wealth of place names. When Lewis named the Marias River after a cousin, Maria Wood, he noted gallantly that the "hue of the waters of this turbulent and troubled streem but illy comport with the pure celestial virtues and amiable qualifications of that lovely fair one." [6] The Judith honored the girl he would eventually marry, and other important streams would bear the names of prominent politicians: President Jefferson, Secretary of State Madison, Secretary of the Treasury Gallatin, Secretary of War Dearborn, and Secretary of the Navy Smith. It was Clark who named Pompey's Pillar after Sacagawea's babe and, like Kilroy, carved his own name on that distinctive two-hundred-foot-high formation, where it may still be seen.

It was in September 1806 that Lewis notified the President of their safe return to St. Louis, having traveled, by his calculation, a total of more than seven thousand miles, a magnificent feat by any standard and a cause for widespread jubilation.

> And, when they returned,
> It was glory well-earned
> That they gave to the national chorus.
> They were ragged and lean
> But they'd seen what they'd seen,
> And it spread out an Empire before us. [7]

4. Thwaites, *Original Journals,* 2:182–183; 2:188, 266.

5. Milo Quaife, ed., *The Journals of Captain Meriwether Lewis and Sergeant John Ordway, Kept on the Expedition of Western Exploration, 1803–1806* (Madison: State Historical Society of Wisconsin, 1916), pp. 242–243.

6. Thwaites, *Original Journals,* 2:130–131.

7. Rosemary and Stephen Vincent Benét, "Lewis and Clark," from *A Book of Americans* by Rosemary and Stephen Vincent Benét (Holt, Rinehart & Winston, Inc. Copyright 1933 by Rosemary and Stephen Vincent Benét. Copyright renewed © 1961 by Rosemary Carr Benét), p. 51. Reprinted by permission of Brandt and Brandt.

Success had been the product of intelligence, expert management—and luck. It had been the right-sized expedition, well-disciplined, physically hardened, and astutely equipped. It had approached the Indians fairly and honestly, without awe and without fear. With a rare open-mindedness it had adjusted to the unfamiliar and the unknown.

This, the first overland trip by whites through what is now the continental United States, marked the beginning of accurate knowledge about the Far West, including Montana. It demonstrated that no practical water route to the Pacific existed, but that the Missouri was safe for navigation; it opened friendly relations with a number of Indian tribes and in the public mind bolstered American claims to the Oregon country; it left no doubt that the Upper Missouri teemed with beaver—all of which would set the stage for the next chapter of Montana history. But even more precious was the special relationship Lewis and Clark would come to have for Montanans; they would become less national than state heroes; favorite sons (and daughters) as it were, whose epic journey only incidentally crossed other areas.

Even before the odyssey was completed, the upriver men were at work exploiting the fur harvest. Coming downstream in 1806, soft-spoken and venturesome John Colter would leave the expedition to go back up with a handful of fur traders, in the process inaugurating a series of new ventures typical of the reckless breed of mountain men who would dominate the Montana scene for the next forty years or so. The blue-eyed Colter would range through the Yellowstone country (known for a time as Colter's Hell) and would join the Flatheads in the Beaverhead Valley against their traditional enemies. Once, captured by the Blackfeet, Colter was stripped naked, given a sporting head start, then pursued by their fleetest runners armed with spears. Running for his life, after six miles Colter outdistanced the Indians and escaped by diving under a mass of driftwood and subsequently walking seven days in his birthday suit to a fur post on the Big Horn.

Colter was one of a hearty stock of entrepreneurs attracted by four-legged wealth into the very heart of Montana. The soft, thick beaver pelt, or plew, was relatively small and light; it had long been in demand for the making of stylish coats and hats; when eastern supplies dwindled, the industry moved westward to more remote and virgin stands, with dogged fur hunters ranging out from a number of invasion bases. In the southwest, Taos was the center for a vast area. To the north, the proud banners of the Hudson's Bay Company waved over Canadian posts, whose fur men penetrated into Montana. (Observers said that the initials H.B.C. stood for "Here Before Christ," though in actuality the concern dated only from 1670.) Led by David Thompson, both an explorer and superb geographer, operatives of the rival British Northwest Company, headquarters in Montreal, ranged into western Montana after 1808, establishing their main post at Saleesh House, near what is now Thompson Falls. After years of bitter rivalry, these two British firms merged in 1822 and would continue to direct thrusts as far as the crest of the Rockies from Fort Vancouver on the Oregon coast and until the early thirties, when trade boundaries were defined by mutual agreement, would provide stiff competition for upriver Americans penetrating from St. Louis.

St. Louis's interest began with Colter and the ambitious effort in 1807 by the Spaniard Manuel Lisa to establish a post at the juncture of the Yellowstone and the Big Horn. This ultimately led to the establishment of the St. Louis Missouri Fur Company, supported by men whose names would be legendary in the fur trade: William Clark; Andrew Henry; the Chouteaus, Pierre and Auguste. Pushing to the Three Forks in the heart of Blackfoot territory in 1810, the company was forced out by hostile Indians; reorganized after Lisa's death, it made another assault, establishing a base at the mouth of the Big Horn, only to be compelled to retreat again. After a lull during and following the War of 1812, came new efforts to open the Upper Missouri, beginning in the spring of 1822, when Andrew Henry and William Ashley, the lieutenant-governor of Missouri, advertised in St. Louis for a hundred enterprising young men to head upriver in search of furs. Among those answering the call were Thomas Fitzpatrick, Jim Bridger, and Jedediah Strong Smith—all among the immortals of the fur era. Later known as the Rocky Mountain Fur Company, the Ashley-Henry outfit used a new approach: rather than establish posts to which Indians would bring pelts to trade for trinkets, guns, or liquor, it would employ white trappers to gather the furs and turn them over to agents at an annual rendezvous, thus eliminating expensive construction of vulnerable forts and giving a new mobility to follow the beaver. Sound in principle, the idea would persist, but opposition of the Arikira, Sioux, and Blackfeet from time to time would close the river lifeline, forcing the fur brigades to take to the open stretches farther south.

But concerns like the Missouri Fur Company, the Rocky Mountain Fur Company, and the Columbia Fur Company were short-lived. They competed not only with the British giants but with one of the prime examples of early corporate power in the United States, John Jacob Astor's million-dollar American Fur Company, which eventually would dominate the Upper Missouri fur traffic. From his office in New York City Astor directed policy in a gutteral German accent, ruthlessly crushing "the opposition," as the rivals were called, and building up the strength of "the company," or more specifically its western department, the Upper Missouri Outfit, as it was known. Establishing a line of posts all the way upriver (Fort Union at the mouth of the Yellowstone, Fort Piegan—later Fort Benton—at the mouth of the Marias, and Fort Cass at the mouth of the Big Horn), the American Fur Company fought, crushed, or absorbed its competitors and relentlessly forced them to the wall. Its methods included violence and intimidation, underselling goods and overpaying for furs, the use of political influence, and reliance on the whiskey trade. Modernizing carefully, Astor introduced the steamboat in the early 1830s to cut transportation costs and to impress the Indians; he bought and sold on global markets; and he carefully organized his ever-expanding home territory to maximize efficiency and allocation of responsibility. When the company absorbed its rivals, often it assimilated able and experienced men like Robert Stuart or Kenneth Mackenzie who would be key in Upper Missouri operations for a quarter of a century. From the pool of unemployed created by the merger of the British titans, the American Fur Company shrewdly acquired vital personnel, including Jacob Berger, an old hand whose influence among the Blackfeet enabled the firm to enter the last great virgin beaver country in the Upper Rockies in 1830–1831.

The American Fur Company foreshadowed future developments. It was the first example of eastern corporate capital boldly and without scruple exploiting western resources—a theme which would persist in Montana, whether in furs, railroads, or mining. The company lingered, though the farsighted Astor sold his interest in 1834. By the mid-thirties the heyday was clearly over. The trade continued but at a trickle of its former self, with a growing emphasis on buffalo robes. Already being trapped out, the beaver was saved from extinction only by changing fashions—the popularity of the silk hat on Broadway and Regent Street.

The medium through which absentee entrepreneurs exploited the Upper Missouri was the "long knives," the fur men, a relatively small advance guard of the westward movement. With names like John Colter, Alexander Ross, John Work, Joshua Pilcher, Jim Bridger, and the Sublette brothers, the fur men came to know every geographic nook and cranny. Some were country boys from east of the Mississippi; some raw arrivals from Europe, especially the Emerald Isle; many were Missouri "graybacks," many were half-breed "pork eaters" of French Canada. Some worked for a set annual fee; others, the elite of the profession, traveled at will with their own horses and equipment and sold their furs on the open market. Many married Indian women, thus cementing tribal relations momentarily, although native spouses would be left behind when they left the mountains. While they came to know and to understand the Indians, they were also the means by which tribal ways were shattered. They prostituted Indian women, plied the men with illicit whiskey, introduced dread diseases, and left the Indians dependent upon white trade.

Picturesque in long hair and greasy buckskins decorated Indian style, with the distinctive odor of bear grease made more pungent by lack of contact with water, the traders and trappers became romantic symbols of a restless breed of free spirits who, said Bernard Devoto of an earlier generation, pulled the wilderness around them like a robe. When they moved on, they left little in the way of permanent settlements: only Fort Benton survived the fur period. But evidence also indicates that many were typical hard-working Jacksonian men, expectant capitalists who were committed to free enterprise and the proposition that the vast West must fall under American institutions, not those of monarchical Britain or capricious Mexico. In spite of danger and privation—and sometimes bankruptcies—they persisted; with their trade goods and their bags of "possibles" they carried with them the spirit of exploitation and discovery. As they ransacked every hole and corner of Montana, they traced the streams to their sources, crossed and recrossed the high mountain passes, and explored wilderness previously known only to the Indians. These were the real pathfinders, who passed on their knowledge by maps drawn with a stick in the sand or with charcoal on a buffalo hide. These were the men who would often serve as guides or scouts for government reconnaissance parties, military columns, or companies of emigrants. They were part of the cutting edge of the frontier and of them a contemporary wrote in 1847:

> From the Mississippi to the mouth of the Colorado of the West, from the frozen regions of the North to the Gila in Mexico, the beaver-hunter has set his traps in every creek and stream. All this vast country, but for the daring and enterprise of these men, would be even now a *terra incognita* to geographers. . . .[8]

With the fur trade came an exposure to Christianity, first through the nominal French Catholics ranging south into western Montana, David Thompson, who expounded Church of England doctrine, or white-educated Spokane Garry, who preached vigorously to visiting Flatheads. It was the Flatheads, beginning in 1831, who persistently sent delegations to St. Louis to learn

8. George Frederick Ruxton, *Adventures in Mexico and the Rocky Mountains* (London: Murray, 1847), p. 241.

more of the white man's way of life and whose perseverance finally brought the handsome, friendly young Belgian Jesuit Pierre-Jean De Smet to found St. Mary's Mission in the Bitterroot Valley in 1841. An amazing fund raiser, the stocky, muscular De Smet would cross the Atlantic sixteen times. With an Italian, Father Anthony Ravalli, he emphasized agriculture, built gristmills and sawmills, vaccinated the Flatheads against smallpox, served as an effective mediator, and in general promoted a working Christianity that his wards at first accepted with enthusiasm. Once, when De Smet lamented persecution of the Church in Europe, Chief Victor proposed inviting Pope Gregory XVI to live in the safety of the Flathead tribe! But Indian traditions stretching back over time died hard; the Jesuit teaching of one God, one wife, no alcohol, no punishment by whipping, and farming rather than hunting, all violated past usages. The last straw came when De Smet announced he would visit their bitter enemies, the Blackfeet, in hopes of establishing a mission among them. By 1850, St. Mary's was so disoriented that De Smet sold the property to pioneer settler John Owen for a trading post. Other efforts would follow in a few years, and eventually St. Mary's would be relocated, but Montana was simply too far off the beaten path to be important missionary ground and would so remain until the call of gold echoed through its mountains.

Meanwhile, occasional visitors appeared. Some came in official capacities, as in 1853–1854 when the survey crews of Isaac Stevens, including young George B. McClellan of later Civil War fame, would lay out the route for a possible transcontinental railroad across Montana. Evidence indicates that rather than brave subzero temperatures in the high Rockies, McClellan's men simply faked some of their figures. More practical and more immediate was the work of Lieutenant John Mullan and the Army Engineers who ran a wagon road from Fort Benton across to Fort Walla Walla, beginning it in 1859 and completing it four years later.

Other travelers might be motivated by scientific curiosity or by a spirit of adventure. One of these was a thin, excitable man of fifty who could swear like a trooper in his stiff Prussian accent. He was Alexander Philip Maximilian, Prince of Wied-Neuwied, a scientist of some reputation who had won the Iron Cross in the Napoleonic campaigns. In the summer of 1833, accompanied by the young Swiss artist Karl Bodmer and a servant with the improbable name of Dreidoppel, he pushed upriver under the auspices of the American Fur Company all the way to the Marias, the heart of Blackfoot country. Wearing a white slouch hat, a black velvet coat "rather rusty from long service," [9] and a pair of greasy old pants, Maximilian took a penetrating look at the people as well as the flora and fauna of the Upper Missouri and would write a valuable and engaging account of his journey.

Two decades later the Irish baronet Sir St. George Gore would include Montana in his monumental "hunt of hunts," an adventure which covered six thousand miles, cost an estimated half-million dollars, and bore little resemblance to sportsmanship. With a fantastic ensemble of retainers, wagons, and equipment, including a large green-and-white-striped tent, Gore by his own count killed 2,000 buffalo, 1,600 deer and elk, and 105 bears as he moved in lordly fashion through Colorado, Wyoming, Montana, and the Dakotas. In the winter of 1855–1856 he camped on the Tongue River; when he departed down the Yellowstone in the spring, he gave the name Glendale to a creek in east-central Montana, a name later corrupted to Glendive.

At Fort Benton in the summer of 1857 John Owen met a young New Yorker named Belknap, who was not satisfied with touring Europe and "bagging Monkey in Brazil . . . but Must cross the Rocky Mtns and see the Waters of the Columbia." [10] Owen himself was a major pioneer figure in Montana and would cross the Rockies not once but many times, making thirty-four

9. Bernard DeVoto, *Across the Wide Missouri* (1947; Boston: Houghton Mifflin, 1964 ed.), p. 136.

10. Seymour Dunbar and Paul C. Phillips, eds., *The Journals and Letters of Major John Owen* 2 vols. (New York: Edward Eberstadt, 1927), 1:175.

trips through the Northwest between 1851 and 1864. Born in Pennsylvania, he had been with the army in Oregon but in 1850, together with his Snake wife, Nancy, had appeared in the Bitterroot Valley. Purchasing St. Mary's Mission for $250, he enclosed it first with a high timber wall, later by one of adobe. From Fort Owen, as he renamed the place, he conducted a trade in furs, but he became much more than an ordinary trader. A friend and strong personal influence among the Flatheads, Owen planted crops and orchards and made his post the center of early settlement in western Montana.

Visitors who enjoyed Owen's hospitality thought his small library excellent. They took pleasure in ruminating with him on the anniversary of Jackson's defeat of the British at New Orleans or in remembering the birthday of "The Immortal Washington" by dancing "Nearly all Night." Christmas and New Year's invariably brought "Some of the good things of this World"—mince pies, brandy, or "a Very Nice Egg Nogg." One New Year's was celebrated by dancing and feasting "for the last past ten Nights," according to Owen, adding with a twinkle that a one-armed fiddler was the hit of the season. "The Ladies would liked to have Known on What he hung his bow." And the Fourth of July always received special notice: the Stars and Stripes were run up, a howitzer fired, a round of drinks poured for the hands, and on one occasion a colt born that day was named Independence. On the other hand, at least once when Owen was away, there were complaints that the great national holiday was not being properly observed. "The American flag has not been seen as a Bloody Englishman is in charge," grumbled a patriotic employee. "I suppose if he had a flag with god save the Queen on it or much less hur Back Side it would have gone up with the Sun." [11]

Thus even in the remote wilderness, from Lewis and Clark on, men did not forget home and traditional ties. Not that life, even at Fort Owen, provided many diversions. In general it was a humdrum, often harsh and sometimes dangerous existence, broken only occasionally by visitors or an opportunity to cele-

11. Dunbar and Phillips, *John Owen*, 1:233, 90, 114, 187, 228, 237.

brate. John Owen himself represented a link, a tie between two phases of Montana's historical growth. He was in a position to see both the end of the fur trade and the coming of the major gold rushes.

3

The Mineral Frontier

Gold Fever Raged,
with Silver and Copper Complications.

*J*OHN OWEN died insane in Pennsylvania in 1889. He never lived to see the State Seal of Montana. *"Oro y Plata"* was its motto, inscribed beneath the symbols of a plow and miner's crossed pick and shovel. A more farsighted designer would also have included the word *"Cobre,"* for in the long run copper would be more important to the state than gold and silver. Of the nearly three billion dollars' worth of minerals produced in Montana by the mid-twentieth century, roughly two-thirds has been copper, one-fifth silver, and something over one-eighth gold. But of whatever kind, it was mining that overnight attracted thousands of people, established a more enduring economic base than the fur trade promised, and brought a quickening exploitation of resources and despoilation of the environment.

Gold was the first of the siren metals. Who made the first discovery in Montana is not clear. Rumors of finds in the fur-trade era are undocumented, but on a Sunday in mid-February 1852 John Owen wrote in his diary, "Gold Hunting found some." But his calm entry for the next day, "Making Rails," indicates that it was unimportant and that he had better things to do.[1] About the same time, a half-blood named François Finlay, working for the Hudson's Bay Company, found traces on what was later called Gold Creek in the Deer Lodge Valley, but nothing came of it. Returning from California, James and Granville Stuart wintered in the same area and, prospecting with an old spade and a breadpan, uncovered a little gold before unfriendly Indians prompted them to leave in 1858. The brothers called this "the first real discovery of gold within the state," and soon returned to prospect in a small way. By 1862, at the mouth of Gold Creek, their ranch was the hub of a small settlement of some forty-five persons, many of them interested but not very successful in mining. Gradually, to the wonder of the Stuarts, the trappings of civilization became visible, especially as households like the Burchetts', with their sixteen-year-old daughter, began to appear. "Every man in camp has shaved and changed his shirt since this family arrived," Granville noted.[2]

If the Stuarts themselves found little gold, like John Owen, they were well located to see Montana history in the making. Important discoveries elsewhere in the West set men adreaming. Silver in Nevada in 1859, gold in Colorado the same year and in Idaho in 1861 and 1862, kindled the imaginations of the restless, and soon prospectors curved northward from the Pikes Peak diggings heading for the Salmon River mines, or they came up by water to Fort Benton, then overland over the rough Mullan Road. Old-timers like Owen watched with interest as these "worn weary pilgrims in Search of the Auriferous Sands" passed by. "Gold Gold Nothing is talked of but Gold," said he. "When will it End." [3]

For Montana it had just begun. In typical fashion, these emigrants prospected as they moved on. One such group from Colorado, headed by John White and bound for the Idaho fields,

1. Dunbar and Phillips, *John Owen,* 1:42, 43.

2. Paul C. Phillips, ed., *Forty Years on the Frontier as seen in the Journals and Reminiscences of Granville Stuart* 2 vols. (1925; Glendale Cal.: Arthur H. Clark Co., 1957 ed.), 1:136–137, 213.

3. Dunbar and Phillips, *John Owen,* 1:258, 334.

wintered in the Deer Lodge Valley, and in late July 1862 White himself struck gold on Grasshopper Creek, a tributary of the Beaverhead. By fall, when the Stuarts visited the booming new camp at Bannack and decided to open a butcher shop, some four hundred people were on the scene. By the following spring, gold production at Bannack was clearly declining. The Stuart brothers closed down their business, returned to Gold Creek, but were soon drawn with hundreds of others to new diggings at Alder Gulch along the Stinking Water, the stream Lewis and Clark had majestically called Philanthropy Creek and later Montanans would dub the Ruby. Originally called Varina, after the wife of Jefferson Davis until a Union judge renamed it with a single stroke of the pen, Virginia City was the center of fourteen miles of crowded, feverish activity, with money practically lying around waiting to be picked up. The Stuart brothers hustled over, establishing themselves in blacksmithing and general merchandising.

Meanwhile, ever-optimistic prospectors fanned out, some into the Yellowstone Valley to work Emigrant Gulch despite Crow opposition; some to Confederate Gulch in the Big Belt Mountains, where "Wooly" Johnson vowed neither to shave nor cut his hair until the South won the Civil War; others penetrated the Prickly Pear Valley, where, in the summer of 1864, the so-called "Four Georgians" (at least one of whom was familiar with the Peach State) made important strikes in Last Chance Gulch. Here the major settlement emerged as Helena, which old-timers claimed erroneously was named after Helen of Troy—a tradition continued by a popular jingle.

> Helen-a; after a darling, dizzy dame,
> Of much beauty but spotted fame;
> In pronouncing the name, understand me well,
> Strong emphasis should be laid on Hel.[4]

In time, over $30 million in gold would be taken out of the area. With relatively easy access to the head of navigation at Fort Benton, Helena would become the entrepôt and develop an

4. Quoted in Vestal, *The Missouri*, p. 327.

agricultural hinterland in the Prickly Pear Valley to furnish goods and foodstuffs to numèrous satellite mining camps like Marysville, Rimini, or Radersburg.

To these, and dozens of other mushroom but often short-lived camps flocked hopeful gold seekers by the thousands. Some followed the trail of the fur traders. Belching steamers with raucous whistles and jangling bells puffed up the Missouri where bullboats had gone before and tied up at Fort Benton to discharge passengers and cargo—10,000 people and 8,000 tons of cargo in the peak year 1867. At Benton countless freight wagons transshipped goods, and passengers caught coaches or made arrangements to work their way to the mines. Many came by overland routes. Between 1862 and 1867 eight wagon trains brought at least 1,400 people from Minnesota across the north with organized protection from the "noble red Feller," as one traveler put it.[5] Farther south was the long, indirect road that followed the Oregon Trail to Fort Hall, then cut north over the Idaho-Utah trail. From this stemmed various shortcuts, including that of John Bozeman who in 1863 cut four hundred miles off the route when he marked a trail from Fort Laramie across the base of the Bighorns and the Yellowstone Valley to Virginia City. But because it cut through Sioux hunting grounds, the Bozeman Road invited persistent Indian attacks, and makeshift gravestones multiplied along its way before it was closed down. Eventually as the railroad pushed west across Wyoming in the late sixties, the trip became much less dangerous and arduous, although travelers who left the train at Corinne, Utah, and rode the stage north to Montana seldom forgot the experience. "That engine of torture jerked, kicked, plunged, and pitched us about," wrote one who experienced the journey. ". . . I spent most of the night bounding about the coach like a pea on a drum. . . ."[6]

By whatever route and mode of conveyance they might come,

5. Quoted in Helen McCann White, ed., *Ho! For the Gold Fields: Northern Overland Wagon Trains of the 1860's* (St. Paul: Minnesota Historical Society, 1966), p. 189.

6. Windham Thomas Wyndham-Quin Dunraven, *The Great Divide* (London: Windus & Chatto, 1976), pp. 375–376.

the energetic, hopeful newcomers scoured the mountains and valleys for precious metal. Across the pages of Montana history would flash countless mining camps, many, like Red Mountain City in the sixties, to wither as quickly as they sprouted. Many came later. In the Little Belts, Neihart had its brief day in the 1880s, then sagged, to recuperate at the time of World War I. On the eastern slope of the Judith Mountains, Gilt Edge prospered in the nineties, peaked in 1908, then coughed and died. Altyn, a self-contained strip within Glacier National Park, would flourish momentarily after 1898. But regardless of when or where they were located or whether the lure was gold or silver, Montana's early mining camps had much in common.

Their populations were diverse and cosmopolitan. Eastern tenderfeet rubbed elbows with "yon-siders," as the Californians were called and the "self-risers," as veteran prospectors in general were labeled. Yankee abolitionists and former slaveholders from Dixie swung picks together, but fought their own war on the side. All nationalities were represented, from the Heathen Chinee of Bret Harte to the beefy German girls who danced in the hurdy gurdies at a dollar a throw, whiskey thrown in. Early Beartown had seventeen saloons, but it also had a general store owned by two partners, one a Spaniard and one a Frenchman, neither of whom could understand the language of the other. These were fluid, mobile populations, ready to move at the slightest rumor of precious metal, be it in the Black Hills, the Sonoran desert of Arizona, or the beaches of Nome.

The raw mining towns were much alike, physically cut from the same pattern and often tucked into out-of-the-way places in such a way as to bear out a standard maxim of prospectors:

> A good silver mine
> Is above timber-line,
> Ten times out of nine! [7]

The original makeshift shelters—tents, dugouts, or lean-tos— soon gave way to log houses, usually with dirt-covered roofs; eventually came frame, brick, or even stone structures with the

7. *Engineering and Mining Journal* 11 (April 11, 1871): 232.

inevitable false fronts—what a Helena visitor in the 1880s called "Queen Anne in front and Crazy Jane behind." [8]

Natural scenery to the contrary, mining camps were not necessarily pleasant. At Virginia City miners soon denuded the gulch of the green alders that gave the diggings its name. As they ransacked the earth, they left "great·deep holes and high heaps of dirt" even in the streets, so that Virginia looked "as if an enormous Hog had been uprooting the soil." [9] Bannack was little better. "If there is such a place as hell," wrote one onlooker in 1863, "this must be the back door to it." [10] Often the newcomer could smell or hear the camp before he actually arrived. Tailings discolored the streams; unsightly dumps and grotesque rusted machinery dotted the landscape. Pounding stamps and dull booms of blasting—the heartbeats of mining—could be felt as well as heard. Sanitation facilities were abominable. Butchers like Conrad Kohrs let their hogs forage around their shops in Bannack and threw their offal out the back door. As elsewhere, horse manure, at the rate of five tons per year per animal, was taken for granted in all seasons. With time, as smelters were erected in camps like Butte, sulphur or arsenic fumes mingled with the stench of privies in a malodorous affront to the nostrils and created a wasteland devoid of vegetation that Dante might have described. Men in Montana to "git and git out" displayed a depressing kind of ruthlessness and thoughtlessness toward both the immediate environment and natural resources in general.

Whatever else they were, early Montana mining camps were active settlements. Virginia City reminded one young woman of a beehive; Helena was smaller than anticipated to one newcomer, "but it is the busiest place I ever saw." [11] "If 'labor is

8. Almon Gunnison, *Rambles Overland* (1884; Boston: Universalist, 1891, 4 ed.), p. 87.

9. Sarah Raymond Herndon, *Days on the Road: Crossing the Plains in 1865* (New York: Burr Printing, 1902) pp. 260–261: Andrew F. Rolle, ed., *The Road to Virginia City: The Diary of James Knox Polk Miller* (Norman: University of Oklahoma, 1960), p. 75.

10. Quoted in White, *Ho! For the Gold Fields*, p. 83.

11. Andrew Fisk, in White, *Ho! For the Gold Fields*, p. 218.

worship,' " said another, of Bannack, "this is a most worship-
full community. . . ." [12] Quick wealth attracted not only miners, but those who would "mine the miners" in ways both essential and iniquitous. There were fortunes to be made in
providing goods and services: in banking, freighting, merchandising, or even farming. There were fortunes to be made even
more rapidly in less staid fields. It was well known that mining
was boring and thirst-raising work, especially among younger
men away from families ties. Water was excellent for baptizing
infants or for sluicing out gold, easterners were told, "but it
don't go for a steady beverage up here, where the air is so
thin." [13] More fitting was stronger stuff, described by one as
"140 rod—fire proof tangle leg" [14] and by another as "farina-
ceous food, taken in a concentrated and liquid form out of a
black bottle." [15] It was pure chance that the first building in
Virginia City was a bakery and the second a saloon. Drinking
places soon outnumbered bakeries twenty to one, as bad whiskey flowed like the waters of the Stinking Water itself. Probably
the toughest place in Bannack was Cy Skinner's Elkhorn saloon, with a huge set of antlers on the outside and the scalp of a
Bannack chief over the bar.

Early Virginia had at least a dozen gambling dens manned by
slick practitioners of the art. Invariably the "light ladies who
followed the heavy money" were promptly on the scene, their
cribs and crude parlor houses an integral part of the camp. So,
too, were the dance houses, in which the girls were not necessarily prostitutes. Indeed, often soiled doves found that there
was more money to be made on the dance floor "than in their
usual professional positions," as Dan Cushmen puts it.[16] And

12. Emily R. Meredith, in Clyde McLemore, ed., "Bannack and Gallatin City in
1862–1863: a Letter by Mrs. Emily Meredith," *Frontier and Midland*, 17 (Summer
1937): 285.

13. Alexander K. McClure, *Three Thousand Miles through the Rocky Mountains*
(Philadelphia: J. B. Lippincott, 1869), p. 278.

14. Andrew Fisk, in White, *Ho! For the Gold Fields*, p. 233.

15. Dunraven, *Great Divide*, p. 53.

16. Dan Cushman, *Montana—the Gold Frontier* (Great Falls: Stay Away, Joe Publishers, 1973), p. 64.

more than one of Montana's first families could trace its lineage
back to the hurdy-gurdy or dance-hall girls.

As elsewhere, Montana mining camps were noted for their
initial lawlessness and turbulence, though this aspect of western
life has been grossly exaggerated. Undoubtedly, gold and silver
attracted a good cross-section of the scum of several continents,
but this differed only in degree from more established towns farther east. What is most remarkable is not that the undesirables
existed, but rather the speed and the thoroughness with which
law-abiding citizens brought them under control. In what has
been called Montana's "first successful uplift movement," [17]
vigilantes virtually eliminated Henry Plummer's outlaw band at
Bannack and Virginia City, shooting or hanging at least twenty-
two late in 1863 and early in 1864. Although spectacular, this
"hemp" period was brief and not without parallels in other
camps. Crime and violence invariably brought spontaneous reaction; as large bodies of population shifted rapidly ahead of the
machinery of organized government, responsible citizens took
matters into their own hands, then petitioned Washington for
creation of a new territory or state.

Surprising, too, is how quickly "civilization" came to the
mines; how early Montanans sought to emulate the patterns of
cultural and social activity they had known before. If Virginia
City folk paid undue homage to John Barleycorn and perhaps
cheered too lustily when their bare-knuckled favorite Con Orem
"bruised & mashed to a jelly" the face of his pugilist opponent,
they also stomped their feet enthusiastically when "The Hunch-
back" and "The Marble Heart" played at the New People's
Theater. If they spent too much time (and dust) "bucking the
tiger" at the faro table, they still found time to organize singing
classes, literary societies, and mock legislatures. If greenhorns
were appalled at the number of saloons in Alder Gulch, they
must also have marveled that dancing and French lessons were
available. If they complained that the Sabbath was ignored—
that "every store, saloon, and dancing hall was in full blast

17. Jerre C. Murphy, *The Comical History of Montana* (San Diego: Scofield, 1912),
p. 1.

. . . and indeed every business is carried on with much more zeal than on week days," the formalities of religion were not far behind.[18] The first sermon at Bannack was reputedly by a black preacher in the spring of 1863; two Methodists evangelized among three hundred busy miners at Norwegian Gulch that same summer; and others by fall were chastising the sinners in Virginia City. There the slight, mild-mannered and tubercular Thomas Dimsdale not only taught school but served as Episcopal lay reader, though some chauvinists complained of his Oxford accent and the fact that he prayed loyally for the Queen and ignored the President. Civilization and crudeness overlapped; progress was well-nigh unbelievable, wrote a participant in 1864, "but truth and the marvelous go hand in hand when Young America finds a good gold gulch." [19]

As they moved about the West and within Montana from one mining center to another or from short-lived camps with names like Ophir, Argenta, or Atlantic City, miners brought with them technology and institutions. With them they carried the basic mining codes and courts, based on Germanic and Spanish-Mexican traditions, that Californians had earlier established to fill a void. Meeting informally in the new diggings, they set down rules defining mineral claims, their means of acquisition and transfer. They created extralegal courts to hear claim disputes or even criminal matters. When legal government was effectively secured, they wrote these codes into law; and in their interpretations, as in the statutes themselves, Montana courts would follow the California construction. As a prelude to genuine national mineral legislation, Congress in 1866 would recognize the local codes and in 1872 would begin to write their provisions into a more unified set of federal statutes.

In most districts, early mining and milling methods varied little. They were simple, individualistic approaches calling for a low investment of capital and a high commitment of hand labor. The first discoveries were usually "poor man's strikes," placer

---

18. Rolle, ed., *Road to Virginia City,* pp. 94, 77.

19. Entry for November 11, 1864, James H. Morley Diary, Montana Historical Society.

deposits, from which gold was recovered by the classic but inefficient processes of panning or the use of rockers or sluice-boxes. As the miners themselves admitted, this "is no child's play." Newcomers were surprised to find gold seekers knee-deep in mud and water, shoveling dirt. "My God, is that the way you get gold?" one asked.[20] Free-milling quartz found in outcrops on or near the surface could readily be crushed in a stamp mill and the gold separated with mercury—again with high loss of precious metal. But the days of these elementary techniques were short: in most regions, free-milling ore was scarce and the gold-bearing gravels of the streams were quickly exhausted, often within a year or two.

In a typical district, like Last Chance Gulch, some quartz mining overlapped the placer, but until capital and transportation were available, it was of necessity limited. Shafting or tunneling by hand was slow, arduous work—"Mighty cold—wet—muddy and disagreeable." Striking rock or water made it impossible and even a young vigorous man found that "tending the windlass is *some* on the *muscle.* . . ." [21] To follow outcroppings deep under the surface required capital; tunneling and shafting were expensive, with thousands of board feet of timber required to shore up the interior; blasting was costly as well as dangerous, even when power drills replaced hand drills; ventilation, moving ore underground, and hoisting it to the top demanded heavy outlay. Sometimes, at depth, gold was in combination with other elements and difficult to handle, although there were always peddlers of fantastic "sure-fire" new processes who sought to capitalize on such refractory or "rebellious" ores, usually with negative results that retarded, rather than hastened the industry's development.

This situation was compounded when the depression of 1873 brought financial despondency, which lasted most of the decade and by the slowness with which rail transportation came to the territory. Through most of the seventies Montana mining remained in the doldrums, awaiting the capital and improved

20. Mark D. Leadbeater, in White, *Ho! For the Gold Fields,* p. 46.
21. Andrew Fisk, in White, *Ho! For the Gold Fields,* p. 224.

freight facilities so vital to deep-level quartz operations and to complex refining and smelting. With the 1880s and 1890s came capital, railroads, and new technology, all of which brought expansion and development to the mineral industry. Along with gold, silver became an important metal. Montana's first major silver strike came at Argenta in 1864, and by 1868 three smelters had been opened, one by William A. Clark, who was destined to become a key figure in Montana mining and politics. But silver was often in combination with sulphur or another metal—copper in the Butte area, for example—and required reduction to a rich concentrate and then smelting. When capital became available in the 1880s, Butte was augmented as a silver producer by other districts. One centered upon Philipsburg, named for Philipp Deidesheimer, who superintended an early smelter there and was best known as the deviser of "square set" timbering on the Comstock Lode. Near Philipsburg important mines like the Hope and the Speckled Trout flourished, and a few miles to the east the Granite Mountain Mining Company would take out more than $22 million, and the Bi-Metallic Mining Company more than $7 million between 1882 and 1889. Silver boomed at Elkhorn, at Neihart, and at Independence high in the Absaroka Range until the panic of 1893 brought prices crashing and caused at least temporary closure of most major producers in the state.

The mid-nineties brought a new gold technology. In May 1895 at Bannack, long since deserted by serious gold seekers, a "Large concourse of people" watched the christening of the vessel *Fielding L. Graves*. "Cheers rent the air as the boat slid gracefully from its ways and floated on the waters of Grasshopper creek." [22] This was the launching of the "first connected-bucket dredge to be built and successfully operated in the United States;" [23] it was the beginning of one of the important mass-production technologies that would revolutionize mining,

22. *Dillon Examiner*, May 22, 1895.
23. Charles J. Lyden, *The Gold Placers of Montana* (Montana Bureau of Mines & Geology Memoir No. 26; Butte: Montana School of Mines, 1948), caption opposite title page.

in this case placer mining, around the world. A self-contained unit floating on its own hull, the electrically operated *Fielding L. Graves* scooped gravel from the river bottom by means of 500-pound buckets, processed it within the apparatus, and dumped the tailings in an unsightly ridge, as it moved itself slowly. Well into the mid-twentieth century, lineal descendants of the *Graves* would dominate the production of gold in the state. Their efficiency was such that, according to one advertisement, "One large Dredge Boat does the work of twenty-five-hundred pick and shovel men of the placer Mining days." [24] This meant that ground in Pioneer District in the north end of the Deer Lodge Valley, which had been mined by hand in the sixties, worked by hydraulic methods in the early seventies, then reworked laboriously by some eight hundred Chinese who washed gold manually, carrying waste away in baskets, could now be dredged with profit, at least until the Forest Service cut off the source of fuel wood. Alder Gulch was completely reworked by the huge floating monsters, the largest of which cost $296,000 and dredged to a depth of fifty-four feet.

But from any point of view, dredging was large-scale corporate enterprise, which, like silver and copper, required substantial capital. When this occurred and mining went from simple processes sustained by blister-and-callus labor to highly sophisticated and expensive operations, the independent miners were cast adrift. Many went their way, panning new streams and dreaming new dreams; but many became company workers, three-dollars-a-shift miners mucking ore into one-ton cars or part of a double-jack drilling team, one man holding and turning the drill, the other striking it rhythmically with an eight-pound sledge at fifty strokes a minute. Or, after the middle seventies, they might become pneumatic-drill specialists, experts with a Burleigh, Ingersoll, or some other brand of "wiggle-tail" of the sort that was beginning to put the double-jackers out of business.

Corporate mining brought its own problems. It gave free license to the mine promoter, that imaginative and persistent

24. *Montana-Idaho Gold Dredging Co.* (Butte?; n. pub., 1910?), p. 5.

midwife to the transfer of property to combinations of capital. Men like Samuel Hauser were busy hawking Montana mines and trying to attract New York capital as early as the mid-sixties. Typical of the shrewd entrepreneurs who could judge men and mines and who had access to capital when opportunity arose, Hauser did well in promoting, organizing, and owning interests in successful mining and smelting enterprises. Perry McAdow, one of the early settlers, despite being partially paralyzed and confined to a wheelchair, also had the golden touch at Maiden and elsewhere. He knew a good mine when he saw it, and he could put his hands on capital. Even more successful would be the copper kings William A. Clark and Marcus Daly at Butte and Anaconda. But, in general, these were neither run-of-the-mill investors nor original discoverers of mining property. Tommy Cruse was an exception. A frustrated California gold seeker, the rough-hewn Cruse located the Drumlummon near Marysville, naming the mine after the parish in Ireland in which he was born. Eventually, in 1883, he sold the Drumlummon to a British company for $1.5 million, proceeded to build a fine house in Helena, branched out into banking and ranching, underwrote the Montana capitol bond issue, and would leave behind an enduring monument in the splendid St. Helena Cathedral. But for every rags-to-riches story, there are far more of discoverers who sold out for a pittance to men who subsequently made a fortune from the property. At Rocker near Silver Bow, for example, Robert McMinn found gold but sold his claim for $200 before he realized what he had; over the next five years, the mine yielded a quarter of a million dollars. At Butte old Bill Parks struck a vein of copper so pure it could be "shipped to hell and back for smelting and still make a profit." [25] But he sold out for a mere $10,000 and relaxed while the new owners took a million dollars from his claim on the "richest hill on earth."

Corporate mining brought problems of absentee ownership. Sometimes "Jolly Dog" managers were sent out, high-living relatives of directors who knew little of mining. Some were dis-

25. Montana Writers' Project, *Copper Camp*, p. 29.

honest, like the manager of the Gilt Edge Mining Company, " a tricky piece of human furniture," [26] who absconded with all the bullion from the mill in 1893; or the crooked superintendent at Maiden who skipped with the profits of McAdow's Spotted Horse mine a year later. If not the man in charge, perhaps some other official or employee might cut deeply into the profits. The Reverend C. C. Frost, treasurer of the Hope mine at Butte, defaulted with company funds and disappeared; an amalgamator for the Vestel Company mill on Silver Creek systematically robbed the firm of between $40,000 and $100,000 before he was caught in 1880; one company at Cable City in 1883 alone lost an estimated $50,000 by "high-grading"—that is, simple theft of valuable ore by miners who carried it off in their lunchboxes, their pockets, or in special bags under their clothes at the end of their shift.

It is frequently charged that outsiders exploited the resources of Montana for their own profit, that they plundered and looted and left the land wasted and ravaged. To some extent this was indeed true. Placer and deep-level mining pock-marked the hills and valleys; smelters and refineries left Butte "a nightmare of a country"; "as ugly as home-made sin"; in later years, monster dredges churned through alfalfa fields, threatened to chew up Helena's golf course, and, wherever they went, left "the kind of furrow that an enormous, obscene, unhousebroken worm might leave—an encrusted seam of broken earth, with mud and rocks lying across a winding trail like excrement." [27]

However that may be, if Montana mines made profits, which was not always the case, such profits were not always drained off. Likely only one in every ten or a dozen companies organized to work Montana mines returned dividends. Men like Coleman the mustard king and former President Grover Cleveland, who saw their money go down the drain in a shady investment

26. Quoted in Muriel Sibell Wolle, *Montana Pay Dirt* (Denver: Sage Books, 1963), p. 357.

27. Archibald Gordon MacDonell, *A Visit to America* (New York: Macmillan Co., 1936), p. 176; John Edward Hicks, *Adventures of a Tramp Printer, 1880–1890* (Kansas City, Mo.: MidAmericana Press, 1950), p. 236; John Gunther, *Inside U.S.A.* (New York & London: Harper, 1947), p. 159.

in the western part of the state, did not feel that they were exploiting Montana, any more than did the several hundred shareholders of the Anglo-Montana Mining Company, Ltd., who plunged into Lewis and Clark County in 1886 with a capital of $600,000 and were bankrupt within two years. At the same time, Montana benefitted greatly as mining progressed. Non-miners followed each mineral boom; mining camps demanded services, goods, and foodstuffs, thus giving rise to farming, cattle raising, and a variety of crafts. Money taken from the mines was often channeled back into other parts of the economy, directly or indirectly. Wisconsinite John Blake, for example, one of the 1864 emigrants, found a nugget in Last Chance Gulch worth $2,300, which he used to study dentistry in Philadelphia, then returned to Helena to practice and raise prize stock until his death in 1927. Entrepreneurs like Sam Hauser, Tommy Cruse, or Anton Holter plowed their mineral proceeds into diversified Montana fields; William A. Clark did likewise, and even included the purchase of a seat in the United States Senate.

Large-scale corporate mining supported communities and a variety of auxiliary industries. If the profits of the Drumlummon flowed overseas to more than three thousand British investors, Cruse was well paid for his property, and for many years it was a primary economic support of the town of Marysville, where it directly employed three hundred men, and indirectly almost the entire fifteen hundred inhabitants were dependent one way or another on its operation. Every going mine was a market for large quantities of quicksilver, chemicals, blasting powder, candles, and machinery, not to mention timber for fuel and for shoring up the inner workings. At one time the Butte copper mines consumed an estimated thirty to forty million board feet per year—enough to fill 3,700 railroad cars and valued at a million dollars. Another thirty million board feet went to fire the smelters. Litigation was also an auxiliary industry. Claims overlapped: "Everybody's spurs were running into everybody else's angles," it was said. A mediocre property—a mine "as barren as a mule"—was simple, but a successful one produced a harvest of lawsuits directly proportional to the value of its ores. Often litigation became a form of legal blackmail on the part of abutting neighbors who wished to be bought out at their own prices. Legal fees must have drained much of the profits of both sides. Lawyers' expenses for the Montana Company, Ltd., owner of the Drumlummon, in its more than twenty years of running litigation with the St. Louis Mining and Milling Company came to more than $400,000, certainly a boon to the legal profession.

Montana's mineral development fitted the temper and model of nineteenth-century national economic growth. It was part of what historian Vernon Parrington has called the Great Barbecue, the rapid, often ruthless exploitation of resources with little planning or thought of implications. It would provide much of the copper for the new electrical era and soon for the automotive age. Its contributions of precious metal would augment an antiquated and inflexible banking system, which could not in itself meet the expanding needs of industry and transportation. Its gold and silver helped muffle the impact of the depressions of 1873 and 1893 and contributed to American ability to finance imports.

The mining boom speeded up the clash with the Indians, as thousands of gold seekers tramped across Indian lands, and required renegotiation of treaties to move the Indians farther away. Sheer numbers and persistence gave miners a more immediate impact on a region than did the more slowly moving and widely dispersed farmers and cattlemen. But, more than anything else, mining quickly drew large numbers of people to the Montana wilderness and, directly or obliquely, provided an economic base. Some of the hell-roaring camps of the boom eras matured into modern regional centers like Helena, which at peak was a town of impressive mansions and half a hundred millionaires, another argument against total exploitation by outsiders. A few, like Butte, would continue to be dominated by the industry, with underground methods giving way to open-pit and its prosperity copper-plated. Others, Virginia City and Bannack among them, capitalize on past brilliance, no longer gauging their worth in heavy bullion but by the number of out-of-state cars and tourists roaming their refurbished streets. But most of the once-flourishing camps are marked, if at all, by weathered gravestones and lonely but still eloquent ruins.

4

The Range Cattle Industry

"The Best Grazing-Grounds in America"

N the wake of the moccasins of the fur hunters and the cowhide boots of the gold seekers came the high-heeled riding boots of the cattlemen. While the cowman's boot is still very much a part of the Montana picture, it was most dominant in the era of the range-cattle industry—the years from the 1870s to the early 1890s, when the use of free government grazing land flourished. The range-cattle industry was not indigenous nor limited to Montana, of course; it thrived wherever enterprising westerners were in a position to exploit the public domain. But in the cold reaches of Montana it reached its most dramatic expression.

From a few scattered livestock around fur-trading posts or along the Oregon Trail, newcomers would begin building herds in the western valleys. Major John Owen ran a few head around his fort in the 1850s, and when James and Granville Stuart arrived in the Deer Lodge Valley in 1858, they found a number of hardy pioneers already there with several hundred head of cattle and horses. Prominent among them was Richard Grant, a Scots-

James Sanks Brisbin, *The Beef Bonanza, or, How to get Rich on the Plains* (Philadelphia: J. B. Lippincott, 1881), p. 90.

man of Falstaffian proportions who had once been a factor for the Hudson's Bay Company, and his family. With his sons, especially John Grant, he traded for footworn livestock along the trail between Fort Bridger and Salt Lake City and in the fall drove the animals into the sheltered western valleys, where they generally thrived and were driven back in the spring to be sold to westbound emigrants. The Stuarts, too, began to traffic in these pre-owned cattle, to use the parlance of modern used-car dealers.

The sudden influx of thousands of gold seekers in the early sixties greatly expanded the market for beef, giving old-timers and new arrivals alike profitable new possibilities. Visitors to the Deer Lodge Valley in 1862 commented on John Grant's herd, which they estimated at from a thousand to four thousand head. "He does not winter feed," said one, "but lets them graze thro' the winter—& we never saw larger, better, or fatter cattle anywhere. . . ." [1] Soon Johnny Grant would sell his ranch and herd to a newcomer with vision and drive, Conrad Kohrs. Having run away from Holstein at the age of fifteen, Kohrs had been a seaman, a raftsman on the Mississippi, a butcher, and a sausage salesman, and had followed the call of gold to California, British Columbia, and the Salmon River. He drifted into Montana on foot in 1862; he became owner of a shop in Bannack when the proprietor left with unseemly haste. From this combined butcher-shop–slaughterhouse, Kohrs would build an empire in cattle. Using borrowed money and credit, he established shops in Virginia and Last Chance Gulch, selling wholesale as well as retail and trading vigorously for livestock. Expanding into ranching, Kohrs would long dominate the cattle trade of western Montana and would migrate with it eastward. He is said to have owned 90,000 head at one time and to have shipped thirty trainloads to Chicago in a single season.

Others, too, were both important and typical. D. A. G. Floweree (his friends pronounced it "Flurry") was a Missourian who had made the trip to California when he was seventeen. Tradition has it that he was a member of the ill-fated Walker fil-

---

1. Quoted in White, *Ho! For the Gold Fields,* p. 67.

ibustering expedition to Nicaragua in the 1850s and escaped death only with the aid of a lovely señorita. In 1864 Floweree had been helping run a gambling house at Last Chance Gulch, but within a year was buying cattle brought in from Missouri and subsequently herds from Oregon and Texas. In time, he moved to a spread on the Sun River, where he prospered. To those who knew him, "Uncle Dan" was a shrewd, honest bargainer who would be successful enough to grow grapefruit in Florida as well as beef in Montana.

Robert Ford had come out of Missouri as a bullwhacker on the Santa Fe and Oregon trails, eventually reaching the Deer Lodge Valley as captain of a wagon train. After several years of freighting in Montana, he bid on and received the government contract to provide hay for the cavalry at Cow Island. With the profits he bought cattle from Colorado, the nucleus of a major herd, which after 1872 ranged out of his ranch near the Sun River crossing of the stage road from Fort Benton to Helena.

An important innovator also was Nelson Story, a Pike's Peaker who had done well in the Alder Gulch diggings and who in 1866 invested in a herd of six hundred longhorns, which he trailed north from Dallas over the Bozeman Road to a ranch near Livingston. Indian troubles would seal off this particular route for some time, but the venture was a pioneering one: in later years the movement of Texas trail herds onto lush Montana grasslands would be an integral part of the expanding range-cattle industry.

In the early years, cattle growing in western Montana depended mainly on local markets—the mining camps, army posts, Indian annuity goods, perhaps railroad construction workers in the late sixties. But lacking rail links to the transcontinental line for years, owners were forced to drive any surplus four hundred miles to railheads in Wyoming or Utah, an undertaking that took two months and entailed considerable risk as long as the Indian question was unresolved. In 1874, in the aftermath of the depression of the previous year, grown steers were bringing ten dollars a head, according to a Deer Lodge editor, and there was a surplus of some 17,000 on hand. With all land north of the Marias and the Missouri and south of the

Yellowstone set aside for the Indians, ranchers like Kohrs, Ford, and Floweree were moving herds onto well-watered natural pastures along the Sun, the Marias, or the Smith, but it was clear that easy access to market depended on surmounting the Indian barrier.

This was the beginning of a major transition—a shift to more northern and eastern ranges and a tremendous boom in the cattle industry, not merely in Montana, but throughout much of the Great Plains and the intermountain West. Within a decade the cattle-raising part of the United States became larger than the cultivated portion. Expanding industrialization and urbanization required larger food supplies for metropolitan areas; the extension of western railroads linked supply and markets; federal policy toward land use was lenient, just at a time when pressures were shrinking Indian holdings and the slaughter of the buffalo was leaving rich grazing grounds free for occupation by ranchers.

At the end of the seventies, beef prices were good, a fact reinforced by numerous ballyhoo artists who wrote of both advantages and profits from the upper ranges. Montana's climate was superb for livestock. Its bunch grass was the finest in the world, according to journalist, Indian war correspondent, and railroad propagandist Robert Strahorn. Cured in a "mild, pure atmosphere," it gave incomparable flavor to beef or mutton. On Montana ranges, suggested Strahorn, cattle could shift for themselves—"grow while their owner sleeps"—and come off in the spring ready for market. "A steady profit of twenty-five percent per annum," he said, "is really a common result." [2] In complete agreement was General James Brisbin, a Bull Run veteran who would spend nearly a quarter of a century in western army posts and whose book on how free grass created instant millionaires touted Montana, "that majestic, wild and solitary land," as having "the best grazing-grounds in America." [3]

No large investment was necessary: under the Homestead Act of 1862, 160 acres were easily available for the nucleus of a

2. Strahorn, *The Resources of Montana,* p. 22.
3. Brisbin, *The Beef Bonanza,* p. 90.

small spread. With judicious selection and an eye to control of all-important water, an aspiring rancher might graze his animals on free government grass which lay all around. To be sure, he might have to wink at illegalities, like the fencing of more than a quarter of a million acres of public land in Montana by 1887 or the kind of subterfuge and unlawful entry necessary to take full advantage of specialized land laws drawn up by Washington congressmen who failed to understand the West and its needs. Since federal lands were illicitly occupied, it would take mutual consent to resolve conflicts between ranchers. To this end, Montanans conceived the idea of the "law of customary range," recognized in the statutes of 1877, to sanction acquisition of public land by occupation and notice given in newspapers. Interlopers like J. H. Conrad of Fort Benton, who refused to recognize the concept, would be ostracized socially and economically.

Many of the older Montana ranchers north and west of the Yellowstone grazed quality stock. Kohrs brought some of the first Herefords to the Sun River ranges; T. C. Power imported Aberdeen Angus from Quebec; Orr and Poindexter raised purebred Durhams near Watson. But unless ranges were naturally limited by streams or steep divides as in the west, the upbreeding of stock was difficult. As the boom developed on the more eastern grazing lands, without barriers and few fences, it was impossible to prevent the haphazard union of everybody's son with nobody's daughter. There, at first the Texas longhorn predominated. Driven up over the long, dusty trails, sometimes by Texans who stocked new Montana ranches with them, the raw-boned longhorns were too scrawny to be ideal beef cattle. A New York newspaper once claimed that all the meat on one of them would go into one of the horns. But they were tough, could forage for themselves even on the snow-covered northern ranges and put on weight. More and more, however, as expansion progressed in the eighties, the Texas longhorns were being replaced by midwestern "pilgrims" of a far less hardy and self-sufficient nature.

When the big boom came, Granville Stuart was part of it. In partnership with Sam Hauser of Helena, A. J. Davis of Butte, and Erwin Davis of New York, Stuart formed the firm of Davis, Hauser & Company in 1879. With a capital of $150,000, he spent the next summer looking for a range in central and eastern Montana. He was as far east as Miles City, then a center of about 350 inhabitants, 20 saloons, even more whores, and, according to one observer, "as many thieves as any town of its size in the world. . . ." [4] The place had its beginnings as an "army brat" of a town, called into being primarily to sell pop-skull whiskey to the soldiers at Fort Keogh. When the railroad reached it, Miles City would be the center first of the buffalo-hide traffic and then of livestock shipment. North of the town Stuart saw where the buffalo hunters had been at work with their big Sharps rifles and Winchesters, the bottoms "literally sprinkled" with the carcasses of dead animals, "all murdered for their hides which are piled like cord wood all along the way. 'Tis an awful sight," he said.[5]

At the foot of the Judith Mountains in the central part of the territory, Stuart found his range. On Ford's Creek he and Reese Anderson erected ranch buildings and a corral close to a thousand acres of hay land, part of which he obtained with soldiers' scrip. At about the same time Fort Maginnis was established nearby, and part of the hay land was lost to the army, but proximity to the military was convenient and even profitable. By fall 1880 Stuart was running five thousand head of cattle driven in from Oregon and sixty horses on the new range, and the enterprise began to prosper despite an especially severe first winter, which added another three percent to the normal ten-percent losses attributed to predators, both two- and four-footed. Blackfeet tried to run off horses nearly every night, and finally the exasperated Stuart, with a show of force at his back, told the Indians to "rattle your hocks out of here" or he would wipe them out.[6] Guts, a healthy herd, good management, and natural shelter helped Stuart to avert the kind of disaster which befell a

4. Quoted in MHS, *Precious Metals,* p. 157.

5. Phillips, *Forty Years on the Frontier,* 2:104.

6. E. C. Abbott, *We Pointed Them North* (New York: Farrar & Rinehart, 1939), p. 154.

British outfit that season when it trailed five thousand head from Texas to the mouth of Otter Creek in southeastern Montana, only to have most of the cattle perish.

Meanwhile other ranchers moved in. The Power brothers and Charles Beldon brought two herds into the Judith Basin; Conrad Kohrs and his partner put three thousand head on the range at Willow Flat. At Armell's Creek, not too far from Stuart, Scottish-born James Fergus located in 1881. A millwright earlier associated with Illinois and Fergus Falls, Minnesota (which bears his name), Fergus was a well-read and fiercely independent thinker, who brought with him to Armell's Creek "the largest and best selected library" of any Montana stockman of his day—even more impressive than Stuart's three thousand volumes.[7] Soon the Davis-Hauser-Stuart enterprise—the DHS outfit—merged with Kohrs, that "big, long-legged old Dutchman," [8] incorporating as the million-dollar Pioneer Cattle Company in the spring of 1885.

As demands for northern and eastern rangeland intensified, so did pressure for reduction of Indian land holdings. At the same time cattle operations became larger, more speculative, more geared to a quick profit. So much Scottish and English capital came into Colorado, Wyoming, and Montana ranching that Congress in 1887 prohibited foreign concerns from acquiring title to land in the territories. In the southeast, the Hashknife outfit of the Continental Land and Cattle Company had a large herd along the Montana-Dakota line. The DeHart Land and Cattle Company ran eight thousand head out of Rosebud Creek. At the extreme eastern end of the territory, Pierre Wibaux, scion of a wealthy French family, forsook the family dye and textile business and brought his bride to live in a sod house when he established a ranch on Beaver Creek. And so it went. Yet in the long run, with such exceptions as Wibaux and the DHS outfit (the latter paid the owners half a million dollars in seven years), not many in Montana's boom cattle companies showed consistent good returns. Eastern and European capital often primed the

---

7. *Progressive Men of the State of Montana* (Chicago: A. W. Bowen, n.d.), p. 9.
8. Abbott, *We Pointed Them North*, p. 248.

economic pump, and if profits failed to materialize, investors shifted to other western investments.

The Northern Pacific Railroad, which reached the lower Yellowstone by 1881 and was completed two years later, was vital to the industry. Even so, high rail costs and poor shipping facilities sometimes prompted cattlemen to band together to fight for improvements. Cattle-rustling was an intermittent problem, with Stuart estimating losses from this source at from three to five percent annually, and commenting with dry wit:

> Near our home ranch we discovered one rancher whose cows invariably had twin calves and frequently triplets, while the range cows in that vicinity were nearly all barren and would persist in hanging around this man's corral, envying his cows their numerous children and bawling and lamenting their own childless fate.[9]

When this situation continued, Stuart and his neighbors threatened to hang the fellow if his cows had any more twins.

It was to handle such problems and to insure control of livestock on the open ranges that cowmen organized the Montana Stockgrowers' Association. Cattle were too scattered to be easily protected by the normal agencies of law enforcement, so the Stockgrowers' Association stepped in to hire range detectives and to establish ground rules for co-operation in roundups and other areas of mutual concern. Normally the association exerted indirect political pressure, but when 429 members met in Miles City for its second meeting in 1884, conservatives like Stuart had to reason carefully with the radicals, who wished to raise an impromptu army and mete out harsh justice to livestock thieves. Even while Stuart was at the meeting, rustlers made off with a number of his horses—a mistake on their part, it turned out. Soon vigilantes were at work (some called them "Stuart's Stranglers"), cleaning out thieves along the mouth of the Musselshell and hanging at least fifteen men in the process, midst cries of anguish over the "arrogance of the cattle kings." When Indians subsequently crossed from Canada to pilfer stock, the ranchers dealt as summarily with them. All the while their

9. Phillips, *Forty Years on the Frontier,* 2:195.

spokesmen, especially Granville Stuart, were busy in the legislature, seeking protection for their interests.

Open-range cattle ranching was a risky business, the cowman gambling, as Stuart said, "with the trump cards in the hands of the elements." [10] By the summer of 1885, in part because of cancellation of stock leases on Oklahoma Indian lands, more than 100,000 head of cattle and numerous bands of sheep had been squeezed onto the ranges of central Montana. Extreme drought in the following summer foreshadowed trouble. Forage was poor, and cattle prices, steadily dropping from the peak of 1882, declined again on Chicago markets, and fell further when some owners liquidated their herds. Others, like Conrad Kohrs, leased land in Canada or on the Crow reservation, or made arrangements to "board out" stock on shares to small farmer-ranchers.

In the fall of 1886, observers noticed that the cattle's coats were heavier than usual; they noticed wild animals moving south early; and for the first time in years they saw Arctic owls in the Judith Basin. November and December brought heavy snow, melted by a chinook in early January but followed by more and more snow and then a raging blizzard late in the month. Temperatures plunged to forty-two below zero at Fort Maginnis, near Stuart's ranch, and to fifty-five below near Havre. Cattle drifted before the storm until they came up against range fences, then froze to death. In vain they pawed at the deep snow to get at the dry grass underneath; but the eastern "pilgrims" foraged badly; they and indeed many of the long-horns perished. Owners worked hard but found it impossible to protect their stock or even to gauge the extent of their losses, although they could guess. At the OH Ranch in the Judith Basin, Charlie Russell painted on a card a picture of a gaunt steer hunched in the cold, a wolf biding his time expectantly, captioned it "The Last of 5,000," and mailed it off without another word to indicate to the owner in Helena how his cattle were doing.

Came the spring thaws, the grim remains were all too appar-

10. Phillips, *Forty Years on the Frontier*, 2:227.

ent. Coulees were littered with the carcasses of dead animals, and soon the scavengers of buffalo bones reappeared, collecting dry bones—the price on the market, a dollar a ton. Granville Stuart was sick at heart. "I never wanted to own again an animal that I could not feed and shelter," he wrote later.[11] The stock still alive were in wretched shape. Their angular frames, as Ernest Osgood likes to say, resembled the insides of Gothic cathedrals. The next summer in the sweltering heat along the Box Elder, with the sweat pouring off his face, an old cowhand looked up soberly at the sun and said, "Where the hell was you last January?" [12]

The actual rate of loss is difficult to know. Stuart estimated that Montana ranchers lost $20 million because of the storm and that the DHS lost 66 percent of its cattle. Kohrs believed that half of his herd was destroyed and probably an overall range of from 30 to 50 percent is realistic. Absentee owners lost most heavily. In ordinary times a 10 percent mortality rate was considered normal in Montana, but frequently managers' reports to eastern or European owners padded the book count, showing one percent losses and carrying more cattle on paper than they actually had. Now came an opportunity to charge off in one lump losses accumulated over five or six years: the elements, not bad management could take the blame. No wonder one manager is supposed to have reported a loss of 125 percent!

Dry seasons on the plains prompted cattle sales in Kansas and Nebraska, with prices continuing low. Some Montanans gradually recouped. Conrad Kohrs borrowed without security from a Butte banker to buy nine thousand head of Idaho stock and made a successful recovery. Pierre Wibaux obtained fresh capital in France, bought cattle at depressed prices, and by careful trading and specialization would, by 1900, be back on top with forty thousand head. But many others, especially the corporate venturees, liquidated their holdings and got out of the business.

For most of those who continued, the range-cattle industry as they had known it before was ending. Significant changes came

11. Phillips, *Forty Years on the Frontier*, 2:237.
12. Quoted in Abbott, *We Pointed Them North*, p. 218.

as a result of the circumstances which seem to have converged in 1886–1887—drought, bitter winter, depressed prices, and overcrowding. Now the federal government would crack down on illegal fencing of the public domain. Sod-busters with visions of waving fields of golden grain would push out onto the ranges, and free use of government grass would become increasingly difficult. Cattlemen now turned from the open public lands to smaller home-owned or leased units fenced with barbed wire. The size of herds dropped sharply, on the average from 8,000 or 10,000 head to 1,500 or so, as owners became concerned with new sets of questions—the building of barns and sheds for shelter, irrigation, and cultivation of feed crops.

The cowhand became less a legend and more a man for all seasons, not that he was ever the romantic figure who galloped through the dime novel or across movie and television screens, saving more women and more gold than the Salvation Army and the U.S. Treasury combined, as historian Walter Webb once said. The lot of the real cowboy has always been dirty, dusty, often dull, and occasionally dangerous—all at $30 a month and keep. As the cattle industry changed, he rode fence and did blister work with shovel and wire-stretcher; he irrigated, mowed and stacked hay, and pitched it to the critters through the winter; he doctored screw worms and performed a thousand-and-one prosaic tasks never envisioned by the Hollywood cowboy, not even Gary Cooper, who came off a Montana dude ranch into the public limelight. If an era was ending, it would be a gradual transition extending well into the twentieth century; and cattle would remain one of the foundation blocks of the Montana economy.

When publicist Robert Strahorn referred to Montana as the "land of the golden fleece," he was not alluding to the faro dealers in Helena but to the wool industry.[13] Sheep followed cattle in western regions, usually with some time lag, and Montana was no exception. By the mid-seventies, when one grower drove 3,500 sheep into the territory from Nevada, sheepmen had firmly established themselves. Governor Benjamin Potts

13. Strahorn, *Resources of Montana*, p. 28.

raised sheep on the side and was reputed to have made $10,000 in less than a year on an investment of $12,000 in them. When the Northern Pacific reached Miles City in 1881, Nick Bielenberg was there with 6,000 of the woolies ready to ship, and the town clearly established itself as the largest shipper in the area. Sheep raising expanded tremendously in the eighties; it went from half a million in 1884 to almost a million two years later. Mobility was vital. Like cattlemen, sheep growers depended upon the open range and subscribed to the customary-use concept, but, more than other stockmen, they shifted their bands from winter to summer range and back again. The familiar figure in this continuing migration was the much-maligned sheepherder. In the old world he was a man who commanded some respect. "Behold the gentle shepherd with his fleecy flock," might be a typical reaction, while in Montana more likely it would be "Look at that crazy blankety-blank with his woolies!" [14] Cattlemen especially allowed that he was strange; indeed, some insisted that eccentricity was a prerequisite for the job. But the herder's life was not easy, and his responsibility was substantial. His life was lonely, except for his dogs; his diet was limited but broader than the "sheep, lamb, ram, and mutton" his detractors listed as his sole menu; every few weeks he moved his herd and his distinctive wagon—his early-day trailer home.

Writers of "shoot 'em up" western history have made much of the clash of sheepmen and cattlemen over the use of public grasslands; like violence in general, this has been much overplayed. To be sure, some cowmen did charge that the "hoofed locusts," as naturalist John Muir called sheep, ruined the range so that cattle would not use it, a charge seemingly refuted by the fact that a number of large operators in Montana ran both sheep and cattle on the same ranges and used the same watering spots. No doubt there were conflicts between the two interests, usually for possession of range, and sometimes settlement meant bloody heads. In question was federal land being used illegally; hence neither wished to test his case in court.

14. John G. Neihardt, *The River and I* (New York: Macmillan, 1910), pp. 91–92.

Generally speaking, sheep brought good profit. It cost less to stock a range with them, and they could reach grass where cattle could not. Usually they survived the elements well, but rugged winters were not selective: sheep as well as cattle went. Cornelius Hedges, one of the promoters of the Montana sheep industry, lost 1,240 head in the storms of 1887. "Went home crushed & didn't sleep at all," he confided in his diary.[15] But Hedges and sheep growing both came back strong. As the range-cattle industry began its decline, sheep production expanded. By 1900, the state had six sheep for every head of cattle, a total of more than six million, a figure that would decline over the next few decades because of periodic disturbances in the wool market, the steady growth of demand for mutton, and adaptation of growers to fenced lands.

In an era in which horses are a luxury, not a necessity, it is easy to forget that, up to World War I at least, horse raising was a major industry. Some of Montana's cattlemen—Nelson Story, for example—in the 1880s ran almost as many horses as cattle. Horse ranches dotted the territory. When Benjamin Potts left the governorship, he went into horse raising at Townsend with the son of President Benjamin Harrison. To the east, Miles City became the major center for horse sales. Despite a slump in the nineties, it provided army horses for the Spanish American War, the Boer War, and World War I. In the summer of 1912, when homesteaders were swarming into the eastern and northern parts of the state, Miles City had at least six major sales: one in June lasted four days, and in it six thousand horses changed hands. By 1918 Miles City was the largest horse market in the world. Then came Henry Ford's Model T, sharply slicing into local transportation, which old dobbin formerly had to himself. Montana continued to be livestock country, but no longer would range cattle dominate. By the 1890s farmers would be pushing in, a small cascade which would grow to a torrent in the early twentieth century.

15. Quoted in Thomas Edward White, "Cornelius Hedges: Uncommon Hero of the Common Life" (M.A. Thesis, Montana State College, Bozeman, 1963), p. 84.

5

Control of the Indians

*"A Lower Must Yield
to a Higher Civilization."*

ONTANA was the setting of one of the final chapters in the long, ofttimes sordid, sometimes dramatic story of white-Indian relations in North America. When the miners arrived, it was one of the last portions of the country still inhabited by "wild" Indians; a substantial part of its land was still in tribal hands; and as the two cultures clashed head-on, it was the scene of sporadic violence in the 1860s and more formal warfare in the 1870s, with the turbulence practically ended by 1878. For the most part it was an old drama, this last chapter of what Helen Hunt Jackson sentimentally called "A Century of Dishonor," recast and played out on a new stage against the backdrop of the northern plains and Rockies, but its basic themes were familiar: increasing white pressures, corruption of the natives, broken promises, shrinking tribal land holdings and in the end subjugation and assignment to a cultural never-never-land.

Although the number of Montana Indians was never great,

Message to the Legislature, January 25, 1883, *Governors' Messages* (Helena: George Boos, 1883).

and they were scattered and disunited, they were also among the most warlike tribes in America, especially those ranging on the eastern side of the Rocky Mountains—the Blackfeet, Gros Ventre, Assiniboin, Crows, and Sioux. Military men recognized them as the finest cavalry in the world—wily, savage, and superb fighters by any standards. From the time they were old enough to ride, war was a part of their way of life; young Sioux or Blackfeet majored in battle and minored in horse stealing, both traditional and honorable pursuits. Stemming from the exclusive nature of tribalism itself, intertribal warfare was a vital force in their life-style long before the whites ever reached the upper plains. Crows and Sioux were deadly enemies; Flatheads lived in dread of the merciless Blackfeet; and numerous Indian alliances were directed at protection against other tribes. These traditional enmities fragmented the Indians on the northern plains and explain why some—the Crows, for example—would align themselves with the whites against ancient foes. They were not merely "mercenaries," as suggested by writers purporting to give "the Indian's view" of history.

By treaty until 1871 and by executive agreement thereafter, it was federal policy to whittle down Indian land holdings and restrict tribal movement to specified areas. In exchange, Uncle Sam provided annuity goods and equipment and the trappings of a practical education to enable the Indian's moccasined feet to tread the white man's path. One of the earliest treaties for Montana, that of Fort Laramie in 1851, limited the hunting grounds of a number of important tribes, among them the western Sioux, the Gros Ventre, the Assiniboin, the Blackfoot, and the Crow. Four years later the Flatheads were among several western tribes signing the Hell Gate Treaty, agreeing to accept goods and shop, school, and hospital facilities in exchange for a reduction of land. By the same treaty, the Blackfeet were reserved an immense block north of the Missouri River, from the Rockies to the mouth of the Milk, with the area between the Yellowstone and the Missouri as common hunting ground and neutral terrain. At the time, these arrangements seemed practical; soon the discovery of gold would make them unworkable.

First came a trickle, then a small stream of whites bound for the Idaho camps; with the gold strikes in Montana proper, this became a torrent across the hunting reserves. Moreover, from the Indian point of view, these vastly expanding encroachments had a distressing air of permanency about them, although white officials made it clear that the newcomers were not interested in tribal holdings. "We assured them that there was no such intention on the part of their Great White Father," an agent to the Blackfeet said, "that the whites now had by far more land than they could cultivate or know what to do with." Yet only a year later, the agent for the Flatheads worried that proximity of the new Montana goldfields would "soon produce collision between the races, unless prompt and effective measures are taken. . . ." [1]

Even as gold seekers migrated across Indian lands, those heading for Montana formulated stereotyped views of their dusky brethren. At worst, Indians attacked white travelers or drove off their livestock. They begged both food and whiskey, and more than one group of emigrants were offered Gros Ventre women at night in exchange for such commodities. One group was petrified with fear in 1867, when the wagons were halted by mounted Indians near the Milk River. While the captain of the train turned "white as a sheet," Nick Hilgers saved the day by ordering out the brass band, which paved the way to a friendly council with a rattling version of "Yankee Doodle." Later the captain could report that the Indians had been dealt with "rigidly and fearlessly" and that the party had "thrust them from our path." [2]

But slight contact established Montana Indians as lazy, half-naked savages, obstacles in the way of civilization. Some whites saw them as a missionary challenge, but usually not those closest to the scene. "But they are Indians and Indians they will ever remain," snorted John Owen. "To Christianize,

---

1. Quoted in *Annual Report of the Commissioner of Indian Affairs . . . 1862*, p. 323; Quoted in *Annual Report . . . 1863*, p. 572.
2. White, *Ho! For the Gold Fields*, p. 247.

Civilize & Educate the Indian is a farce long Since Exploded.'' [3] Arguing that the grizzly was superior to the Indian because he had a good hide and because he worked for his living, the editor of the *Montana Post* in 1865 pointed up the typical western and Montanan point of view.

> The copper-colored banditti make pack horses of their own women, ravish and enslave all of ours they can lay their hands on, and dry the scalps of our plundered and murdered people in that nest of abominations, an Indian wigwam. . . . It is because we of the mountains know what an Indian is and feel what he does, that we hate him and desire his death.'' [4]

Men of Southern and Northern backgrounds alike might unconsciously be able to transfer their negative feelings about blacks to the native Americans, in whose veins ran evil incarnate:

> —There ain't no trusting an Injun;
> He's a catawampous cuss,
> And when he's a doin of suthin bad,
> He's a wishin ''twas suthin wuss.[5]

Given such attitudes as these and with the opinion common that the Montana Indian "must yield to the advancing tide of Anglo-Saxon supremacy," as an 1882 guidebook put it,[6] it was inevitable that the overwhelming tide of white settlement would soon inundate tribal society.

Reduction of the tribes resulted not merely from superior numbers of whites, but also from the impact of disease, alcohol, and military action. Back in the fur-trade era, horrible unchecked epidemics of smallpox, measles, or syphilis decimated entire camps because Indians lacked any inborn immunity. When the tribes were confined to smaller reservations, the consequences were even more disastrous. Perhaps the worst single scourge was in 1837, when the American Fur Company steamer

3. Dunbar and Phillips, *John Owen*, 1:262.

4. *Montana Post*, June 10, 1865.

5. *Helena Herald*, July 8, 1873.

6. *The Yellowstone Valley and Town of Glendive* (St. Paul: Pioneer Press Co., 1882), p. 8.

carried the deadly stowaway smallpox upriver to eventually take the lives of an estimated seventeen thousand persons among six tribes, including the Assiniboin and the Blackfeet, leaving villages silent and full of rotting corpses.

From the beginning of white contact, whiskey had contributed to a gradual decline of the Indians; settlers and especially some of the unsavory types who followed the mineral booms and who, like the Indians, "need care and attention" by the government, took up where the fur traders left off. Their ware was a lethal concoction of alcohol, river water, tobacco, and red pepper (Mark Twain, who was prone to exaggerate, would add a dash of strychnine, soap, and boil with sagebrush). In the Deer Lodge Valley, the Stuart brothers often complained about drunken Flatheads; and a Blackfoot agent in 1864 grumbled that there "is hardly a boat going up the Missouri but a large portion of the cargo is made up of whiskey, and this leaks out astonishingly in going through the country." [7] Under the nonintercourse acts, such traffic was strictly illegal, but efforts to stifle it met opposition from Fort Benton merchants, and Indians continued to travel "to the Alcohol Springs," as one observer put it,[8] much to their own detriment.

More directly, the white men's bullets took their toll, but not fast enough nor cheaply enough to suit many Montanans. The Commissioner of Indian Affairs in 1868 estimated that it was costing the federal government $1 million for each Indian sent to the Happy Hunting Ground. At times, when federal troops were scarce, Montana citizens were not unwilling to take to the field as volunteers, for there was profit to be made from plunder and from outfitting such enterprises.

As settlement expanded, the tribes grew restless, even the Flatheads, who, Father De Smet had proudly boasted in 1859, had never spilled "a drop of white man's blood." [9] The Black-

---

7. Quoted in *Annual Report of the Commissioner of Indian Affairs . . . 1862*, p. 324; Quoted in *Annual Report . . . 1864*, p. 416.

8. Andrew Garcia, *Tough Trip through Paradise, 1878–1879* (Boston: Houghton Mifflin Co., 1967), p. 21.

9. Quoted in *Annual Report of the Secretary of War . . . 1859*, p. 99.

feet in 1864 were "the most impudent and insulting Indians" their new agent had ever met. Were it not that their treaty soon expired, he remarked, he would recommend payment of their next annuity "in powder and ball from the mouth of a six-pounder." [10] Chief Justice Hezekiah Hosmer believed in 1865 that there would be the "very d——l to pay unless the government sent troops. The Blackfeet, he noted, had killed a dozen men at the mouth of the Marias, and the governor had "made a great fizzle" of getting volunteers to protect the route between Helena and Fort Benton. "We had more Generals and Colonels, etc. etc. than there were in the Army of the Potomac, trying with beat of drum, a great display of flags, and a most melancholy waste of cheap whiskey, to raise 500 men." Only 30 were recruited, plus "about 90 of the hardest looking specimens of horse and mule flesh you ever laid eyes on," and the whole effort collapsed.[11]

Meanwhile, in 1866 federal troops were stationed in the territory. Fort Buford, at the mouth of the Yellowstone, guarded the entrance to Montana; Camp Cooke was located on the south bank of the Missouri, near its juncture with the Judith River. Farther south, garrisons were established to protect the Bozeman Road: Fort Phil Kearny just east of the northern Big Horns; Fort Conner near the upper Powder, re-manned as Fort Reno; while just within the southern boundary of Montana, Fort C. F. Smith was built on the Big Horn River. In 1867, Fort Shaw was established on the Sun River and a cavalry post constructed in the Gallatin Valley—Fort Ellis. But the army was more impressive on paper than in actually keeping peace. Garrisons were small, spent too much time in "moral combats with the Legions of Bourbon," according to one officer,[12] and were badly located for effectiveness. With respect to deployment of troops on the Missouri River, James L. Fisk wondered late in 1866, "what earthly object there can be in this present fancied disposition of

10. Quoted in *Annual Report of the Commissioner of Indian Affairs . . . 1864*, p. 444.

11. Hezekiah Hosmer to Samuel Hauser (Virginia City, June 24, 1865), Hauser MSS, MHS.

12. Quoted in MHS, *Precious Metals*, p. 73.

paid military forces." [13] And difficulties with the Sioux soon forced abandonment of the Bozeman Trail and the closing of Forts Reno, Phil Kearny, and C. F. Smith in August 1868.

Meanwhile, Montanans were thrown largely on their own for protection, with an increasing number of depredations in 1866 and 1867, especially among the Piegans in the north. "I am afraid but little freighting will be done here next spring, without these gentlemen are whipped during the winter," wrote the chief clerk of the Blackfoot agency. [14] In 1867, while Governor Green Clay Smith was in the East and while the legislature was urging Congress to abolish the agency system and put Indian affairs in the hands of the War Department, Acting Governor Thomas Francis Meagher, an Irishman of considerable charm, ambition, and military experience, set out to make political capital of the unstable Indian situation. An impassioned revolutionist in the Young Ireland movement, Meagher had been sentenced to death, then banished to Tasmania, whence he escaped and made his way to the United States. A dazzling orator and a charismatic figure, he had led the Irish Brigade—those Sons of Old Erin making up part of the 19th Regiment—through half a dozen major battles of the Civil War. Now, using as a lever the killing of John Bozeman by renegade Blackfeet along the Yellowstone, Meagher sought War Department authorization to raise eight hundred volunteers to protect the Bozeman Valley. "Not an hour to be lost," he telegraphed. [15]

The department was slow to move, though the commander of the District of the Missouri, of which Montana was a part, gave a nebulous response, which Meagher construed as approval, and he promptly proceeded to outfit and provision troops at exorbitant prices, issuing government vouchers to eager local merchants. Some 150 or 200 men were recruited, most attracted by

13. Quoted in "Expeditions of Captain Jas. L. Fisk to the Gold Mines of Idaho and Montana, 1864–1866," *Collections of the State Historical Society of North Dakota,* 7 vols. (1908), 2:460.

14. Quoted in *Annual Report of the Commissioner of Indian Affairs . . . 1866,* p. 199.

15. Quoted in Robert G. Athearn, *Thomas Francis Meagher: An Irish Revolutionary in America* (Boulder: University of Colorado Press, 1949), p. 160.

the idea of booty or by the need for a stiff policy toward the natives. "The Indians have to be chastized," wrote one volunteer, "& we are going to give them the best in the shop." [16] But there was little contact with the Indians; duty was mainly patrolling communication lines and waiting. As for Meagher—a man who never found a bar he did not like—he reportedly "kept full of whiskey" and "had a merry time in Virginia City" while preparing to take to the field.[17] Instead, he accidentally drowned and found a watery grave in the Missouri. Meanwhile the returned governor, Green Clay Smith, took command, but soon disbanded the militia. Many militiamen decamped with quartermaster and commissary goods, along with 250 horses and mules, and those waiting for proper discharge found no funds and had to take what they could get in rations and horses. At the end of the "campaign," General William T. Sherman was embarrassed to receive warrants owed to Montana suppliers for a total of $983,303.11, a figure challenged by an army inspector, who found ample evidence of padding and overcharging that seemed to bear out the charge of a Helena resident that this "biggest humbug of the age" was "Got up for A Speculation" and to advance Meagher's military career.[18] Ultimately, Montana settled for a little over half a million dollars.

Intermittent raids by Piegans between Helena and Fort Benton in 1868 and 1869 put pressure on another governor, James Ashley, to call out a regiment of volunteers, but Ashley resisted, believing that the success of his administration depended upon keeping the peace. New military posts were established: Camp Cooke, at the mouth of the Judith, was abandoned for a more suitable location at Fort Benton; Camp Baker (later Fort Logan) was built on the Smith River, sixty miles east of Helena. Depredations increased, with the *Helena Herald* estimating that from January to October 1869, at least a thousand horses had

16. Quoted in MHS, *Precious Metals,* p. 57.
17. Herman Francis Reinhart, *The Golden Frontier,* ed. by Doyce Nunis (Austin: University of Texas Press, 1962), p. 264.
18. Snavely to U. S. Grant (Helena, March 1, 1870), Bureau of Indian Affairs Letters, National Archives.

been stolen and fifty-six settlers killed. Word came down from General Philip Sheridan: "If the lives and property of citizens of Montana can best be protected by striking the Indians, I want them struck. Tell Baker to strike them hard." [19] Baker was Major Eugene M. Baker, who moved with troops from Fort Ellis against the Piegans on a January morning in 1870, with the mercury at forty below. Striking up the Marias in search of the band of Mountain Chief, Baker, by mistake, hit the camp of Heavy Runner, who was friendly to the whites, burning it to the ground, killing 173 unresisting Piegans—including 53 women and children—and forcing another hundred out into the cold. But even a case of mistaken identity could be lauded by his superiors, who believed this command "entitled to the special commendation of the Military authorities and the hearty thanks of the Nation. . . ." [20]

Clearly, Montanans in the early 1870s supported Baker's action. They urged more federal troops or companies of volunteers, "to rid the country of the desperate Sons of b——s" on the Milk River and elsewhere.[21] Governor Benjamin Potts was concerned about the Crows, but especially about the Sioux, who were becoming increasingly prickly as pressure upon them mounted. "The opening of the Country from Bozeman to Bismarck I regard as absolutely necessary to the prosperity and growth of Montana," Potts told the Secretary of the Interior early in 1875. "We can have no peace until the Sioux Indians on the Yellowstone are whipped; no other policy will answer the purpose." [22] Soon the governor would have his war against the Sioux.

After the closing of the Bozeman Road in 1868, the Sioux had been reassured by treaty of the Black Hills, plus a much larger hunting ground. But the discovery of gold on Sioux lands, verified in 1874 by an expedition headed by George Cus-

19. Quoted in J. P. Dunn, *Massacres of the Mountains* (New York: Harper, 1886), p. 443.
20. Quoted in MHS, *Precious Metals,* p. 60.
21. A. J. Simmons to Samuel Hauser (Helena, January 4, 1871), Hauser MSS.
22. Potts to Columbus Delano (Virginia City, March 27, 1875), Potts to Delano (Helena, August 6, 1875), Bureau of Indian Affairs Letters, National Archives.

ter, led to white infiltration. After vainly attempting to keep the gold seekers out, the federal government threw up its hands in despair, opened the Black Hills to miners who wished to take the risk, and watched gold seekers pour in by the thousands. When the younger braves slipped off to join non-treaty Indians, authorities ordered them back, despite treaty rights permitting them to hunt. Both Sitting Bull and Crazy Horse refused, whereupon the Indian Bureau dumped the problem in the lap of the army in the spring of 1876.

The Hunkpatilas, Crazy Horse, has been called "one of the great soldiers of his day and generation"—"the bravest of the brave." With Sitting Bull, the combination medicine man–warrior, he had harassed the whites on the Bozeman Road and those surveying for the Union Pacific Railroad. He had fought a series of battles with Custer in the Yellowstone Valley. Now, in 1876, three military columns moved against the Sioux and their Northern Cheyenne allies: one, under General George Crook, moved north from Fort Fetterman; another, led by Colonel John Gibbon, came east from Fort Ellis; while a third, commanded by General Alfred Terry, started west from Fort Abraham Lincoln below Bismarck. Part of Terry's command under Lt. Colonel Custer, whom the Sioux called "the Chief of all the Thieves" since his Black Hills expedition, was sent south along the Rosebud to prevent retreat into the Big Horns.[23] The impatient "Boy General" moved too soon and with 264 of his men became part of the American legend. The enemy were "as thick as bees," and Custer's own, the Seventh Regiment was "entirely used up," as a diarist with Gibbon's wagons said.[24] But in the end, the Sioux and the Northern Cheyenne were forced back to their reservations, and a punitive campaign by Colonel Nelson Miles ("Bear Coat," the Indians called him) and his Fifth Infantry ("walk-a-heaps") effectively broke Sioux power in 1876–1877, except for Sitting Bull's band, which fled to Canada until 1881.

A year after the Custer debacle, the Nez Perce under young

23. Alvin J. Josephy, Jr., *The Patriot Chiefs* (1961; New York: Viking Press, 1969 ed.), pp. 259, 292.

24. Quoted in MHS, *Precious Metals*, p. 79.

Chief Joseph gave settlers in western Montana a fright they would long remember. A peaceful people, bitter over the loss of their traditional Wallowa lands in the region where Idaho, Oregon, and Washington converged, the Nez Perce had been driven by injustice into hostility. Fighting troops under the one-armed "Christian general," O. O. Howard, they slipped eastward over the Lolo Trail into Montana, bringing women, children, horses, cattle, and baggage with them. Warned by telegraph, Missoula troops and a couple of hundred volunteers threw up a log fort across the eastern end of the route. But the volunteers faded away, and the Indians moved easily around "Fort Fizzle," as the site was called, and on leisurely into the Big Hole Valley, where they were hit by Gibbon and units from Fort Shaw. Giving an excellent account of themselves, they proceeded through Yellowstone Park, capturing tourists en route but failing to enlist Crow support, fought a skirmish near Billings, crossed the Missouri at Cow Island, then, feeling secure, went into camp at the foot of the Bear Paws, only forty miles short of the Canadian border. But again they were outflanked by the "singing wires" of the telegraph which summoned Miles from Fort Keogh. After a hard fight, the Nez Perce gave in, and Joseph is supposed to have given his famous lyrical surrender speech which kindled the imaginations of so many Americans: "Hear me, my chiefs. I am tired; my heart is sick and sad. From where the sun now stands I will fight no more, forever." [25] Whether Joseph actually uttered these words or not is immaterial; they were attributed to him and made him the symbol of and endowed upon him the responsibility for the strategy and success of that magnificent retreat, deserved or not; and the words gained sympathy for his people. But he never returned to the high, grassy plateaus of the Wallowa country; he died in exile on the Colville reservation in Washington.

If Montana's Indian wars came to an end with this episode, the tribes were already at the mercy of the whites and were being forced to adapt, to accept new values, whether they

---

25. Quoted in Joseph K. Howard, ed., *Montana Margins* (New Haven: Yale University Press, 1946), p. 48.

wished or not. By destroying the buffalo, the invaders left the Indians dependent upon the federal government. Not by accident did the Indian-head nickel have the bison on the other side: providing food, clothing, and shelter materials, the great shaggy beasts were an integral part of the Indian way of life. At the time of the Civil War there were an estimated 13 million buffalo left. The great northern herd ranged through the Powder River country and into Canada. Travelers in 1866 encountered "an innumerable herd" on the Milk River "and remained in it for six days, the buffalo surrounding us on all sides as far as the eye could reach." [26] One member of the party guessed there were 600,000 head; some went as high as 6 million, probably both too much. In 1877 a Montana rancher, returning from driving cattle to the railroad at Cheyenne, had to stop three days and three nights in the Yellowstone Valley to let the northern herd drift by. But ten years later, a Smithsonian Institution expedition to the same area was able to find 25 buffalo only with difficulty. The vast herds were gone.

Sportsmen and professional hunters slaughtered them without restraint; many animals went to feed the railroad builders; but the big carnage came after a Pennsylvania tannery adopted a German method of making leather from the hides. Beginning in the seventies, the hide hunters began to scour the plains, dropping the buffalo by the hundreds with their .45 or .50 caliber Sharps, Spencer, or Henry rifles at a thousand yards and leaving the carcasses to rot.

> The buffalo skinner stacks the reeking pelt;
> One stench of rotting carcass drowns the plain;
> Buzzard and coyote, and fly have smelt
> The offense, but all their scavengery is vain
> To sweeten any breeze. . . .[27]

One visitor in the summer of 1881 noted a "large party of butchers" killing buffalo about twenty miles north of Fort Keogh at the rate of about a hundred a day and thought it "a

26. Quoted in White, *Ho! For the Gold Fields*, p. 189.
27. From Edwin Ford Piper, "Once On a Time," *Barbed Wire and Wayfarers* (New York: Macmillan, 1924), pp. 6–7.

burning shame and a disgrace" that "this infamous and damnable traffic" be permitted.[28] Isaac P. Baker, steamboat captain on the Yellowstone and the Missouri, estimated that in the two years 1881 and 1882, his vessels had carried a quarter of a million buffalo hides from Montana.

Soon human scavengers ranged out to collect the bleaching bones to be shipped east for fertilizer, to make handles, or to provide carbon used in refining sugar. Beginning about 1883, the bone trade flourished along the rivers and the railroad. Piled high, ready to be picked up was a

> Mountainous wreckage, shin and back confused,
> Crowned with horny skulls grotesquely menacing.[29]

But nobody stopped the slaughter—and for good reason. From Washington, the Secretary of the Interior had reported in 1873 that he ". . . would not seriously regret the total disappearance of the buffalo from our western prairies, in its effect upon the Indians, regarding it rather as a means of hastening their sense of dependence upon the products of the soil and their own labors." [30] In other words, starve the Indians into submitting to the white man's way of life. General Philip Sheridan, in charge of the Army of the West, once made the same point, when he spoke of the role of the buffalo hunters:

> These men have done in the last two years and will do more in the next year, to settle the vexed Indian question, than the entire regular army has done in the last thirty years. They are destroying the Indians' commissary. . . . For the sake of a lasting peace, let them kill, skin, and sell until the buffalo are exterminated. Then your prairies can be covered with speckled cattle, and the festive cowboy. . . .[31]

All the while, federal policy sought to settle the Indian on smaller amounts of land, throwing open the surplus to white set-

---

28. G. O. Shields, *Rustlings in the Rockies: Hunting and Fishing by Mountain and Stream* (Chicago: Belford, Clarke & Co., 1883), p. 55.

29. From Edwin Ford Piper, "Dry Bones," *Barbed Wire and Wayfarers,* pp. 4–5.

30. Quoted in *Annual Report of the Secretary of Interior . . . 1873,* 2 vols. 1:vi.

31. Quoted in John R. Cook, *The Border and the Buffalo* (Topeka: Crance & Co., 1907), p. 113.

tlement, and whether he wanted it or not, to make of him something he was not. Excluded was the possibility that Indians might prefer their own traditional ways. Why should a tribe abandon age-old customs and give up the hunt in favor of tilling the soil? As Sitting Bull once asked, why should the Sioux have anything to do with a people who makes a brave "carry water on the shoulders and haul manure?" [32] Or why should the Flatheads give any but a negative response when whites, trying to pry them from their beloved Bitterroot Valley, suggested taxing their lands. As an unidentified spokesman for the tribe pointed out, white ". . . laws never gave us a blade of grass nor a tree, nor a duck, nor a grouse, nor a trout. No; like the wolverine that steals your cache, how often does he come? You know he comes as long as he lives, and takes more and more—and dirties what he leaves." [33]

With the Indian's land and his freedom both restricted and his ability to hunt being sorely limited, the federal government was less than effective in providing substitutes and preparing the unwilling charges for their new role. If officials negotiating treaties were ignorant, and, muttered one old-timer, "knew as much about an Indian as I did about the inhabitants of Jupiter," [34] resident agents were frequently not much better. Often they were political appointees, and their positions offered opportunity for graft and corruption. Even outsiders noted the

. . . sudden and wonderful change in the pecuniary circumstances of Indian agents, often from comparative poverty to wealth and affluence, enabling them to build costly mansions, give splendid entertainments, and fare sumptuously every day, and all on simply a living salary of fifteen hundred dollars a year. . . .[35]

32. Quoted in Charles Larpenteur, *Forty Years a Fur Trader on the Upper Missouri,* 2 vols. (New York: F. P. Harper, 1898), 2:429.

33. Quoted in Howard, *Montana Margins,* p. 19.

34. Quoted in George Bird Grinnell, *Beyond the Old Frontier* (New York, 1913), p. 357.

35. Edwin J. Stanley, *Rambles in Wonderland: or, Up the Yellowstone, and Among the Geysers and Other Curiosities of the National Park* (New York: D. Appleton & Co., 1878), p. 23.

Tribes complained, with monotonous frequency, that treaty obligations were not being met, that annuity goods were not suitable or that they were inferior. The Flatheads had no use for "tons of coffee, rice, and Hardbread;" they wanted red blankets, not blue. The musty coffee sent them had been sunk in the Missouri and raised; shawls and flannels were "Miserable flimsey things No Earthly use," said John Owen.[36] According to an army office in 1878, the Crows had received inferior beef, fine light overcoats with velvet collars, Cashmere pants and vest, all of which they traded away immediately. Frequently agents were charged with making large issues of rations on paper but only a fraction in practice.

Even President Grant's Quaker policy—the appointment of agents designated by various religious denominations—did not solve all the problems. Agents needed qualifications besides their "Christian character," it was pointed out by Montanans who complained that "these psalm-singing Methodist ministers" spent more time proselytizing than in practical worldly matters.[37] Probably this is what humorist Bill Nye's Idaho chief meant when he tersely commented, "Ugh! Too much God and no flour." [38] Agents under the Quaker policy were Protestant, but one of the stories going around was of a Jewish rabbi who was so determined to convert his wards, popularly thought to be the Lost Tribes of Israel, that with army assistance he circumcised them "as fast as they were brought in," whereupon the Indians threw their gear together "and leaned toward Canada" posthaste. Hearing that result, goes the story, presidential candidate Horace Greeley promised former Governor Ashley that if he was elected, all his Indian agents would be rabbis! [39]

Even apart from shady dealings of agents, there was money to be made, and legitimately, from the Indians. When the events

36. Dunbar and Phillips, *John Owen*, 2:210, 231.

37. W. F. Chadwick to Martin Maginnis (Helena, November 23, 1873), Maginnis MSS, MHS.

38. Bill Nye [Edgar Wilson Nye], *Baled Hay* (Chicago: W. B. Conkey Co., 1893), p. 235.

39. *Helena Herald*, August 19, 1872.

of 1876 and 1877 brought additional army posts and troops, local entrepreneurs like Samuel Hauser saw economic advantage and urged Montana's delegate to push for Helena as district military headquarters; such a plum, he believed, would double property values. Montanans like Charles Broadwater and Thomas C. Power would profit handsomely from supplying hay to the army, beef to Indian agencies, and from general trade with both. Broadwater kept the post store at Fort Assiniboine; Power financed the trader at Fort Shaw for many years. Power and I. G. Baker both provided capital for the Whoop-Up traders and by 1870 controlled much of the merchandising that flowed north from Fort Benton to the Blackfoot nation, with considerable traffic to the Crows, Gros Ventre, and Assiniboin as well. In his early career, at least, Power would be strongly criticized for selling whiskey, rifles, and ammunition to Indians. Obviously, some Montanans found lucrative business with Indians and the military. In opposing reduced expenditures for Indian affairs and consolidation of agencies in 1877, Power could argue that "the cutting down and abandonment of any Indian agency will hurt Montana—especially those in close proximity as [the Indians] spend considerable money." [40]

Even more central to Indian policy was land. One of the earliest official acts of the first legislature was to complain to Washington that "only a small fragment of land embraced within the boundaries of this Territory" was open for settlement. [41] Montana policy was constant pressure on both Indians and federal government for reduction of the amount of lands in tribal hands, a policy successful in trimming down Indian holdings from almost all its more than 95 million acres to just under 11 million by 1889. Idealistic belief in the Indian as a Christianized agrarian was fine—in the future; but when the time came, it was apparent that the Indian was basically bloodthirsty and improvident and thus disqualified. "We deny the Indian right to the lands," said the editor of the *Montana Post* in 1865, "Robbers

---

40. Quoted in Paul F. Sharp, *Whoop-Up Country* (Norman: University of Oklahoma Press, 1973), p. 221.

41. *Laws of Montana Territory* (1st Session, 1864–1865), p. 721.

and murderers have no such rights." [42] Nor did the Indian till the soil according to the Biblical injunction; destiny had meant the white farmer to put the land to superior use. When the federal government was slow in opening more Indian land, indignant Montanans invoked theoretical arguments on human rights, white only, and the natural functions of government. Or, like frontiersmen of every era, they proceeded ahead of the extinguishment of Indian title, confident and usually correct that official sanction would be forthcoming.

The most flagrant example undoubtedly was the treatment of the Flatheads, a small tribe with a history of peaceful coexistence with whites from the time of Lewis and Clark, and who gave up much land in 1855, retaining some 1.25 million acres of their traditional homeland in the Bitterroot Valley, but with an alternative clause which allowed the President to determine whether it would be better in the long run for them to move to a new reservation on Flathead Lake and the Jocko River. When the government failed in its promise to keep white farmers and ranchers out of the Bitterroot Valley, settlers, in turn, pushed the buffalo herds into Blackfoot country where, without federal protection, the Flatheads found hunting impossible. Soon it became clear that the Bitterroot was too good for Indians, and pressure mounted for their removal—"to protect them from the vices incident to a . . . connection with the Whites," according to Governor Potts in 1871. [43] Admittedly, the whites were trespassers, but by this time they outnumbered the Flatheads three to one, and Montanans argued that their agricultural products were required to feed the territory's growing population. When the Indians, under Charlot, demurred, President Grant declared that the Jocko reservation was indeed more suitable than the Bitterroot Valley and ordered them to move. Charlot still refused to budge. Grant sent Congressman James A. Garfield of Ohio to negotiate, and in the summer of 1872, Garfield brought back a treaty, supposedly signed by Flathead chiefs, including Charlot, consenting to removal to the Jocko. But soon it became obvious

42. *Montana Post,* June 10, 1865.
43. Quoted in MHS, *Precious Metals,* p. 62.

that Charlot had not in fact affixed his X to the original document and that he and his 350 or so followers had no travel
plans. However, Congress by law stipulated transfer of the
Flatheads and threw open the Bitterroot Valley north of the Lolo
Fork to actual settlers. A number of Flathead families did move
to the Jocko lands, and this minority group under subchief Arlee
would be recognized as legitimate recipients of the annuity
goods authorized by the old Hell Gate Treaty. Meanwhile, the
main band suffered; the buffalo vanished, their hunting was
sharply curtailed, and government aid was withdrawn until
1885, when after Charlot had visited Washington, the first supplies in twelve years arrived. Finally, in 1891, a bitter and
beaten Charlot led the rest of his people onto the Jocko reservation, damning the federal government as he did so. "You are
liars," he said. "I do not believe you. My young men have no
place to hunt, they get whiskey, they are bad. My women and
children are hungry; I will go." [44]

The story of other Montana tribes is perhaps less shocking,
but the end results were no different. Lands controlled by the
Crows went in 1851 from about a quarter of Montana, including
much of the rich drainage system of the Yellowstone, to a mere
5 million acres in 1868, an area still "large enough and fertile
enough for a great State," as the governor pointed out a decade
later. [45] One-fourth of the reservation went in 1882, but the
remainder stayed intact, despite Montanans' petitions to open
the lands west of the Big Horn to settlement in order to relieve
the Crows of "the evil influences of the opportunities and
machinations of designing speculators." [46] And how Montana
residents complained in 1884 when 371,000 acres on the Rosebud, just east of the Crow lands, were set aside from the
public domain for the Northern Cheyenne.

Where in 1864 most of the northern and central portions of

44. Quoted in Phillips, *Forty Years on the Frontier*, 2:94.

45. Report of the Governor of Montana, 1879, in *Annual Report of the Secretary of
Interior . . . 1879*, p. 44.

46. Memorial to Congress, in *Laws of Montana Territory* (14th Session, 1885),
pp. 236–237.

the territory were held by the Blackfeet, Piegans, Bloods, Gros Ventres, and Assiniboin, the whites chipped away persistently, and succeeded in opening large blocks in 1873 and 1880, although even at the later date 21 million acres remained in the hands of the northern tribes, and newspapers complained that fully one-third of the entire territory was tied up in reservations inhabited by 18,000 Indians. This included millions of acres of "the finest agricultural and grazing lands to be found on the continent," according to Governor Hauser, who was soon suggesting that for the Indians Oklahoma, "a country further south, with more natural rainfall, would suit them better." [47] Finally, in 1888, the great northern reservation was sharply diminished and nearly 18 million acres thrown open for settlement. A small-scale stampede followed. "Nearly every one in the northern part of the territory who can raise a camping outfit and a cayuse or mule has left or is about to leave for that land of promise," observed a Helena editor, five days after the opening was announced. [48]

Only the year before, under pressure from those who saw that land would be released and from humanitarians who believed that the Indians would benefit, Congress had passed the Dawes Act, which would give individual land allotments. The law was not widely applied in Montana, but over a twenty-year period, the Flatheads would lose more than half their Jocko reservation under its operation, although few Flatheads moved in the process from ordinary tribesmen to rugged, propertied individuals. By 1910, the amount of Montana land in Indian hands was about 6 million acres, roughly the current figure.

By the end of the seventies, only minor military mopping-up operations continued; by the end of the eighties, only minor Indian land-shrinkage operations continued. By the end of the territorial period, Montana's Indians were neither of the old nor the new. Restricted in economic base and in the ability to pur-

47. Report of the Governor of Montana, 1885, in *Annual Report of the Secretary of Interior . . . 1885*, p. 1000; Report of the Governor of Montana, 1886, in *Annual Report of the Secretary of Interior . . . 1886*, p. 833.

48. *Montana Live Stock Journal*, May 5, 1888.

6

Territorial Politics and Government

*"Nothing but Political
Insomnia and Internal Unrest"*

*C*ONGREGATE a hundred Americans anywhere beyond
the settlements, and they immediately lay out a city, frame a
state constitution and apply for admission into the Union, while
twenty-five of them become candidates for the United States
Senate.'' [1] So wrote the veteran newspaperman and western
traveler Albert Richardson, who visited Montana in 1865. Early
Montanans were no exceptions: even though engrossed in the
scramble for wealth, they were very much political animals who
were concerned with stability, protection of property rights, and
a measure of democracy at the local level and with the national
scene as well. Because their interest was strong and they tended
to take their politics personally and vigorously—straight, without a chaser, as it were—the young territory's political history
would be both fiery and acrimonious.

Tradition has it that the left wing of General Sterling Price's
Missouri army was not really defeated in the Civil War but

Congressional Record, 50 Cong., 2 Sess. (1888–1889), p. 822.
1. Albert D. Richardson, *Beyond the Mississippi* (Hartford: American Publishing
Co., 1867), p. 177.

merely retreated upriver and set out to hold Montana for the
Confederacy until stalwart Republicans prevented it. No doubt
this is an exaggeration and distortion, but clearly when President Lincoln, in May 1864, signed the new Territory of Montana into being, the area harbored an explosive mixture of political sentiments. Long linked with St. Louis via the Missouri
River highway, Montana had an obvious and vociferous bloc of
Southern sympathizers, as place names like Dixie or Confederate Gulch would indicate. One of the territory's pioneer women,
Mary Ronan, recalled that when the news of Lincoln's assassi-
nation reached Virginia City, "The Southern girls, by far the
majority, picked up their ankle-length skirts to their knees and
jigged and hippety-hopped around and around the room cheering. . . ." Extremists like Nathaniel P. Langford, who had to
collect federal taxes, believed that "Four-fifths of our citizens
were *openly declared* Secessionists" and that Montana was
"more disloyal as a whole, than Tennessee or Kentucky ever
was." [2] Like the good Republican he was, Langford overstated
his case; but the fact remains that, while reflecting a minority
point of view, "secesh" opinions were no myth but were strong
enough to color the political life of the territory's early years.

At the same time, Montana also had its large group of northern Democrats, critical of the war at times, but loyal. John
Owen, for example, railed against "Mr. Lincoln's reign of
Blood & Terror," but made it clear that he supported the
Union.[3] Branded as traitors and Copperheads by the Unionists,
these northern Democrats often joined with the southern wing to
form a majority. Republicans were also split: the Lincoln
Unionists welcomed northern Democrat support; the Radicals
stood unequivocally for the crushing of the South and equality
for blacks. Especially vocal and spirited, the badly outnumbered
Republican extremists would, for years to come, fan Demo-

2. H. G. Merriam, ed., *Frontier Woman* (Missoula: University of Montana Publications in History, 1973), p. 31; Langford to J. W. Taylor (Virginia City, May 20, 1866),
copy, Nathaniel Langford MSS, Minnesota Historical Society, St. Paul.

3. Dunbar and Phillips, *John Owen*, 1:273, 274.

cratic flames by "Waving the Bloody Shirt"—i.e. re-fighting the Civil War—at election time.

This was the situation in the spring of 1864, when the newly first appointed governor, Sidney Edgerton, set out to organize the territorial machinery from a curtained-off corner of his log cabin in Bannack. Formerly chief justice of the Territory of Idaho, of which Montana had been a part, Edgerton had been instrumental in Washington in breaking Montana away as a separate political unit. In keeping with long established practice, the new territorial government was designed as temporary, until an expanding and maturing population warranted statehood. To aid him (or sometimes to hinder him), the governor would have a secretary, a kind of combined fiscal officer and lieutenant governor; three judges appointed by the President, with dual territorial and federal jurisdictions; an elected legislature; and a delegate—also popularly chosen—who spoke but could not vote in Congress.

Even when naming Bannack the temporary capital, Edgerton's Radical Republicanism came through. Virginia City had too many Copperheads in it, his wife said. The first election of delegate and legislators was fought over the great national issue: unionism versus traitorism, as the Republicans saw it. The Union standard-bearer was Wilbur F. Sanders, the essence of Montana Republicanism for nearly half a century. Lawyer, Civil War veteran, vigilante, Sanders was a master of charm and invective, but he was no compromiser: right was right and wrong was wrong. "His soul was as imperious as ever was Caesar's," a contemporary wrote, "and his tongue was perpetually firing poisoned arrows. . . . He was not always right, but he always meant to be right." [4] But for Sanders, 1864 was the first of four Republican defeats for the delegateship; the combined Democrats elected portly Sam McLean, and the first legislature was split—the council Unionist, the house Democratic, in each case by a single vote.

When the assembly convened in mid-December, Governor Edgerton tactlessly denounced the Confederacy in blunt terms

4. Charles C. Goodwin, *As I Remember Them* (Salt Lake City, 1913), p. 326.

and insisted that all members subscribe to the "Iron Clad Oath" that Congress had prescribed for elected or appointed federal officers, even hinting no oath, no pay. One, John Rogers of Deer Lodge, who had ridden with Confederate General "Pap" Price in Missouri, refused and was denied his seat, but would be re-elected and seated two years later without question. Proceeding with enactment of laws of a general nature, including a ban on blacks testifying against whites in court or in voting, the legislature then adjourned without making provision for the convening of the next assembly. Again, part of the problem was political and linked to the intransigence of a Republican governor and the strong force of Democratic legislators. Edgerton had vetoed a bill to set off election districts and increase the assembly membership because it did not take population shifts into account and that body made no attempt to override, realizing that the districting carried out in 1864, if retained, would be most likely to return a Democratic legislature.

At this point, in the autumn of 1865, Edgerton departed and handed over the reins of government to the dynamic, dramatic Thomas Francis Meagher, a newly arrived secretary and now acting governor, who reaped the whirlwind. Meagher—ambitious and intensively political—was a Democrat and no fire-eating Radical. Neither was he, at first, in complete accord with the Democrats in the territory, many of whom he saw as still "favourers and abettors of treason." [5] What Montana needed, he confided to a friend, was "a strong infusion of . . . Celtic blood to counteract the acidity and poverty of its present population." [6]

Initially, Meagher sided with the Republicans that specific federal authorization was required before another legislature could convene. But soon he admitted that he had misjudged the Democrats: Southern sympathizers and all, they could be relied

5. Meagher to William Seward (Virginia City, December 11, 1865), Territorial Papers Montana, Department of State, National Archives.

6. Meagher to George W. Pepper (Virginia City, January 20, 1866) in *Calendar of the Montana Papers in the William Andrews Clark Memorial Library* (Los Angeles: Southern California Historical Records Survey Project, 1942), p. 68.

upon by the administration. It was the Republicans, especially that "unrelenting and unscrupulous" Sanders, who were the blackguards, he decided.[7] Reversing himself, he called the legislature together using the old districting. That the result was a thoroughly Democratic body made Meagher the center of furious protest, which increased in intensity and bitterness when the "Acting One" also called a constitutional convention in the hopes that Montana could be made a state—and a Democratic state. He had, cried the Republicans, surrendered to the turncoats and "Missouri bushwhackers." Much capital was made of his ill-concealed affair with John Barleycorn ("The legislature met today," one diarist recorded, "the Governor called the House to order the Governor very drunk." [8]) Twice Meagher "lost" his father, one Republican editor charged, and required an "Irish wake" each time.

Meagher called a third legislative assembly to meet in the winter of 1866–1867. Before it gathered, a new governor had arrived to relieve him at least momentarily. A Kentucky Union Democrat and an officer in both the Mexican and Civil wars, the new executive, Green Clay Smith, had served in Congress and had been a contender for nomination as Lincoln's running mate in 1864. While the third assembly convened (some called it the Jeff Davis legislature because of its Democrat composition), Governor Smith, Sanders, and one of the Republican judges who had held it and the prior session illegal, all used their influence in Washington to have Congress nullify all laws of both sessions and authorize the governor to establish new districts and call new elections. Reaction in Montana split along party lines, and nullification was the focal issue of the political campaign of 1867, in which Sanders was pitted against James M. Cavanaugh, a genial Irishman whose wit, eloquence, and sarcasm was matched only by that of his opponent. Cavanaugh swept the polls; only one Republican was elected to the legislature and he was not seated. Swiftly censuring the Republican

7. Meagher to Andrew Johnson (Virginia City, January 29, 1866), Andrew Johnson MSS, Library of Congress.
8. Entry for March 5, 1866, Diary of Neil Howie, MHS.

judges for having dabbled "in the filthy pool of politics," [9] the assembly laboriously re-enacted all the laws voided by Congress, but it was years before the courts laid to rest all the questions arising from the controversy. Four decades later a former delegate still called it "the most unjust act ever perpetrated by the Congress of the United States on a Territory." [10] But basically it had been a political squabble arising from the emotion-charged Civil War era; it had been a matter of which party should control the legislature. In the end, the Republican Congress acted in support of the Republicans in Montana.

The well-liked and vigorous Governor Smith (he had clubbed a drunken Irishman with a fence stake at Fort Benton in 1867) resigned late in 1868 and was replaced by James M. Ashley of Ohio, an abolitionist and advocate of stern Republicanism who had led the fight to impeach Andrew Johnson. As chairman of the House Committee on the Territories for several years, he had an excellent grasp, from the Washington point of view, of the workings of territorial government; and he had been instrumental in the creation of Montana. Almost immediately Ashley was in trouble, first when he challenged the right of the legislature to convene in the winter of 1869, subsequently when he tried to push his rock-ribbed Republican views upon the overwhelmingly Democratic assembly. He appointed a black as a notary public; he insisted, without success, that the territorial election law copy the exact words of the Fifteenth Amendment to safeguard minority voting rights. He became embroiled in a running controversy with the council over territorial appointments. Ashley proposed a list of Republicans acceptable to him; the council rejected it and countered with a compromise roster, part Democrat, part Republican, which the governor declined. Over a period of time, the council had rejected fourteen of his nominations for superintendent of public instruction and eighteen each for auditor and treasurer. Only Ashley's successor could find a solution to the problem.

9. *Council Journal,* 4 Session (1867), p. 231.

10. Martin Maginnis, "Thomas Francis Meagher," *Contributions to the Historical Society of Montana; with its Transactions, Officers and Members,* 10 vols. 6 (1907): 106.

Hardly had Ashley warmed the governor's chair, when President Grant somewhat capriciously removed him, much to the Ohioan's distress. "I came here for the express purpose of making this strong hold of democracy, Republican," he said, and had gambled his political future on achieving that end.[11] Inflexible and unwilling to temporize, he ran smack up against what was a truism, at least for the time being: "Montana is Democratic, and no governor, clique, faction or 'sorehead' can make it otherwise." [12]

But time could dilute Democrat strength and mitigate harsh Civil War antipathies; and an especially able governor, Benjamin Franklin Potts, would be able to work harmoniously with factions of both parties in a kind of no-party arrangement that was much to Montana's advantage. A member of the Ohio senate and friend of both James A. Garfield and Rutherford B. Hayes, Potts had been one of Sherman's best young division commanders on his march to the sea. Because of his enormous physical size, Sherman had called him his "Sample Vandal." [13] When he arrived in Virginia City in the summer of 1870, Potts was amazed to find "a well ordered community" and "as much refinement here among the ladies as you find in almost any of our country towns in Ohio." Like Ashley, he expressed his hope of winning Montana for the Republican party. When, with his help, a Republican was elected delegate in the fall of 1871, he could crow to Hayes, "We have redeemed Montana from the misrule of the left wing of Prices Army [*sic.*] and elected a noble specimen of a man to Congress." [14] But his exultation was premature: not until 1888 would another GOP delegate be sent to Washington.

Potts would serve until 1883, nearly half of the territorial

11. Ashley to Hamilton Fish (Helena, January 23, 1870), Hamilton Fish MSS, Library of Congress.

12. *Daily Rocky Mountain Gazette,* July 21, 1870.

13. John Sherman to U. S. Grant (Washington, March 8, 1869), with endorsement by William T. Sherman, Potts file, Appointment Papers, Department of the Interior, National Archives.

14. Potts to Rutherford B. Hayes (Virginia City, August 31, 1870), Potts to Hayes (Virginia City, August 17, 1871), Rutherford B. Hayes MSS, Hayes Library, Fremont, Ohio.

period. From the beginning he made it clear that he would run not only the executive branch of government but also the party machinery. In this, he was sharply challenged by Wilbur F. Sanders and the influential Fisk brothers and soon came to realize that local Democrat support was as important as that of right-wing Montana Republicans. There were six Fisks, four of whom—all Union veterans—had arrived with the Minnesota expeditions of gold seekers in the 1860s; but it was the eldest, Robert, editor of the *Helena Herald,* the most influential newspaper in the territory, who would lead the bitter anti-Potts campaign for nearly thirteen years. Sanders, whom Potts called "the most unscrupulous man that ever disgraced the legal profession," added his weight, helped lobby for the governor's removal and opposed this "vandal" executive on a number of important issues. The Fisk-Sanders coalition abused Potts scurrilously in the press: this selfish, calculating "Apotheosis of Avoirdupose [*sic.*]" was incompetent: Montanans ought to be ashamed of "this gubernatorial specimen of imbicility," "this pensioner on public alms," whose "intellectual limitations are about those of a Saddle Rock oyster." [15] Potts returned in kind, charging that scoundrels were at him from all sides. Fisk was "a professional blackmailer," a destroyer of the party and "totally without character for truth." Sanders was a mere disappointed office-seeker, "bankrupt in morals, purse and reputation." [16]

One of the issues was party patronage and its control. Montana Republicans believed that they, not a governor appointed from Washington, should have a strong voice in determining such federal appointments as postmasters, Indian agents, U.S. attorneys, or land-office personnel in the territory. Potts, on his part, made it one of his basic creeds to make sure that none "of

15. Potts to Hayes (Helena, December 28, 1878), Decius Wade file, Appointment Papers, Department of Justice, National Archives; *Helena Herald,* September 25, 1873; October 7, December 23, 1874; February 1, 1875.

16. Potts to Zachariah Chandler (Helena, September 1, 1876), Robert E. Fisk file, Potts to Carl Schurz (Helena, November 14, 1878), James H. Mills file, Potts to Schurz (Helena June 7, 1877), Potts file, Appointment Papers, Department of the Interior, National Archives.

the tools of Sanders & Fisks'' received political plums in Montana,[17] and in this was successful on a number of occasions.

Another issue was territorial printing, a lucrative business contracted out to private publishers. Potts complained that Fisk had the lion's share and sought by various means to limit his portion. When the rival *Independent* received more of the work printing laws and journals, Fisk flayed that ''Hippo-Pottsimus'' [18] viciously and kept up a running fight over printing benefits that spanned much of the 1870s.

Another issue came over public support of railroads. By the early seventies, Montanans were splitting in two groups: one in favor of a north-south link to the Union Pacific in Utah; the other backing, as did Potts at first, the east-west Northern Pacific, stalled in 1873 east of the Montana border. In 1872 and 1873, Fisk and Sanders joined with entrepreneur Sam Hauser to pressure Potts into calling a special legislative session to consider territorial subsidies for the north-south line. Hauser, a Democrat who had migrated from Missouri at the time of the Civil War, had substantial holdings in mining, milling, and banking and was one of the most important political manipulators in Montana and was not without influence in Washington. Into the subsidy campaign he put much energy, not a few greenbacks ''& considerable bad whiskey.'' [19] In time, Potts would have business links with Hauser and would support subsidy for the Utah and Northern, but not before the issue had been added to the differences with the Fisk-Sanders coalition for several years. And in the end there would be no subsidy: the Utah and Northern built into Butte on its own in 1880 and before long would link up with the Northern Pacific pushing across from the east.

A parallel controversy raged over the location of the capital. Seated by the first legislature at Virginia City, it weathered several early efforts to remove it to Helena and to Deer Lodge, that

17. Potts to Francis Servis (Helena, September 30, 1876), in James A. Garfield MSS, Library of Congress.

18. *Helena Herald,* March 18, 1876.

19. Edward Stone to Potts (Missoula, December 23, 1872), Benjamin F. Potts MSS, Montana Historical Society.

"little village on the trail to Bear," as James Cavanaugh called it.[20] When, in 1874, voters were asked to decide between Helena and Virginia City, preliminary returns showed a victory for Helena, but at the canvassing board, because of improper forms and transpositions, the votes favored Virginia City. A grand jury agreed; the courts ordered a re-canvass, which was done by Secretary James Callaway in Pott's absence, and Helena was awarded the prize.

The dispute generated strong anti-Callaway opposition. Potts at first supported him, but when the capital moved to Helena and Callaway refused either to resign the secretaryship or to move from Virginia City, Potts turned against him, referring to him as "a drunken little scrub" and urging his removal by the President "as a personal favor." [21] Fisk and Sanders stood solidly behind Callaway and joined him in itemizing a list of grievances against Potts and carrying to Washington their fight to oust him. But Potts waged an aggressive campaign of his own, drew bipartisan support, and won. As Delegate Martin Maginnis put it, "The Governor walked over the course in Washington. The President took him to his bosom and sent him home happy." [22]

Despite bitter opposition, Potts was an effective governor and brought a good measure of political and economic stability to the territory. He preached economy and sound management. When the legislature ignored his recommendation to do away with the laws making it possible to vote officials extra compensation—actions which had plunged the territory $130,000 in debt by October 1872, Potts used his influence in Washington to get congressional prohibitions. Behind the scenes he suggested to friends in Congress where waste might be cut from Montana appropriations and he warned the Secretary of the Interior

20. Quoted in Phillips, *Forty Years on the Frontier*, 2:35.

21. Potts to Rutherford B. Hayes (Helena, July 5, 1876), Hayes MSS; Potts to Hayes (Helena, March 6, 1877), Potts file, Potts to W. A. Knapp (Helena, February 22, 1877), James A. Mills file, Appointment Papers, Department of the Interior.

22. Maginnis to Samuel Hauser (Redwing, Minnesota, June 5, 1877), Samuel Hauser MSS, Montana Historical Society.

against "human vultures" who would divert money from the Sioux.[23]

"Extravagance must be checked and economy exercised," he told the legislature at home in 1873. "No people exist so rich and powerful that prodigality and corruption cannot destroy." [24] By that time his cheese-paring program had already started the territorial debt of $158,300 on a downward trend; already he had re-funded the debt at a lower rate and from time to time would prod the legislature to do so again. Although he could never limit county debts, by 1883 he could announce that for the first time the territorial treasury had a surplus. Part of this was the result of broader tax levies, more efficient collection, and fewer exemptions, but mine owners never did pay their share. Potts was quick to veto money bills he thought excessive and to demand frugality in government operation. According to one story, he rejected a voucher from the warden of the penitentiary for two dollars per convict for toothbrushes. "I consider this item an extravagant and useless expenditure," Potts is supposed to have written. "If the hotels in Montana can get along with one toothbrush, I don't see why the Territorial Penitentiary can't do the same!" [25]

To the end Potts remained a loyal Republican. But he failed to unify his own party and came to depend as much upon Democrat support as upon Republican. He caught the backwash of earlier political battles, which gradually grew less acute; during his administrations there was no longer the bitter, deep-seated, cross-party enmity toward the governor that had existed before. Potts had the ability to give and take and pragmatically accepted the fact that Montana was not a Republican stronghold.

Part of the reason for Potts's success was Martin Maginnis, the "Little Giant of Montana," whose tenure as territorial delegate overlapped much of that of Potts in the governor's chair. A Minnesotan with an impressive war record and proprietor of the

23. Potts to Garfield (Virginia City, September 23, 1872), Garfield MSS.
24. Potts to extra session (April 15, 1873), *Council Journal,* Extra Session (1873), pp. 19, 20.
25. *Helena Herald,* December 24, 1873.

Democratic *Rocky Mountain Gazette,* Maginnis unseated Billy
Clagett in 1872, with Bob Fisk screaming fraud at the ballot box
and accusing Sam Hauser of buying votes. In Washington,
Maginnis proved an able representative; at home a master politi-
cian and an unbeatable campaigner who would serve six conservative terms and whose name would be one of the best known
in the territory. Clad formally in Prince Albert coat and high
hat, with grayish hair and beard trimmed like that of the Prince
of Wales, Maginnis cut an impressive figure when he addressed
the Montana house on one occasion in the late seventies. Montanans liked the story of one of the national Democratic conventions where a nominating speaker referred to Lincoln, Ford's
Theater, and the assassin Booth's words, *"Sic semper tyran-
nus."* Not being able to catch the phrase, one delegate asked his
neighbor what the speaker had said; the companion replied that
he wasn't sure but he thought it was "I'm sick, send for Maginnis." [26]

At the polls, Maginnis was unstoppable. Every two years he
bowled over his opponents with a kind of cyclical regularity,
good politicians as well as mediocre. In succession, he beat
Yale graduate Cornelius Hedges, an excellent debater and fluent
writer; Beaverhead physician Erasmus Leavitt, who made but a
token race; the veteran Sample Orr, who campaigned on an Independent ticket when Republicans failed to select a nominee in
1876; the bare-knuckle political brawler Wilbur F. Sanders, in a
contest in which the GOP still complained of Price's Left Wing
having "Bourbonized" the territory and still damned the Democrats as the party of disunion, singing Civil War vintage songs,
including "Marching Through Georgia," at their rallies; and finally in 1882, the crippled Alexander Botkins, former U.S.
marshal, who ran his race from a wheelchair, and whose supporters subsequently charged fraud and illegal voters—at Wil-
der's Landing, where there were only a dozen voters, they
claimed, Maginnis had received 400, because that many army

26. Quoted in James Blaine Walker, *A Boy Pioneer in the West and Other Reminiscences* (n.p.: n. pub., 1963), p. 62.

MONTANA RANCH

A photographer's essay by Bob Peterson

Photographs in sequence

Neighbor cowboys help during summer cattle-moving.
Inside the barn.
Cowboy during roundup.
Driving a Hereford bull at roundup.
Branding time.
Calf-roping at the rodeo.
Old-timer watching the rodeo.
Barbed-wire fences require constant repair.
Combining grain.
Hay-stacker.
Irrigated grain field, where irrigation ends.
Spillway at the head of the ranch irrigation system.
Dan Leadbetter, manager of the ranch.
Lunch break during roundup.
Whitefaces in the holding pens.

*Photographs taken at Valley Garden Ranch, Ennis,
Montana, owned and managed by Mrs. Winifred Gammie and her daughter and son-
in-law, the Dan Leadbetters.*

mules "in sympathy for their ancestor, the Democratic Donkey, cast a solid vote for Martin." [27]

When Martin Maginnis voluntarily bowed out in 1884, he left an impressive record in Washington. After his first six months, he was elated over his accomplishments. "Naturally I feel 'sot up' and may have the big head bad if my luck holds on," he wrote Sam Hauser.[28] By the mid-1870s, he was the recognized leader of the loose-jointed association of delegates which met informally in the nation's capital. He repeatedly urged statehood for Montana, fought for more appropriations, worked to open Flathead lands to white occupation, and to shrink Indian holds in general. He succeeded in gaining additional military posts, funds for helping clear the Missouri River, and lands for the future state university. At the same time, Maginnis was accused of being the captive of such leaders as Sam Hauser, Charles A. Broadwater, and even Republican Tom Power. Broadwater thought highly of him and told Hauser so in 1874: ". . . you and I can get no man who will watch our interests closer than Maginnis. . . . He is the acknowledged ablest Delegate in Congress, and with twice the snap I ever gave him credit for." [29] That he indeed did much for such patrons is undeniable, but many stalwart Republicans, including Bob Fisk, had to admit in 1882 that Little Mac had served Montana well and was to be preferred over any other Democrat. What was most important was that Governor Potts was able to co-operate with him and with the Democratic power behind the throne, Sam Hauser, to give effective government by a coalition of interest groups cutting across party lines.

Potts's successor was handsome, dashing John Schuyler Crosby, scion of an old aristocratic New York family, who had fought in the Civil War and had served under Sheridan against the Indians. Independent of mind, he had no qualms about step-

27. Alva Josiah Noyes, *In the Land of Chinook* (Helena: State Publishing Co., 1917), p. 134.
28. Maginnis to Hauser (Washington, May 14, 1874), Hauser MSS.
29. Broadwater to Hauser (Washington, April 6, 1874), Hauser MSS.

ping on toes, including those of Wilbur F. Sanders; nor was his political philosophy much different from that of other newly arrived governors. "I am having a hard fight out here between a lot of thieves, drunkards & vicious democrats," he wrote the Attorney General early in 1883, "but I feel thoroughly confident that if I have the support of the administration I can make this Territory thoroughly Republican." [30] Impulsive and at times moralistic, he made free use of the veto power, in the process earning the enmity of stockmen, and he forced resignation of the secretary after revelation of an unsavory divorce scandal. Members of the legislature would call Crosby "the dawdling dandy from the bank of the Arno," referring to his previous consular appointment in Italy, but he did an excellent job during his brief stay. The *Missoulian* made a fair appraisal when it called him "a pretty good Governor, notwithstanding the fact that everybody can't boss him." [31]

After him came "large, healthy-looking, well preserved" [32] B. Platt Carpenter, earlier defeated for lieutenant governor of New York, whose administration was as brief as it was uneventful. A new President—a Democrat for a change—swept him out in 1885 and replaced him with one of Montana's own, Sam Hauser, who had conducted a behind-the-scenes campaign to block Maginnis's drive for the post. Hauser's appointment brought cheers "for the first Territorial resident appointed Governor of Montana," [33] and brought to fruition a long battle waged by locals. Throughout the territorial era, Montanans, like other westerners, had complained that the system imposed upon them nonresident "pilgrims and Carpetbagger" officials— "political convicts" and hangers-on with party influence but who "have no interest in common with the people and are as ignorant of their wants as are the Esquimaux of orange

30. John Schuyler Crosby to Benjamin H. Brewster (Helena, April 15, 1883), Source-Chronological Files, Montana, Department of Justice, National Archives.
31. Quote in *Helena Herald*, August 16, 1884; J. U. Sanders, "Hundred Governors Rule Montana in Two Centuries," *Contributions*, 9 (1923): 363.
32. *Weekly Independent*, January 8, 1885.
33. *Helena Herald*, July 6, 1885.

groves." [34] For the offices of governor, secretary, and judges, nonresidents outnumbered resident appointees three to one; and since such "hot-house specimens" often proved "too frail to stand transplanting," [35] the turnover was great. Yet, as Samuel Hauser's career indicates, home-grown politicians were not necessarily the best officials.

Time bore out the fears of some who believed he would find the job "an obstruction and an annoyance;" certainly he considered it a bore and no great matter. Republican Cornelius Hedges wrote many of his reports and much of his message to the fifteenth legislature, and Hauser spent about as much time in New York and Washington on private affairs as he did in Helena. To be sure, he showed sympathy both to mine owners and to cattlemen, but his role in proposing legislation was not great, and he resigned after a year and a half without having made any real impact. According to Hauser, he recommended Maginnis as his successor, apparently as part of a political deal which would return delegate Joseph K. Toole to the Congress and Hauser to the Senate once statehood were achieved. But, somehow, Maginnis was bypassed in favor of Preston H. Leslie, ". . . a Kentucky colonel, by gad, suh," who "scooped the persimmons," as one editor put it.[36] Hard-working, but never a real leader, Leslie served two years, bothered few, and was generally ignored by the legislature. When he was replaced in 1889 by Benjamin F. White, pioneer merchant, banker, and the first mayor of Dillon, the new governor represented a compromise among territorial Republicans. He was a caretaker: statehood was but a few months away; it was White's role to steer the ship through the organizational waters. He had not sought the job, but he had taken it with one of the same aspirations as most of his predecessors—namely, he said, "to increase our chances for making Montana a solid and reliable Republican state." [37]

34. *Weekly Independent,* June 20, 1878.
35. *Congressional Record,* 50 Cong., 2 Sess. (1888–1889), p. 82.
36. *Semi-Weekly Inter Mountain,* December 19, 1886.
37. White to Russell B. Harrison (Dillon, April 2, 1889), Russell B. Harrison MSS, Lilly Library, Indiana University, Bloomington.

But the people of the territory had been Democratic. Only two of Montana's delegates had been Republican—Clagett in 1871 and the last, Thomas Carter, in 1888. Democrats also dominated the legislatures. After the first session, in which the council was unionist by one vote, Republicans did not hold a majority in either house until 1885; only once—in the sixteenth and final session—did the GOP command both houses. As might be expected, voters sent more lawyers, ranchers, and mining men to the legislature than any other group. Nor were they old men. As Bob Fisk remarked in 1881, "Most of the members are young and vigorous, and but few grey hairs are seen in either House." [38] Political experience was at first limited, but time built up a solid core of veterans. Granville Stuart in 1884 could point with pride to his five terms: Alexander Mayhew of Deer Lodge would be speaker of the house six times.

Although scoffers were frequent, labeling the legislature as "one of the standard amusements of the city," and grumbling of the members that "about all they do is drink whiskey and play Billiards," [39] the territorial lawmakers reflected the wishes of their constituents. In the early years, until limited by Congress, the assembly voted many private charters and privileges, especially for toll roads and bridges. As Governor Ashley pointed out in 1869, a team and wagon between Helena and Corinne, Utah, paid more than forty dollars in such charges. Much of the legislation was imitative, rather than innovative. "Montana is the young daugher of a young mother—the child of Colorado," an early visitor noted. Along with early Pike's Peakers were a substantial number from Missouri ("Are you a grammarian?" "Why no. I'm a Missourian.").[40] Thus it is not surprising that Montanans copied their laws or substantial parts of their laws from those of these regions. Yet some, like the statutes dealing with probate, civil practice, and education, were

38. *Helena Herald*, February 14, 1881.

39. McClure, *Three Thousand Miles*, p. 410; "Jack" [no other name] to James Fergus (Virginia City, February 23, 1867), copy, Allis Stuart Collection, MHS.

40. Albert D. Richardson, *Our New States and Territories* (New York: Beadle & Co., 1866), p. 73.

notoriously bad until replaced with new ones drawn primarily from California models. In the 1870s, the growing number of migrants from the east and Midwest "left their footprints on the statutes," as the *Helena Herald* put it.[41]

Whatever the precedents for its action, the Montana territorial assemblies were not leaders in modern social legislation. They proceeded cautiously, blending tradition, trial and error, and local political pressures. Indeed, in a number of statutes they mirrored a racism latent even at the end of the period. It took the threat of Congress to remove the restrictive phrase "all white male citizens" from the election laws in the sixties; it took court decisions to overturn the laws levying discriminatory license fees on male laundrypeople (invariably Chinese) and forbidding aliens to hold title to or take profit from mining property. The school of law of 1872 allowed separate schools for black children at the discretion of trustees, and Helena sanctioned such a school in 1876 for "the little bevy of colored children in town." [42] There and at Fort Benton, segregated schools existed and were a warm issue until Helena rejected the idea in 1882 and the legislature repealed the law a year later. But racism was slow to die. Here and there were still former slave owners like the one near Bozeman who minced no words, even in the mid-eighties. "God Almighty made the niggers black and unthrifty," he said, "and do what you will you can never make them anything else." [43] At the tail end of the territorial period, Lewis Hershfield, banker and popular head of the local Republican machinery, was blocked for the governorship by tactics that were both personal and anti-Semitic. "Haven't we plenty of Christians in the country without having to select a Jew?" some Montanans were asking.[44]

The legislature could always override the governor's veto, of course, and in the earlier years, the Democrat-dominated assem-

41. *Helena Herald,* December 23, 1880.

42. *Helena Herald,* August 26, 1876.

43. Quoted in Edward Marston, *Frank's Ranche; or, My Holiday in the Rockies* (London: Sampson, Low, Marston, Searle & Rivington, 1886), p. 148.

44. Louis Walker to Russell B. Harrison (March 14, 1889), Russell B. Harrison MSS.

bly used other tools to thwart the Washington-supplied Republican officials. One device, until Congress expressly prohibited it, was to augment salaries, revoking the stipend when officers became particularly irritating—as when two of the judges ruled adversely in the "Bogus Legislatures" fiasco of 1866–1867. In that instance, the justices were also denied fuel and stationery and were "sage-brushed" by the legislature, which re-drew the court districts to assign the offenders to the least desirable parts of the territory—an action Congress would also soon ban.

When the assembly sat, the usual lobbyists were on hand: newspaper editors seeking printing contracts, railroads looking for bond or other subsidies, drummers working for repeal of commercial license laws, and a host of others, but in the long run the two most important pressure groups were cattlemen and the mineral industry. The power of mining interests was apparent from the beginning. If mine property was taxed at all, it was over heavy opposition and on advantageous terms—on the net proceeds, plus a nominal direct levy on patented claims equal to the original purchase price from the United States, a most lenient arrangement that prevailed from 1879 through the territorial period and left mine operators shouldering less than their share of the burden. Cattle growers fought the idea and made mine taxation a major issue in the constitutional convention of 1884. Mines were wasting assets—their value decreasing as they worked—but they were vital to the economy, argued the champions of low mineral taxes. "An old cow is capable of having so many calves," countered James Fergus. "You can't fool a poor old man. Our cattle are just like your mines, and horses and cattle get worn out just like your mines do." [45] Five years later, when Montana came into the Union, it left the taxation of mines relatively unchanged, not because of a conspiracy, but because mining men, like other business people, acted in their own self-interest.

Though stockmen lost on the tax question, they could not be ignored completely and played a decisive role in prompting

---

45. Discussion of February 4, 1884, Proceedings of the Constitutional Convention, microfilm copy, MHS.

much legislation concerned directly or indirectly with their own pursuits: for example, water law, limitations on movement of diseased livestock, bounties for predators, stringent penalties for theft or failure to record marks and brands and the principle of "customary range," giving pseudo-legal sanction to illegal private use of the public domain. Spokesmen like Granville Stuart believed that "the miners have always shown a very narrow & unjust prejudice against us," and called his fellow cattlemen together to discuss "what Legislation is necessary to protect our interests." [46] Stock growers were particularly incensed when Governor Crosby in 1883 failed to sign a bill to establish a board of livestock commissioners with extremely broad powers to appoint inspectors to protect against depredations at public expense—a measure one critic called "An Act to create the office of Head Gamekeeper, Chief Fire Warden and Boss Cow-Boy in the Territory of Montana, in the interest of, and for the sole use and benefit of the impoverished cattle owners of said Territory." [47] The so-called "cowboy legislature of 1885 (the fourteenth assembly), in which stockmen comprised a third of the membership, marked the peak of the cattle growers' power in the territorial period, and even then, as Stuart pointed out, only five of the eighty-five laws enacted pertained to the livestock industry. But that this important interest group did not dominate was due to the counterbalance of the mineral industry; and both did much to shape legislation.

Practically from the moment the territory was created in 1864, some Montanans were campaigning for statehood. Territorial status implied an inferior political position, the denial of fundamental rights of Americans, a status of "colonialism," they argued. Admission to the Union would put an end to "carpetbag" officials imposed from Washington; allow expansion of an inflexible judicial system; remove special limitations on debt, taxation, and alien land ownership; and above all give voters a

---

46. Granville Stuart to R. S. Ford (n.p., February 4, 1883), copy; Stuart to Conrad Kohrs (Fort Maginnis, May 2, 1882), copy, both in letterbook 2, James & Granville Stuart MSS, Beinecke Library, Yale University.
47. *House Journal,* 13 Session (1883), pp. 243, 244.

more direct voice in government. Not only would they be able
to help elect the President and send voting members to the national Congress, they would also assist at the distribution of the
loaves and fishes at the state level. Without statehood, contended Montana's delegate, "there is nothing but political insomnia and internal unrest." [48]

The movement began early. Realizing that Montana "would
take rank among the staunchest of the President's Democratic
supporters," and not disinterested in a Senate seat for himself,
Thomas Francis Meagher called a constitutional convention
which met in Helena in 1866, ". . . sired by the Acting One,
and damned by the people," according to an opponent. [49] More
political than serious, the convention sat for six days, drew up a
constitution which subsequently disappeared, and members remained in their seats for a Democratic caucus.

Following this meaningless escapade, the legislature from
time to time petitioned Congress for statehood, and an occasional bill would be introduced in Washington and defeated.
After the census of 1880 showed 39,159 people in the territory,
an increase of more than 90 percent over 1870, the momentum
picked up. One of the prayers of the chaplain of the lower
legislative house in 1881 was a divine appeal for admission; me-
morials to Congress became more blatant in tone; and in 1883
the assembly provided for a constitutional convention early in the
following year. There in Woody Paynter's new building in Helena, forty-five elected delegates fashioned a basic document
under the chairmanship of William A. Clark, already rising rapidly in the mineral world. When the final constitution was
drawn up for signatures, it represented a good deal of scissors-
and-paste work: its preamble came from Massachusetts, its judi-
ciary section mainly from California, other portions from Ala-
bama and Minnesota "and probably more from Colorado than
from all the rest together." [50] Governor Crosby thought the
constitution "a good one," but long on legislation and short on

48. *Congressional Record,* 50 Cong., 2 Sess. (1888–1889), p. 822.
49. *Montana Post,* April 14, 1866.
50. *Helena Herald,* February 11, 1884.

taxation.[51] Although the electorate approved it by a margin of four to one, delay hurt, and in 1885 it went to a split Congress, the Senate Republican and the House Democratic. An attempt to pair Democrat Montana with Republican Dakota failed; an amendment to attach Montana to a bill for Washington, also GOP, was quickly voted down by the Senate.

Debate over Montana statehood continued into 1887 and 1888, but despite favorable committee reports, delaying tactics prevented action. With at least one house of Congress Republican from 1881 to 1889, admission of a Democratic state was not likely until popular pressures were so great that neither party could refuse. By the summer of 1888, that point was at hand: at their national conventions, both parties adopted planks calling for admission of Montana, Dakota, Washington, and New Mexico; for good measure, the Republicans threw in Idaho, Wyoming, and Arizona, but nobody would touch infidel Utah. Montana's claims were not judged individually but were merged with those of other territories to be determined on a basis of political expediency. When the electorate in November sent Republican Benjamin Harrison to the White House and a GOP majority to both houses of Congress, the old lame-duck session of the Fiftieth recognized the inevitable and approved an enabling act for the Omnibus States—Montana, Washington, and the two Dakotas, an accomplishment called by Delegate Toole "the grandest act of this administration and in the extent of constitutional government conferred is unparalleled in the history of the republic." [52] Amidst paeans of self-congratulation, Montanans set about writing a state constitution. With Clark again presiding, the convention blended much of the document drafted in 1884 with the California constitution of 1879 to produce an acceptable compromise which limited legislative power and exalted the executive, but contained safeguards to prevent corruption of both—safeguards which time soon proved ineffective.

The new constitution was adopted by an overwhelming margin, but election of the first state legislature saw extensive

---

51. Crosby to Maginnis (Helena, February 13, 1884), Maginnis MSS.
52. *Congressional Record,* 50 Cong., 2 Sess. (1888–1889), pp. 821–822.

political jockeying and charges of vote irregularities, especially
complaints of the "Dago Vote"—ignorant, ineligible foreigners
"marched to the polls and voted like cattle," [53] again an omen
for the future. But when President Harrison proclaimed Montana a state on November 8, 1889, adding the forty-first star to
Old Glory, most residents saw a new era at hand. Ended were
twenty-five years, five months, and twelve days of "territorial
vassalage"; restrictive "gyves and fetters . . . have fallen
away," rejoiced the editor of the *Helena Herald*.[54] But some of
the nostalgic old-timers expressed only regret. "Now she's gone
to hell," one of them remarked.[55]

53. *Helena Herald*, November 19, 25, 1889.
54. *Helena Herald*, November 8, 1889.
55. Quoted in Frank B. Linderman, *Montana Adventure* (Lincoln: University of Nebraska Press, 1968), p. 44.

7

The War of the Copper Kings

"They Never Bought
a Man Who Wasn't for Sale."

CONOMIC warfare and relentless, bare-knuckle politics would dominate the late nineteenth and early twentieth centuries in Montana, as massive shock waves generated in Butte and Anaconda would reverberate throughout the state and even beyond. Central in this arrogant, if colorful, "War of the Copper Kings" were tough, worthy opponents: frosty William A. Clark, described as a "tight white starched little man," [1] a Presbyterian pincher of pennies whose fanatical ambition and ruthlessness more than offset his lack of humor and the more personal vices; Marcus Daly, a ruddy, stocky, gregarious broth of an Irishman, already well known for his keen nose for ore and his shrewd, never-say-die attitude; F. Augustus Heinze, handsome, genial, and unscrupulously sure of himself, even to the point of taking on the Company—the gigantic, Standard Oil-backed Amalgamated Copper Company. The clash of such strong personalities and of corporate giants would bring unprecedented turmoil to the "russet hills" of Butte, make shambles

Quoted in Montana Writers' Project, *Copper Camp,* p. 39.

1. Joseph Kinsey Howard, *Montana High, Wide, and Handsome* (New Haven: Yale University Press, 1943), p. 58.

95

of political alignments, and help rivet the "copper collar" on Montana's legislature for years to come.

From the moment Daly rode into Butte on a hot summer day in 1876 he was on the make. Acquiring the Anaconda mine, he joined with California capitalists to form the Anaconda Gold and Silver Mining Company; and as the silver content of the ore gave way to increasingly rich copper, he seemed to sniff the age of copper and electricity just around the corner, just as he understood the importance of low freight rates and mass-production refining. Tradition has it that he shut down the Anaconda, then bought out at bargain prices panicky neighbors who feared his vein had pinched out. Next he sought out a smelter site with adequate water, and by 1884 Anaconda's new plant on Warm Springs Creek, twenty-six miles northwest of Butte, was belching forth its arsenic-laden smoke—fumes that reportedly turned the wash green on the line and so impregnated grass that local cattle had copper-plated teeth. By 1885 Anaconda produced thirty-six million pounds of copper; other Butte mines owned by Boston firms or by the tough-minded Clark turned out another thirty-two million pounds. Farther east, seventeen competing Lake Superior copper mines produced seventy-seven million pounds and by selling at low prices attempted to drive western producers from the field. But despite depression in Butte and some closings in Arizona and Utah, Anaconda hung on grimly and by 1888 had beaten the Michigan combination.

Meanwhile, in Paris, French brass magnate Hyacinthe Secretan eyed the Michigan-Montana price war wistfully and made a bold move to corner the world copper market. He failed, but raised copper prices substantially before he lost control and saw prices plunge to a nickel a pound. To prevent massive dumping of the huge surpluses left in their hands, European bankers joined with copper producers to control output and to peg prices at twelve cents a pound for five years. Not only did Anaconda weather this international storm, it doubled its capacity, and by 1902 its ultramodern Washoe smelter would be handling 4,000 tons daily at the concentrator and 1,000 tons at the furnaces.

At the same time, a bitter personal feud developed between Marc Daly and William Clark, two men some thought were born to hate each other. In the 1888 election, Democrat Clark ran for delegate, undoubtedly with his eye on a future seat in the United States Senate. In a biting, intensively personal campaign, Clark was accused of trying to buy his way into office with a hefty "boodle bar'l," [2] but his opponent, Silver Bow lawyer Thomas Carter, won a surprising victory. As the stunned Clark appraised the results, he saw conspiracy and the touch of fellow-Democrat Marcus Daly. Clark had assumed that the Irish would give solid support. After all, as an old Cornishman noted, "they not honly 'ave two votes heach on Helection day, but thee buggers vote seven years hafter they 'ave been dead hand buried." [3] But this time, with Daly's urging, they went for Carter. A liberal use of whiskey and cigars was apparent, and some coercion. Daly forces intimidated and instructed employees of Anaconda, the Northern Pacific, and the Montana Improvement companies how to vote. Apparently Daly—because he, Sam Hauser, and others connected with the Montana Improvement Company were under indictment for trespass on public timber lands—was convinced that a Republican would be more influential in Washington. And Carter, at least, succeeded in getting the suits deferred.

In 1890, in an *opéra bouffe* situation stemming from disputed election returns, Montana sent two sets of senators to the nation's capital, but the GOP-dominated Senate seated Republicans Wilbur F. Sanders and Thomas C. Power, while rejecting Democrats Clark and Martin Maginnis. This seemed only to whet Clark's political aspirations: when Sanders's short term ended in 1893, Clark made every effort to gain his seat, and Daly fought him stubbornly. Newspapers on both sides charged fraud and bribery; but after fifty days of balloting, the legislature adjourned in deadlock, leaving Montana represented by only one senator for two years.

While Clark and Daly wrangled, the impact of depression and a national third-party movement swept over the state. The Populist or People's party was officially born in Omaha, Nebraska,

2. *Helena Herald*, November 5, 1888.
3. Montana Writers' Project, *Butte Copper*, p. 49.

in 1892. The offspring of agrarian discontent and cheap-money advocates, its platform called for striking reforms: a graduated income tax, a land policy restricted to actual settlers, postal savings banks, the initiative and referendum, federal control of railroads and communications, and most significant to Montanans, the free and unlimited coinage of silver and gold at a ratio of sixteen to one.

Free Silver looked toward both an inflated dollar and higher metal prices. In 1889 silver had dipped to ninety-three cents an ounce, but the price climbed again temporarily after Congress in 1890 doubled the amount of silver purchased by the federal government. Farmers and others in debt believed that unlimited amounts of cheap silver in the monetary system were desirable. Montana mine and smelter people, obviously directly concerned with silver prices again on the decline in early 1892, joined hands with laboring men and agrarians to run a slate of Populist candidates later that year. Among these was the first woman admitted to the Montana bar, in 1889, Ella Knowles, who ran a good losing race for attorney general. Ironically, this "Portia of the People's Party" subsequently went to work for the man who defeated her, then married him!

The panic of 1893 and the depression that followed brought additional converts to the Populist cause. National in scope, the crisis was no doubt aggravated to some extent by Congress's repeal in 1893 of the Sherman Silver Purchase law, an action which sharply reduced the amount of silver bought by the government and sent prices spiraling even lower. By 1894, silver was down to sixty-three cents an ounce, and the Montana mineral industry was floundering. Demands for beef and grain did not deteriorate as rapidly as those for silver, so eastern Montana suffered less, but all around the state silver mines closed down. The Wickes plant suspended operations and was dismantled; suddenly the town of Cerlew was "almost too dead to skin;" [4] at Granite, a long blast on the steam whistle signaled the end of major mining and smelting employment and began an exodus of some three thousand people practically overnight.

4. Linderman, *Montana Adventure,* pp. 85–86.

Wagons that hadn't been used for ten years, creaked and screeched down the incline. Bandboxes, babies and bull dogs brought up the rear, and so it kept up all day and all night—a continual stream of almost panic-stricken people, leaving, perhaps forever, their home on the mountain.[5]

By 1894 most of the large silver producers were silent, though those like the Drumlummon, with other metals as well, still operated. Copper was not so hard hit; indeed its position was strengthened; although Butte experienced a rash of holdups and burglaries attributed to hard times. With some 20,000 unemployed, some companies leased mines to workers on a percentage basis. Those impolitic enough to strike—as were some of the employees of the Northern Pacific Railroad—were quickly discharged. Sometimes municpal governments hired the jobless on public works, but the dwindling price of silver and of revenue made this increasingly impossible.

During the crisis the bottom went out of the egg market, and egg prices in Helena plummeted to ten cents a dozen. The doors of Sam Hauser's First National Bank of Helena and of the late Charles Broadwater's Montana National Bank were closed for six months, though a public meeting of two hundred local business and professional men expressed full confidence and called for an immediate slashing of school and city government expenses. Banks elsewhere closed temporarily, but most reopened. Times were tough, but the state managed to pay its warrants on time and no county or town defaulted on its interest payments, although the citizens of Walkerville petitioned for dissolution of their incorporated status because tax income was insufficient to meet indebtedness.

After the fashion of Jacob Coxey's national "army," William Hogan sought to raise a force of five hundred unemployed people to march on Washington and present the President with a "petiton with boots on," i.e., to demonstrate the need for federal action in this economic crisis. In April 1894 Hogan's rag-tag-and-bobtail regiment seized a locomotive and a number of railroad cars at Butte and headed eastward, with warm and en-

5. Quoted in Wolle, *Montana Pay Dirt,* p. 252.

thusiastic welcomes at Bozeman and Livingston. But at Billings, Hogan's heroes clashed with the marshal and his deputies, and a citizen was killed before the deputies withdrew. As Hogan continued east, Governor John Rickards telegraphed President Cleveland, who ordered troops from Fort Keogh to apprehend the miscreants at Forsyth. Ultimately Hogan would spend six months in jail, but sympathetic Helena residents provided transit for the rest of his "army" to Fort Benton, whence it floated down the Missouri in flatboats, determined to reach the White House.

Meanwhile, politics as usual continued: Clark and Daly raked each other, and the Populists added recruits. In 1894, not only hard times, but the location of the state capital, always a thorny matter, became a central issue. Originally, the constitutional convention, with Clark presiding, had provided for a popular election on the question in 1892, an election, it transpired, at which nine-tenths of Montana's registered voters turned out, and which put Helena and Anaconda on the ballot in a special contest scheduled for the fall of 1894. Evidence seems to indicate that Helena businessmen agreed to support William Clark for the Senate in exchange for help in retaining the capital at Helena. Daly, on the other hand, campaigned hard to move the seat of government to Anaconda. As usual, it was a bitter and spirited struggle, with lavish use of cash and hard drink by both factions. Cowboy poet D. J. O'Malley ("When the Work's All Done this Fall") was enlisted by Daly forces to pen a parody of the popular song, "After the Ball."

> After the Fall is over,
> After the voting's done
> There will be great rejoicing
> When Anaconda's won.[6]

But voters decided to keep the capital at "Her Hogogracy of Last Chance Gulch," as one sour Missoula editor dubbed Helena,[7] where a thousand cheering inhabitants met Clark's special

6. John I. White, "D. J. 'Kid' O'Malley. Montana's Cowboy Poet," *Montana* 17 (July 1967): 66.

7. *Montana Silverite,* quoted in C. B. Glasscock, *The War of the Copper Kings* (New York & Indianapolis: Bobbs-Merrill Co., 1935), pp. 125–126.

train and pulled him by hand in a carriage through the streets, and a drunken night it was.

In the general election of the same year, a promising young Republican named Joseph Dixon "waved the bloody shirt" and won a county post; three Populists went to the state senate, and thirteen to the house. Soon Dixon admitted hard times for the GOP in Montana; he remembered "when the blizzard blew in 1896 and almost wiped us out of existence." [8] The "blizzard" was William Jennings Bryan, who had taken the cause of Free Silver to his bosom, and swept the state for the national Democratic party and a fusion ticket of Populists and Democrats headed by Robert B. Smith, who won the governorship, while the "Popocrats" took the house. But inevitably, because the Democrats had stolen their loudest thunder, Free Silver, and fusion had undermined their organization just as the Clark-Daly feud created intense havoc, Populist power waned. Free Silver was never achieved, but in Montana, the party cemented a distrust of the East and of corporations that would endure; it also pointed up a lack of party regularity—a characteristic that was neither new nor easily discarded; and it helped lay the groundwork for subsequent progressive reforms.

All the while, the itch of little William Clark to sit in the Senate had not grown less. In the 1898 primary and in the general election for legislators, pro-Clark charges and countercharges flew like the overripe tomato that hit visiting millionaire J.P. Morgan as he rode through the streets of Butte in Fat Jack Jones's open hack. Daly was accused of using repeaters, "herded like sheep," to vote the "Dalycratic" ticket. On election day, complained a Clark organ, "every irresponsible loafer and bum in the city was shouting for Marcus Daly and jingling in their pockets the price of their votes." [9] Daly men won, in spite of fraud and "the lying and thieving tactics of the Clark forces," countered the *Anaconda Standard*. [10]

8. Quoted in John W. Smurr and K. Ross Toole, eds., *Historical Essays on Montana and the Northwest* (Helena: MHS, 1957), p. 237.

9. *Butte Miner,* November 9, 1898, quoted in Montana Writers' Project, *Copper Camp,* p. 48.

10. *Anaconda Standard,* quoted in Montana Writers' Project, *Copper Camp,* p. 49.

But ice-water flowed through Clark's veins, and he was far from beaten. As the new legislature went about its business of selecting a U.S. senator early in 1899, a member from Flathead County dropped a bombshell. State Senator Fred Whiteside produced four envelopes containing a total of $30,000 and charged that Clark had reached into his long purse to buy his way to the Senate, purchasing votes like eggs, it was said, by the dozen. Turmoil followed: Clark was denounced by pulpit and press; a St. Paul, Minnesota, cartoonist depicted a thousand-dollar bill— "the kind of bill most frequently introduced in the Montana Legislature," [11] and a grand jury was empaneled to investigate. There was talk that the statement attributed to one of Clark's sons—that "the old man" would be sent either to the Senate or to the poor house—might well be amended to include "penitentiary," but the jury found insufficient evidence.

Finally, on the eighteenth ballot, eleven Republican assemblymen swung over, and Clark was elected. All night long, bands blared forth, rockets were shot off, and free champagne flowed in Helena, but the question of bribery could not be ignored, especially when Daly carried it to Washington, where the Senate Committee on Privileges and Elections heard more than ninety witnesses on the goings-on in the statehouse. It was clear to the committee that Clark had spent at least a third of a million dollars on his own election, which it then declared null and void. With the decision pending, Clark had resigned. Immediately, while Montana Governor Smith, a Daly man, was decoyed to California, the lieutenant-governor appointed William Clark to the now vacated Senate seat! Clark made no attempt to take the post, but returned home, he said, to vindicate himself. Through alliances he succeeded in winning control of the state Democrat machinery in 1900, though it cost a pretty penny, and was elected to serve a full term in the U.S. Senate. Before Clark claimed his seat, Marcus Daly was dead—some said of a broken heart. Clark himself admitted that it was all a terribly costly business, but not necessarily immoral. After all, he is supposed to have said, "I never bought a man who wasn't for sale." [12]

11. *St. Paul Dispatch,* quoted in Glasscock, *War of the Copper Kings,* p. 175.
12. Quoted in Montana Writers' Project, *Copper Camp,* p. 39.

As a senator, he was undistinguished but no worse than many others, yet the stigma of a bought office never left him. Noting that Clark was so thin in evening clothes that he "just seems the handle for his yellow mop of curly hair and whiskers," the wife of a Texas congressman in 1907 quoted a current saying in Washington that "if you took away the whiskers and the scandal there would be nothing left of him . . . ." [13]

In the meantime, young Fritz Heinze had been making a name for himself. When he arrived in Butte in 1889, he carried a diploma from the Columbia School of Mines, but was not heavily burdened by scruples. Working at first as an underground surveyor, Heinze coolly appraised the inner workings of the "richest hill on earth" and remembered what he saw. Next, he built a smelter to cut into the near monopoly of Daly and Clark, acquired control of the Rarus Mine, adjoining property of the Boston and Montana Consolidated Company, and settled back to play a dangerous game.

One of his trumps was the so-called law of the apex, confirmed as far back as 1866 by federal statute, which gave the locator of a mineral vein the right to follow it, "with dips, angles and variations," downward to any depth beyond its sidelines, provided that its top or apex was enclosed within the endlines of the location. Another high card was Heinze's ownership of a pet county judge, William Clancy, a key figure described by a contemporary as "a huge, unkempt, ursine type, with a long tobacco-and-soup-stained beard, a rough pioneer wit, and no dignity whatever." [14]

Using the vagaries of the apex law, Heinze followed the vein through the sidewall of the Rarus into the adjacent Boston and Montana ground, taking out rich ore twenty-four hours a day before the owners discovered what was going on and sought an injunction to halt the incursion. This was the first of a long series of encroachments and legal suits with Clancy, the curbstone lawyer and bummer never swerving in his loyalty to Heinze as he handed down decisions.

13. Ellen M. Slayden, *Washington Wife: Journal of Ellen Maury Slayden from 1897–1919* (New York & Evanston: Harper & Row, 1963), p. 91.

14. Braley, *Pegasus Pulls a Hack*, p. 59.

In 1889, when Daly reorganized Anaconda as the Amalgamated Copper Company, a gigantic holding concern dominated by Standard Oil and incorporating into its holdings many properties, including the Boston and Montana, Heinze jauntily waded into the new opponent. Having discovered, surveyed, and gained title to a tiny unrecorded triangular fraction of ground the size of a large living-room, he calmly announced that three major mines—the Apex, the St. Lawrence, and the Neversweat—all apexed on it; and Clancy enjoined the owners from working these, pending legal settlement of title. But when the Amalgamated closed down in protest, throwing three thousand miners out of work, Clancy, fearing mob action, quickly dropped out of sight momentarily, but revoked the injunction and the Amalgamated reopened.

Both Heinze and Clark wooed labor with adoption of the eight-hour day; they co-operated closely in 1900 to achieve the legislature receptive to Clark and the election of the malleable judges so important to Heinze's plans. No wonder Clark-hating Marc Daly could refer to Heinze as "a blackmailer, a thief and a most dangerous and harmful man to the business and property interests of Butte." [15] Clark would soon sell out to the Amalgamated, however, but Heinze continued his slashing attacks. An eloquent orator who ingratiated himself with the average working stiff, Heinze skillfully blasted the soulless "kerosene trust" in particular and foreign monopolies in general. He was David against Goliath, he inferred; champion of the little man, committed to do battle with corporate evil. "They will force you to dwell in Standard Oil houses while you live," he told the man in the street, "and they will bury you in Standard Oil coffins when you die." [16]

All the while he systematically poached on Amalgamated underground property, hoisting high-grade ore from them through his own shafts, while his lawyers and judges enjoined the firm from operating its own mines, and litigation backed up in the

15. Quoted in David Lavender, *The Rockies* (New York: Harper & Row, 1968), p. 328.

16. Howard, *Montana*, p. 84.

courts. From time to time, underground warfare erupted, as partisan crews bashed each other's heads, shot off powder, or wafted smoke or ammonia fumes through ventilating shafts in efforts to oust the opposition. Unable to cope with Heinze's tactics and unsuccesssful in efforts to buy his judges, the Amalgamated, in October 1903, resorted to indirect pressure: it simply closed its mines and plants throughout the state, in the process idling some 20,000 men. Despite Heinze's moving indictment of the company from the steps of the Silver Bow County courthouse, approaching winter and mounting public unrest forced Governor Joseph K. Toole to call a special legislative session to consider a "fair trial" bill, adoption of which was considered vital by the Amalgamated. Such a measure would permit either party in a civil suit to gain a change of venue merely by charging the presiding judge with prejudice. After a blistering session, which included allegations of bribery and "even fistic encounters among lobbyists," [17] the "fair trial" law passed. Now clearly the Copper Trust was in the saddle; Heinze's tame judges had been bridled, and both the governor and the legislature had responded to company pressure. Heinze saw the handwriting on the wall; early in 1906 he sold out to the Amalgamated for $10.5 million, agreeing in the process to drop the 110 lawsuits then pending. Retiring to the East to play the Wall Street game, Fritz was forced to the sidelines when he went "belly up" in the panic of 1907, and it was big copper who helped break him.

But Heinze had struck a responsive chord among the Montana rank and file; to many, he became a kind of folk hero. He had fought the company singlehanded and made a fortune. But when he made his peace, the Amalgamated was free to consolidate its hold: in 1910 it acquired Clark's mines and smelter and, with subsidiaries, merged to become the Anaconda Copper Mining Company. After 1915 it was no longer tied to Standard Oil. It had emerged as a new, independent giant, controlled from Wall Street, and in turn dominating Montana's economy and politics. If Clark and Daly had perverted journalism and compromised

17. Linderman, *Montana Adventure,* pp. 131–132.

8

Progressivism versus The Company

From The Sixth Floor
of the Hennessey Building.

F the War of the Copper Kings overlapped at least part of the Populist Crusade, it was also superimposed upon several other broad national movements that carried Montana along with them. When the Spanish-American War erupted in the spring of 1898 and the country flexed its imperialistic muscles, Montana "was the first state in the Union to respond to the call," according to Governor Smith.[1] Townspeople at Missoula postponed their Easter services to see troops from Fort Missoula off to the war. The Twenty-fifth "is a dark regiment," wrote a local editor, but "not a white feather will be shown." [2] The governor was overwhelmed by those who wanted commissions, and according to one wag was "considering a proposition to send a regiment in the field composed entirely of brigadier generals." [3]

Under federal auspices the Montana National Guard was mus-

1. Message to legislature, 1899, *Messages and Public Documents of Governor Robert B. Smith, 1897–1901* (Helena: State Publishing Company, 1900), p. 57.
2. *The Missoulian,* quoted in *The Missoulian Bicentennial Edition,* July 2, 1976, p. 44-A.
3. *The Dillon Examiner,* April 20, 1898.

tered in as the First Montana Volunteers and sent not to Cuba but to the Philippine Islands to help put down Aguinaldo's native insurrection after the Spanish were defeated. ''The glory & honor gained in killing these reptiles falls as flat on us as rice cooked without salt,'' wrote one disgruntled young officer.[4] Equally as unromantic was the campaign history of another Montana outfit. From town after town, the boys sang ''A Hot Time in the Old Town'' as they marched off to join the Third Regiment of the U.S. Volunteer Cavalry, Troop F from Missoula, Troop L from Butte, Troop I from Miles City, and Troop M from Billings. But the men of the Third Regiment spent the war fighting flu, typhoid, and chiggers in the swamps of Georgia.

At home, Montana women did Red Cross work, raised money for Christmas boxes, presented each recruit with an American flag, in general ''inspiring the brave boys to a high degree of patriotism.'' [5] Dr. Mary Atwater volunteered as a nurse, but was disappointed when she was never called to service. In Missoula, a rousing Fourth of July celebration became near-pandemonium with the news that Commodore Schley had destroyed the Spanish fleet off Santiago. The town of Libby celebrated American victories in Cuba by shooting off dynamite; later it honored local servicemen with a Grand Ball and Supper at Neff and Plummer's Hall. And soon the ''splendid little war,'' as Secretary of State John Hay called it, was over. With a quota of 524, Montana had furnished a total of 1,366 men; most came home, though some died in action in the Philippines and more perished from disease.

Hardly were the boys out of khaki when the nation was caught up in a new reform era covering roughly the first decade and a half of the twentieth century. Urban-centered, middle-class, and directed by vigorous young leaders, progressivism reflected faith in the belief that intelligent people were capable of advancing human society; that wise, efficient use of natural

4. MHS, *Precious Metals,* p. 89.
5. Mary L. Alderson, ''A Half Century of Progress for Montana Women'' (typescript, 1935), p. 30. MHS.

resources would abolish poverty; that direct participation in government was the key to purifying politics and opening the door for true social justice. With states like Wisconsin and Oregon leading the way, progressives sought to clean up government, at first on the local level, then at the state level, pushing for means by which voters would be given a more direct vote in the political process—the recall, referendum, initiative, and popular primary. They also sought legislation on such questions as safety, child labor, workmen's compensation, and the eight-hour day. On the national scene they fought for pure food and drug laws, the firmer regulation of trusts, the direct election of senators, woman suffrage, and prohibition.

It has been contended that progressivism in Montana meant little; that it was "full of sound and fury," as Shakespeare's Macbeth would say, with little practical results save one meager tax revision; that the unique and dominant role of Anaconda largely blunted the reformers' aims.[6] While few would argue that Anaconda confined its operations to the mining and smelting of copper or that Montana was in the vanguard of social and political change, neither would they deny that the reform spirit of progressivism left the state unchanged. The company to the contrary, Montana was making many of the same gains as forward-looking states elsewhere in the period. And she would produce a set of progressive leaders in Joseph M. Dixon, Thomas J. Walsh, Burton K. Wheeler, and Jeannette Rankin, who would achieve national as well as local distinction.

A transplanted Southerner and a Missoula lawyer and editor, Joseph M. Dixon had served as county attorney and as a member of the legislature, an experience he believed "worth a year at Harvard University." Elected to Congress as a Republican in 1902 in part by the Heinze split in Democrat ranks, Dixon early came under the magnetic spell of Theodore Roosevelt. "I think Teddy and I will get on together," he once told his wife in one of history's massive understatements. A protégé of House Speaker "Uncle Joe" Cannon, he used Cannon's in-

6. K. Ross Toole, *Montana: An Uncommon Land* (Norman: University of Oklahoma Press, 1959), p. 226.

fluence to open the Crow and Flathead reservations to whites, despite Flathead opposition, in the process, "trading my hope of Heaven, almost." [7] This kind of success, his public aloofness during the Copper Wars, his closeness to Roosevelt and his praise of the President's antitrust action against the meat packers, all made him extremely popular and assured his re-election to a second term. By 1906, he was sent to the Senate as a balance to the veteran Thomas Carter.

The effective, if somewhat cynical and demanding "Uncle Tom" Carter (some called him "Slippery Tom"), had been territorial delegate, the first representative from the new state, U.S. senator from 1895–1901 and elected again in 1905. Of him, one legislator could say, "I liked him immensely, and did not believe in him at any time." [8] A former chairman of the Republican National Committee, Carter had important contacts. At home he was one of the Old Guard, closely identified with business interests and unable or unwilling to recognize the progressive currents of his own time and state.

Even while Dixon was in the House, he and Carter clashed over federal patronage in Montana; with the two in the Senate together, the conflict sharpened and broadened. While they might agree on a protective tariff for wool, hides, sugar beets, coal, lead, or other state products, they split on fundamental progressive issues. Carter would stand pat; Dixon damned the monopolies, especially the railroads; called for corporate, inheritance, and income taxes; and espoused the cause of woman suffrage, direct election of senators, and direct primaries. Indeed, the first serious effort in Montana to introduce a direct primary system was an extension of the Dixon-Carter struggle for control of state party machinery. Legislation to this end would benefit Dixon, and Carter, for the time being, blocked the move.

Since the legislature still chose United States senators, Carter, whose term would expire in 1911, ran indirectly in the 1910

7. Quoted in Jules A. Karlin, *Joseph M. Dixon of Montana,* 2 vols. (Missoula: University of Montana Publications in History, 1974), 1:31, 46, 58.

8. Linderman, *Montana Adventure,* p. 134.

election to build assembly support. His primary opponent was Thomas J. Walsh, a tough young lawyer who had campaigned for the capital at Helena in 1894 and who had joined the Free Silver Crusade in 1896. Already Walsh had made a name for himself in legal cases involving election law, public land policy, and railroad rates. He had run for Congress in 1906 as a progressive Democrat, but was beaten. But he was regarded as a friend of labor, as a conservationist emphasizing local controls, and as in favor of the extension of popular democracy. During the 1910 campaign, he was openly reformist, and hit Carter's reactionary views hard; in so doing he ran up against Anaconda and allied businesses who saw him as a maverick difficult to control. While Carter sought to manipulate corporate support, denying he was beholden to any interest group, his fellow Republican and senator, Joseph Dixon, thumped the tub for progressive legislation but gave him practically no support. The new legislature split, but clearly what Big Copper decided on the sixth floor of the Hennessey Building in Butte was important in Helena, where its lobbyists maintained convenient "waterholes" in the major hotels. In the 1911–1912 assembly, according to member Burt Wheeler, "the Democrats controlled the House, the Republicans controlled the Senate, and the Company controlled the leaders of both." [9] Neither Walsh nor Carter was named to the Senate, although President Taft appointed Carter to the International Waterways Commission, whence he continued the rivalry for Montana patronage.

By this time, Theodore Roosevelt and his protégé Taft had split, Roosevelt assuming the mantle of leadership for the progressive wing of the Republican party. Joseph Dixon took charge of the preconvention campaign, toured Montana with Roosevelt in 1911, and waged a bitter fight for control of the state's GOP delegation. But the "Great Amalgamated Steam Roller" captured the delegation for Taft, just as Taft recaptured the nomination in Chicago. Two weeks later Roosevelt supporters met in the Windy City to form a new Progressive party.

---

9. Burton K. Wheeler, *Yankee From the West* (Garden City: Doubleday & Co., 1962), p. 84.

Roosevelt gave a roaring speech: "We stand at Armageddon, and we battle for the Lord." [10] He felt as strong as a "bull moose," he said, and the party had an unofficial new name.

Nominally, at least, Joseph Dixon served as Teddy's campaign manager. He also declared open war upon the company at home, campaigning vigorously for his Senate seat on a slogan of "Put the Amalgamated Out of Montana Politics." But when the returns came in, the results were clearcut. Roosevelt ran well in the state, but because of the GOP split, the Democrats swept the boards, all the way from Woodrow Wilson, a reformer in his own right, through the entire congressional delegation and both houses of the legislature. With the assembly now bound by the voters' preference, Dixon was beaten in the Senate race by Thomas Walsh, very much a Wilsonian Democrat and an able crusader and harmonizer then on the threshold of an outstanding political career. Dixon continued to work for the Progressive party, but it was clear after the 1914 election that the Bull Moosers, as a political organization, were "as dead as Julius Caesar or Bill Taft." Returning to publishing momentarily, Dixon found printing "a twelve-page paper in an eight-page town" [11] less than profitable. Eventually, after a period of political retirement on his ranch at Flathead Lake, he would return to the fold as governor of the state. But 1912 was the acme of progressivism in Montana. And despite the company, positive advances had been and were being made.

For example, Montana crusaders attacked corruption and malfeasance in municipal office. In Missoula, saddled with a debt of $30,000 and countless political hangers-on, the community cleaned house. Among officials barely escaping indictment were the mayor, three aldermen, and the county treasurer, as the local Neighborhood Club succeeded in bringing in a new commission form of government, a typical progressive reform. Other towns applied the principle of the initiative and referendum, giving citizens greater voice. In Butte the voters revolted against the com-

10. *The Works of Theodore Roosevelt* 24 vols. (New York: Charles Scribner Sons, 1926), 17:231.

11. Karlin, *Joseph M. Dixon*, 1:206, 198.

pany as well as both political parties to elect a Socialist ticket headed by Lewis J. Duncan, an honest, efficient Unitarian minister whose two terms reflected not only the strong radical labor vote but also the reform concern with municipal abuse. Given Heinze's ownership of judges and the machinations of Clark and Daly with party nominating conventions and the legislature, Montana progressives could see a real need to clean up state politics. The state had been one of the first to adopt the Australian secret ballot, which increased the uncertainty that a bought vote would stay bought, though one could never be sure: one defeated candidate for the Butte mayor job grumbled that he had purchased substantially more votes than he actually received! To give the electorate a more direct role and to help set the stage for laws to reform political machinery, progressives advocated the initiative and the referendum—the first to permit voters to initiate new legislation, the second to allow them to pass judgment on statutes already on the books. "Popocrat" Governor Robert B. Smith and his successor, Joseph K. Toole, had both urged these innovations earlier; by 1906 there was strong newspaper support, and by an overwhelming margin of six to one, Montanans adopted a constitutional amendment which provided for the initiative and referendum. The importance of this is not lost by noting that in 1912, when progressivism was at its peak, voters used the initiative mechanism to adopt four separate reform measures: nominations by direct primary, presidential preference primary, popular referendum for election of senators, and a corrupt-practices act.

Many of the progressive measures sought to ameliorate social ills or give consumer protection. A State Board of Health was created in 1901 and a pure food and drug law adopted. Two years later the legislature enacted a comprehensive meat and milk inspection act. Enforcement was another matter, however, as was discovered when the Board of Health sought to enforce laws against pollution of streams by cities. Even more futile were efforts to legally combat the sulphur dioxide, arsenic trioxide, and other toxics spewed out over the Deer Lodge Valley after the Anaconda Company's Washoe smelter opened in 1902. Over the years, the company would spend close to a million dollars negotiating settlements and discrediting claims of farmers whose livestock died from poison-laden grass and hay. Even President Roosevelt's attempts to mediate and finally federal lawsuits in 1910 brought not solution but only procrastination.

Progressive in spirit was the creation of the State Bureau of Child and Animal Protection in 1903, an agency concerned with protection of minors and dedicated to the elimination of child labor, although only eight percent of males between ten and fifteen were in the Montana work force, compared with twenty-six percent nationally. In the following year, voters overwhelmingly set sixteen as the minimum age for mine workers, then added a compulsory school law, which, as elsewhere, proved even more effective than age restrictions in curtailing child labor. In 1907, voters extended the sixteen-year limitation to areas other than mining; at the same time, having listened to Judge Ben Lindsey of Denver speak to the public and the legislature on youth delinquency, they created a juvenile-court system. Such advances had the support of ministerial groups, civic organizations, and the Montana State Federation of Women's Clubs, who were also battling against gambling, drinking, and prostitution, in part to improve the moral atmosphere for the youth of the state.

Labor was strong and well defined in Montana; but so was capital. Thus while the state did not lead in labor reforms, it did come forth with changes in the progressive spirit. In 1904, for example, after Clark and Heinze both had used the eight-hour day to gain miners' support, voters overwhelmingly adopted a constitutional amendment requiring this as the standard workday in mining, public works, and other areas. Mine safety laws were strengthened; and in 1915, the electorate by initiative instituted at least a limited program of workmen's compensation, after earlier efforts had been narrowly defeated. To what extent such reform was progressive and what inspired by labor itself is difficult to determine, for Montana, ironically enough, had one of the strongest radical labor movements in the country. Butte, the Gibraltar of unionism, was the birthplace of the Western Federation of Miners and long an important center of the Industrial

Workers of the World (called the Wobblies), an offshoot in 1905, which was frank and open in its aim to overturn the capitalist wage system and to unify workers under one big industrial union. It was strongest in mining and smelting, but not limited to those areas. The pervasiveness of unionism in Butte was long evident. That town, according to Burt Wheeler, had "even a chimney sweeps union composed of two chimney sweeps." [12]

At the same time, progressivism in the early twentieth century received some reinforcement from the relatively strong Socialist party in Montana's mining and industrial counties—enough so that Eugene Debs could pull nearly 6,000 votes for the U.S. presidency in 1904 and 1908, and more than 10,000 in 1912, the peak year, when Lewis Duncan could draw 12,566 in the governor's race—about half of the winning total of Democrat Sam Stewart. The party gained some farm support, with organizations like the American Society of Equity urging cooperatives, more impartial taxation, and lower railroad rates, and the Nonpartisan League after 1916 coming in from North Dakota with a drive for state-owned banks, elevators, and packing plants. These "Sons of the Wild Jackasses"—as those who kicked over the political traces would later be called—would be aided by the direct primary and would expand more rapidly with the drought and depression of 1917, and undoubtedly they helped foster progressive reforms.

The shutdown of Anaconda's mines during the 1903 Heinze dispute seemed, to many people, to bear out the reformer's belief that big business required control. Much was being said nationally of the "malefactors of great wealth," as Teddy Roosevelt called them, and of the monopolistic and corrupt powers of trusts. When Governor Joseph K. Toole complained to the legislature in 1901 of "the long continued practice of corporate interference in political affairs in this State,"[13] the reference was hardly veiled. The railroads and Anaconda (still Amalgamated) had earned their reputations; soon the new Montana

---

12. Wheeler, *Yankee*, p. 89.

13. *Message of Governor Jos. K. Toole to the Seventh Legislative Assembly of the State of Montana, January 7, 1901* (Helena: State Publishing Company, 1901), p. 33.

Power Company would be added to the list. But it was clear, as Toole himself pointed out, that relief from the trusts must come from Washington, not Helena. One state effort came in 1907, with the creation of a Montana Board of Railroad Commissioners, charged with taking a hard look at rates and services, free passes, and railroad taxation. While the commission made some improvement, real regulation was still in the future. It would be tied to the expanding powers of the Interstate Commerce Commission, just as more substantial controls over business in general would be national and would stem from such progressive legislation of the Wilson administration as the Clayton Anti-Trust Act, the Federal Trade Commission Act, and the Federal Reserve Act, among others.

At the state and national level, progressivism intertwined woman suffrage and prohibition, two movements that went back into earlier history and would be brought to fruition by the broader currents of the twentieth century.

When Montana became a state, only three western territories—Wyoming, Utah, and Washington—had or had had equal suffrage. In the 1880s, female taxpayers were eligible to vote in Montana school elections, to sit on school boards, or serve as county school superintendents, but not to participate in general elections. Attempts to enfranchise women failed in 1876 and in the 1884 and 1889 constitutional conventions, where the issue was a warm one. Members of the 1889 convention listened to silver-maned Henry Blackwell, editor of the *Boston Woman's Journal,* argue the refining and tempering influence of women at the polls; they heard stubborn little Martin Maginnis insist that women would not be independent but would be controlled by ministers of the gospel. Then, as usual, the opponents of "old maids and non-breeders," as the suffragettes were labeled, won out.

But outsiders like Emma Smith De Voe began organizing across the new state for the American Woman Suffrage Association, just as she would do elsewhere in the West. Mary Long Alderson, wife of a Montana farmer and businessman, gave less dramatic but sustained leadership; while Maria Dean, a talented and versatile physician with genuine concern for child welfare and mental health problems, provided much of the spark for the Helena Equal Suffrage Club. It was because of such leaders that suffrage bills came before the legislature with some regularity, and assemblymen were exposed to the standard argument that peace and total enfranchisement went hand-in-hand: only women "can rescue poor, indiscreet and misguided man and lift him to the height about the seething, rotten conditions into which he has got himself." [14] But, in general, the "staid old benedicts and confirmed bachelors" [15] were unmoved, and political strongman Marcus Daly was known in his day as a "powerful enemy of women in Montana. . . ." [16] Bills were consistently defeated or quietly put "to rest among the pigeonholes," even though Governor Joseph K. Toole urged vigorously in 1903 that the suffrage question be submitted to a popular vote: "A new force is demanded in this State to clean out the Augean Stables whose poisonous effluvia ladens the political atmosphere and corrupts the public morals." [17] But the legislature was more concerned with other matters: the struggle between Heinze and the Amalgamated; efforts to increase the tax levy; or attempts to establish a railroad commission, for example.

Yet change was in the air. Progressives like Dixon and Walsh talked suffrage and saw its importance. Thousands of homesteaders flocking in tended to be receptive. Though a bill had been turned back in 1911, the Democratic sweep of the following year was encouraging. Governor Sam Stewart, a big, distinguished-looking man, called for full suffrage, and the assembly, perhaps reluctantly, agreed to set the question before the voters in 1914.

It was Jeannette Rankin and Mary Long Alderson who directed the campaign to educate the public. Rankin, a young University of Montana graduate who had studied in New York

14. *Great Falls Tribune,* October 26, 1902.
15. Quoted in Doris Buck Ward, "The Winning of Woman Suffrage in Montana" (MA Thesis, Montana State University, Bozeman, 1974), p. 46.
16. Ida Husted Harper to Mary L. Alderson (November 14, 1900), copy, Mary Long Alderson MSS, MHS.
17. *Message of Governor Jos. K. Toole to the Eighth Legislative Assembly of the State of Montana, January 5, 1903* (Helena: State Publishing Co., 1903), p. 54.

and practiced social work briefly in Seattle, was one of the "new" women of her day. Where Alderson saw temperance and woman suffrage as "twin sisters," Rankin was single-minded and fought successfully to keep them separate. She knew that the opposition included liquor interests, some immigrants who wished to preserve both their traditions and their drinks, and organized antisuffrage campaigners who argued that woman's place was in the home. Nativism was not a conscious issue, but implicitly it was there. Woman suffrage would increase the proportion of native-born voters.

Energetic, vivacious, and friendly, Jeannette Rankin directed a whirlwind campaign, scouring the state, organizing every county seat for the referendum, and co-ordinating efforts of both local and outside speakers. With winning ways, she sought out the man in the street. When she spoke intensely at Lewistown in a gold velvet suit, she was described as looking "like a young panther ready to spring." [18] She appeared at schools, picnics, and county fairs; but the climax of her work came at the state fair in Helena in September 1914, with a mile-long procession, which included automobiles; floats; horseback riders; labor leaders; "Sacagawea" in costume; more than 600 women in white, yellow, or black; and boy scouts bearing banners "I want my mother to vote." Two months later, in a fairly close election, in which the homestead counties were important, the vote came to Montana women.

In the election of 1916, three women were elected to the legislature, including red-haired Maggie Hathaway, who had given fifty-five talks during the 1914 suffrage fight and who had campaigned for the house in Ravalli County, going by buggy from ranch to ranch. In the assembly, where she was a thoroughgoing progressive, a colleague referred to her as "the biggest man in the House," [19] and in 1920 she was chosen minority floor leader, the first woman in America so honored.

18. Belle Fligelman Winestine, "Mother Was Shocked," *Montana,* 24 (Summer 1974): 71.
19. Harold Tascher, *Maggie and Montana: The Story of Maggie Smith Hathaway* (New York: Exposition Press, 1954), p. 73.

At the same time Maggie Hathaway was being sent to the legislature, Jeannette Rankin was being elected to the United States House of Representatives. Using the slogan "Let the People Know," she ran on a platform which stressed child welfare, publicity for congressional action, and woman suffrage at the national level. The first woman ever elected to Congress, Rankin fascinated the public, an enchantment reflected by Christopher Morley in the *New York Times:*

> We have so many Congressmen
> Whose ways are dark and shady—
> How joyfully we welcome then
> The coming Congresslady! [20]

"A Montana suffragist—right out of the cattle country," wrote a journalist, tongue-in-cheek. "Suppose she packs a .44 six-shooter and trims her skirts with chaps fur." [21] But Jeannette Rankin hardly fit the image. When she made her initial appearance in Congress, she wore "a well-made dark-blue silk and chiffon suit, with open neck, and wide white crepe collar and cuffs" and carried yellow and purple flowers "given her at the suffrage breakfast." [22]

Many of the suffragettes had also been active in the prohibition movement. Montana had from the beginning been wet. Alcohol lubricated the tonsils of dusty miners; it spiced up cowhands' infrequent trips to town; and it was vital for the proper celebration of holidays like New Year's and the Fourth of July. But it was also a commodity viewed negatively by some from the early days of the Stuart brothers, who commented on local "students of toxicology" in the Deer Lodge Valley and wished the whiskey traders would go "to the Blackfoot country or to Hades." [23] The Stuarts themselves were teetotalers but not crusaders. They wished, but others worked to bring dryness.

20. *New York Times,* November 19, 1916. © 1916 by The New York Times Company. Reprinted by permission.

21. *San Francisco Chronicle,* quoted in John C. Board, "The Lady from Montana," *Montana,* 17 (July 1967): 14.

22. Slayden, *Washington Wife,* p. 299.

23. Phillips, *Forty Years on the Frontier,* 1:186, 192.

Governor Green Clay Smith was more attuned to the temperance cause and, after he left Montana, would run for the presidency on the national Prohibition ticket in 1876. Another chief executive, Preston Leslie, was an active marcher in the "Cold Water Army" in the eighties, but his pious recommendations cut no ice with the legislature. When Frances Willard spoke in Butte on behalf of woman suffrage in 1883, she also helped to organize a chapter of the Woman's Christian Temperance Union there, surely an uphill task to anyone who knew the ways of that thirsty camp. Events soon bore this out: in the Union's free library, confirmed tipplers kept themselves in whiskey money by pawning the books. But through the years, the drys worked diligently, fighting what seemed a losing battle. Even when the Prohibition party ran a near-full slate in 1892 with a gubernatorial candidate named J. M. Waters, it was hardly worth the effort.

In the progressive era, national temperance leaders visited the state, sometimes with embarrassing results, as in 1910 when Carrie Nation, hatchet-wielding crusader from Kansas, managed to get herself thrown out of one of Butte's many brothels by an irate madam. But the W.C.T.U. remained ever active, soft-pedaling the suffrage issue, and like the potent Anti-Saloon League, dogging the legislature and pounding the pavement on behalf of local-option prohibition. With counties and townships gradually drying themselves up, the question of statewide prohibition came before the public in a referendum of 1916, and by a substantial margin Montanans closed up their 5,000-odd taverns as of New Year's 1918, joining the parade of legally dehydrated states two years before the national Prohibition amendment went into effect. But, as time would indicate, legality and practicality are often poles apart.

Closely allied with liquor in the eyes of progressive reformers was prostitution and the need to clean up the moral environment for the youth of Montana. Around the state were many red-light districts, but apart from San Francisco's Barbary Coast, Butte's was probably the largest in the country. From 1904 to 1917, it included close to a thousand girls, licensed by the city at $10 a

month, and may have been one of the reasons visitors viewed
Butte as a place of "horror by day and joy at night." [24] Reform
pressure forced segregation mainly into one district, and a new
wave of puritanism that came with World War I closed it completely, not to reopen until the thirties, when "Venus Alley"
was a mere shadow of its former self. Meanwhile, idle Butte
girls demanded justice: prostitutes in Deer Lodge were still actively meeting continuing consumer demands. City fathers did
crack down there and at White Sulphur Springs, action which,
some claimed, undermined the towns' economic bases.

Throughout the nation the main thrust of the progressive
movement would be blunted by the war and the conservative reaction that followed. So, too, was the pattern in Montana.
When the European powder keg erupted in the summer of 1914,
Montanans, like their counterparts elsewhere in the nation, felt
strong, secure, and smug, far from the Old World's bloody
shores. They had more important concerns—homesteading, the
company, woman suffrage, as well as increased prosperity, for
the demands of war-torn Europe for foodstuffs, strategic metals,
and army horses boosted prices, with a positive impact on Montana producers.

Gradually, with German submarine warfare, economic ties,
propaganda, and pro-Ally feelings all playing roles, American
isolation would break down, and in April 1917 the United States
would enter the crusade "to make the world safe for democracy." When Congress considered war, its lone woman member, Missoula's Jeannette Rankin, took a firm stand. With a sob
in her voice she spoke simply, "I love my country, but I cannot
vote for war; I vote *No*." [25] Although one of fifty so balloting,
she was singled out for vilification at home. The *Helena Independent* called her "silly and sentimental," "a dupe of the
Kaiser, a member of the Hun army in the United States, and a
crying schoolgirl." She was a "misrepresentation of the strong-
minded men and women of the best fighting principality be-

24. George Wesley Davis, *Sketches of Butte* (Boston: Cornhill Co., 1921), p. 27.
25. Slayden, *Washington Wife*, p. 301.

tween the Father of Waters and the Western Sea." [26] And many of her cohorts were convinced that her position had seriously harmed the national woman suffrage movement. ". . . every time she answers a roll call she loses us a *million votes*," confided Carrie Chapman Catt. [27]

When the war came, the "best fighting principality" lived up to its notices. Although Frank Linderman's offer to raise a regiment of Indian troops was declined, by the time of the Armistice, Montana had provided 41,133 men. This meant an abnormally high ratio of 796 servicemen for every 10,000 citizens and was apparently tied to erroneous Selective Service quotas, based on an over-inflated projection of Montana's population for 1920.

Montana's old Second Regiment was recalled from duty against Pancho Villa in Mexico and reassigned to France. Many other local boys saw service with the Ninety-first Division, and some, like University of Montana football player Paul Dornblaser, died in Argonne Forest. On the Missoula campus newly completed Simkins Hall, named after another Montana casualty, was first used as a barracks for the Student Army Training Corps, then as an infirmary when the great flu epidemic swept the state. Fort Missoula became a training camp for mechanics.

In towns across the state, Red Cross Auxiliaries rolled bandages, knitted socks and sweaters, and even made nightshirts for the boys in the trenches. Victory gardens sprouted forth, and citizens voluntarily assigned themselves meatless, wheatless, and sugarless days to conserve food under the program directed nationally by millionaire Herbert Hoover. Young Lillie Klein learned to use flour substitutes and, with the ladies at Korn, sewed and raffled off quilts for the war effort. At Glasgow a Ladies Home Guard was formed, and local banks urged people to buy government bonds. A number of Montanans, Maggie Hathaway among them, joined George Creel's corps of "Four-Minute Speakers," carrying the gospel of wartime need and

26. Quoted in Hannah Josephson, *Jeannette Rankin: First Lady in Congress* (New York: Bobbs-Merrill Co., 1974), pp. 76–77.
27. Quoted in Board, "The Lady from Montana," *Montana*, 17 (July 1967): 14.

sacrifice to the public. As a result, Montanans oversubscribed their allotment of Liberty Bonds, even though that quota was based "on the same fictitious basis of population" as man-power.[28]

But there was a price for mobilization of the home front. What happened in Montana bore out Woodrow Wilson's prediction the night before he asked Congress to declare war:

> Once lead this people into war . . . and they'll forget there was ever such a thing as tolerance. To fight you must be brutal and ruthless, and the spirit of ruthless brutality will enter into the very fiber of our national life, infecting Congress, the courts, the policeman on the beat, the man in the streets.[29]

Woe unto those not in complete sympathy with the war effort— the Scandinavians who pursued a neutral course; the Irish who were never pleased with the British alliance; the German-Americans who understandably might not take an anti-German position; the leftist radicals, especially the Wobblies, who for a variety of reasons preached pacifism!

Under the aegis of the Montana Council of Defense, with grassroots councils in each of the forty-three counties, the state was gripped in a wave of superpatriotic, irrational anti-German sentiment of the most hysterical and senseless nature—at least in the eyes of later generations. The Council of Defense applied pressure, not merely to promote the sale of war stamps and bonds, but to purge libraries of books on Germany. One school even clipped German songs out of books, blotted German flags out of its dictionaries, and required its students to spell Germany with a small "g." When the council forbade the use of the German language, this no doubt was one factor in the migration to Canada of the already much-abused German-speaking Mennonites from eastern Montana. On the flimsiest of hearsay evidence state and local councils haled before them those accused of being slackers or of having made seditious remarks;

28. *Message of Governor Jos. M. Dixon to the Seventeenth Legislative Assembly of the State of Montana, January 4, 1921* (Helena: State Publishing Co., 1921), p. 3.

29. Quoted in John L. Heaton, *Cobb of "The World"* (New York: E. P. Dutton & Co., 1924), p. 270.

foreign accents and Teutonic names were automatically suspect as the zealots and superpatriots issued "orders" of near-legislative force.

The state ran rife with rumors of German agents and saboteurs. German airships were sighted; enemy airplanes reportedly flew from secret bases in the Bitterroot Valley. Working hand-in-hand with the already tainted I.W.W., the Kaiser's infiltraters in Montana were accused of poisoning wells, burning crops, and subverting copper production. Although not more than 500 of the 15,000 miners in the Butte area were Wobblies, their pacifist stance made the I.W.W. a special target. Any Wobbly not for the war effort must perforce be against it. In spring and summer, 1917, guardsmen and government raids had finally ended a bitter series of strikes in the lumber industry. In the mines, the I.W.W. had challenged the Butte Mines Union, had been infiltrated by the company, and in 1914, after riots, dynamiting, and martial law, had suffered humiliating defeat. Labor was still tense when the war came and would emerge even more militant after the terrible shaft fire disaster which killed 164 men in the Speculator Mine in 1917. When the company refused to bargain with the new Metal Mine Workers' Union, some 15,000 workers ultimately went off the job, and detectives and goon squads were brought in. On August 1, amid this harassment, acute labor unrest, and actual striking, intense feelings reached a peak when organizer Frank Little, who had made biting antiwar speeches, was taken from his bed by masked men and lynched from the Milwaukee Railroad trestle in Butte. "Good work: Let them continue to hang every I.W.W. in the state," wrote a Helena editor and council stalwart the next morning.[30] That not all Montanans were in agreement was indicated a few days later when 3,000 people marched in Frank Little's funeral procession and watched him buried while they sang "La Marseillaise."

U.S. District Attorney Burton K. Wheeler was one of those who condemned the lynching as "a damnable outrage, a blot on the state and country" and who refused to acquiesce in the hys-

30. *Helena Independent,* August 2, 1917.

terical campaign.[31] A young University of Michigan law graduate, Wheeler had stepped off a train in Butte in 1905, had been cleaned out in a poker game, and had decided to remain at least temporarily. With support of the company, he had gone to the legislature in 1911; subsequently, with the aid of Senator Thomas Walsh, he had been appointed district attorney, a stepping-stone to a more important political office. Joining Wheeler in upholding wartime civil and personal rights was Federal Judge George Bourquin, a somewhat eccentric but admirable and fair-minded man who heard charges and frequently dismissed them for lack of evidence. Out of the tragic, senseless turmoil of the Little episode and the unwillingness of both Wheeler and Bourquin to conduct a zealous witch hunt came a special legislative session early in 1918 to give official sanction to the Council of Defense and to enact tougher laws. Governor Sam Stewart told the assembly:

> The free air of Montana is too pure; too sacred, and too precious a heritage here in this mountain region to be used as a medium by the vicious, the traitorous and the treasonable to breathe forth sentiments of disloyalty against our cause and to extend comfort to the enemies of the country.[32]

Out of the session came a stringent Montana Sedition act, a statute which a few months later would be adopted almost verbatim by the federal government; at the same time, the legislature passed a new Criminal Syndicalism law, all of which made it easier to restrict individual rights in general and sounded the death knell for the I.W.W. in particular. No doubt the broad powers of the Council of Defense were unconstitutional, as state attorney general Sam Ford insisted. And some, like Wheeler, believed that the Anaconda Company used both the council and the wartime legislation primarily to demoralize and destroy organized labor.

With the Armistice, these excesses gradually faded, though

---

31. Wheeler, *Yankee*, p. 140.
32. *Message of Governor S. V. Stewart to the First Extraordinary Session of the Fifteenth Legislative Assembly of the State of Montana, 1918* (Helena: State Publishing Co., 1918), p. 7.

some shaded off into the anti-Red period of the early twenties. The young men returned; or rather, some of the young men returned—939 had given their lives for their country; many others were discharged, with their sixty dollars and railroad ticket, but elected not to come back to Montana, despite the move by the War Mothers of America to have land set aside for veterans who wanted to take up farming. More opportunity loomed elsewhere: the northern farm boom was about to collapse; mining and metal processing were on the wane.

Meanwhile, politics went on as usual. Under fire from the ultra-conservatives, Wheeler resigned the district attorney post, lest his continuation harm Tom Walsh's chances for re-election to the Senate, but in leaving he vowed "to do everything possible to wrest control of the Democratic Party from the Company." But Walsh won handily. As the farm depression deepened, the Nonpartisan League made such astonishing inroads in the state and in the legislature that both parties sought a modification of the direct primary, lest the League capture the primary machinery. But the League forced postponement of a referendum on the question until the election of 1920, when Wheeler led the fight against it. Although asked to run with League endorsement on the GOP ticket, Wheeler eventually agreed to try for the governorship on the Democratic slate, while the Republicans nominated liberal Joseph Dixon, former senator and Bull Mooser. Faced with two progressive types, the company reluctantly decided to back Dixon as the lesser of twin evils; with its slogan "We are opposed to private ownership of public officials," the Nonpartisan League threw its weight behind Wheeler and a rock-'em, sock-'em campaign was on. Wheeler argued that the public ownership of mills and elevators advocated by the league was no more socialistic than public ownership of schools. He denounced the copper interests and their tools. After he avoided possible violence near Dillon by hiding in a railroad-car depot, the company press labeled him "Boxcar Burt" or denounced him as the "red socialist," "Bolshevik Burt." When Wheeler was badly defeated, an editorial in the *Anaconda Standard* shrieked:

BUTTE KICKS OUT THE RED
AND ELECTS AMERICANS TO OFFICE.[33]

A dozen days later, Anaconda closed down three mines, reducing operations by half; soon it announced a wage cut, to "avert a complete shutdown;" and in spring 1921 suspended all mining operations because of depressed copper prices. A story went the rounds of a judge examining a would-be citizen, who insisted that Wheeler was governor of Montana. When corrected, the applicant explained:

> All I know is that all the papers, the bankers and the politicians said that if Wheeler was elected all the mines would close, the banks would foreclose the mortgages on the farms and everybody and everything would go broke. Now, Judge, the mines have closed, the farmers are losing their farms and it looks as if everybody is going broke—so I think Wheeler must be governor.[34]

It soon became apparent that retirement on Flathead Lake had not dulled Joe Dixon's progressive sentiments. His message to the legislature in 1921 was a model reform document in which he focused on the state's financial distress and called for an enlightened tax program, including levies on income, oil, coal tonnage, gasoline, and especially on mineral production. "In the matter of taxation," he insisted, "Montana has lagged in the very rear of all the other states." [35] When he advocated a permanent tax commission to study and revise the structure, a bill to create a body was defeated by what he called "probably the most powerful opposition lobby ever assembled in Helena." [36] Burt Wheeler endorsed Dixon's program before the legislature but could not refrain from chiding the company about "their governor" having stolen his "Bolshevik" program of 1920.

33. Wheeler, *Yankee,* pp. 162, 183.
34. Wheeler, *Yankee,* p. 186.
35. *Message of Governor Jos. M. Dixon to the Seventeenth Legislative Assembly,* p. 17.
36. *Message of Governor Joseph M. Dixon to the First Extraordinary Session of the Seventeenth Legislative Assembly of the State of Montana, 1921* (Helena: State Publishing Co., 1921), pp. 16–17.

The taxation of mines had always been a controversial issue, even back to territorial times. In 1918, hoping to expand tax base revenues, Chancellor Elliott of the University of Montana had urged economics professor Louis Levine to undertake a study of the state tax structure. Suddenly, early in 1919, Elliott ordered Levine to drop the project. It was untimely and inappropriate, he said, and the university might be harmed. Levine refused and was suspended, but his findings, published in the book, *The Taxation of Mines in Montana,* indicated that the mineral industry did indeed pay a disproportionately small share of taxes. After much strife, Levine was technically reinstated, but it was clear that it was in spite of strong pressure behind the scenes.

Thus Dixon's tax proposals in 1921 faced an active, organized opposition. When the regular session failed to respond, he called it back to a special sitting and this time won a small levy on oil production, a "bachelor" inheritance tax, and a license tax of 1.5 percent on the net proceeds of mines. But because mines could deduct overhead and improvement costs, they could easily show no net proceeds, while farmers and ranchers paid property taxes at full value regardless of operating expenses.

Burt Wheeler ran for the U.S. Senate in 1922. Realizing that it could not openly attack him and at the same time hope to elect a Democratic legislature to block Dixon's tax program, the company, which after nine months had reopened its mines, now soft-pedaled its opposition. Given Wheeler's overwhelming rout in the 1920 gubernatorial race, it saw no reason to spend money to help defeat a candidate who obviously had no chance. Some said that Anaconda was mildly supporting Wheeler or at least keeping its hands off because he could harm them less in Washington than at home. However that might be, Wheeler swept the state in a breeze, even some of the "cow counties." As a senator, he would be one of the first to visit Red Russia and for strictly economic reasons to urge recognition of the Soviet regime. When a Red Lodge newspaper denounced him for this and suggested his deportation, Wheeler snapped, "Where would you deport me—back to Massachusetts?'' [37] Sub-sequently, he would be involved in investigating the Harding scandals and in 1924 was the vice-presidential candidate on a Progressive party ticket with Robert La Follette of Wisconsin, a ticket which ran a strong second to Calvin Coolidge in Montana.

Meanwhile, Governor Dixon took the mine-taxation issue to the voters. He ran for re-election in 1924 and the tax measure— a gross tonnage levy—was on the ballot by initiative. While Dixon argued that the hard-hit farmers paid thirty-two percent of the state's total revenue, the mines contributed less than nine percent, the company and its associates condemned him as wasteful and extravagant and whipped labor into line with the threat of cutting back operations. Dixon lost to ''Honest John'' Erickson, but the tax initiative won. Here was a minor tax reform, belated and certainly not onerous to an industry which in 1925 reported net profits three times those of the previous year. That the company was a major political influence in the state is without question. But in spite of it, the same kinds of progressive social and political reforms that were instituted elsewhere leavened Montana government in the early twentieth century.

37. Wheeler, *Yankee*, p. 202.

9

The Homesteader Boom

"Buried Up To His Ears in Debt"

IN the story, a bowlegged old Montana cattleman walked up to a withered old Indian and warmly shook his hand. He didn't know him, he explained to a friend, "but I sure as hell know just how he *feels*. We cowmen run him an' his kind off the ranges an' now the nesters have run us cowmen off." [1] Perhaps the episode never happened, but it might have. In its sentiments and the sequence of occupation of the public lands, it has the ring of authenticity about it. Where the northern tribes once rode in buffalo grass and wild hay brushing their ponies' bellies, stockmen in the eighties grazed their longhorns and their herds of sheep. In time, they too would give way, in many instances, to waves of plowmen, who left the sod "wrong side up," as the Indians insisted, as they brought another era to much of Montana.

From the beginning, going back to the fur posts and De Smet's mission, the local economy was in part agricultural. As soon as miners swarmed in along the Stinking Water and on Grasshopper Creek, settlers around Fort Owen supplied them with vegetables, which, as Owen noted in 1863, "command fab-

1. Linderman, *Montana Adventure*, p. 19.

ulous prices." ² Gradually, to meet the needs of an expanding population, the farm domain spread fingerlike into the fertile valleys of the west, south, and central regions. In the fall of 1868 David Carpenter made the first homestead application in Montana, and in the following spring the first woman filed on 160 acres on Warm Springs Creek. In 1870, when Montana's 84,674 acres of improved farmland produced 181,000 bushels of wheat—enough so that flour need no longer be imported, newly arrived Governor Potts was astounded when he attended the territorial fair in Helena and saw cattle that "surpassed our Ohio cattle shows" and a sample of wheat that yielded 85 bushels per acre, "as fine as any Ohio wheat and vegetables that surpassed anything I ever expected to see.³

Potts was much more conservative than the early professional boosters who wrote of thirty-pound turnips and of oats that ran 160 bushels to the acre, these wondrous sizes and prolific yields induced by a blend of clear mountain water, soils practically wanton in fertility, and a "thrifty, enterprising class of people." ⁴ The high mountains protecting the western valleys gave comparative freedom from insects of all kinds, a claim that would have surprised Thomas Harris at Fort Owen, who battled crickets all summer in 1867 to save his 1,400 cabbage plants and in a single day killed five large wagon boxes full of the invaders. Or, if some of the pamphleteers did acknowledge an occasional insect, they denied any possibility of wholesale destruction as in the prairie states. Besides, one contended, "most wheat-growers agree that they can well afford to lose every third crop as long as yields and prices remain so favorable in the good years." ⁵

But as farmers all over the country learned, prices in the two decades following the depression of 1873 were seldom favorable. After completion of the Northern Pacific Railroad in 1883,

2. Dunbar and Phillips, *John Owen,* 1:296.

3. Benjamin Potts to Rutherford B. Hayes (Virginia City, October 8, 1870, Hayes MSS.)

4. James Handly, *The Resources of Madison County, Montana* (San Francisco: Francis & Valentine, 1872), p. 33.

5. Strahorn, *Resources of Montana,* p. 21.

Montana grain growers were part of the American productive system, competing with farmers the world over, with prices determined by various factors, none within their control. As the depression lingered into the mid-seventies, farmers and former miners, too, pushed from the older southwestern counties into the valleys of the Smith, the Sun, and the Yellowstone, where land was cheap and where cultivation as well as stock growing was possible. Thus for the next twenty years, at the same time the range-cattle industry was developing, so also was farming, especially in the well-watered basins ringed by the Belt, the Judith, and the Snowy mountains. From the east, settlers followed the railroad up the Yellowstone and into the valleys of its tributaries, with towns like Glendive, Billings, and Livingston catering to sod-busters, as well as cowpokes. Even as early as 1882, a young clerk from Illinois out to make his fortune in the West was surprised that all the good land fifty miles or so from Bozeman was already taken up.

The number of farms grew steadily—from 851 in 1870 to 5,603 in 1890 and 13,097 by 1900, just as their size also increased regularly—from 164 acres in 1870, to over 350 acres in 1890 and nearly 886 acres by 1900. Irrigated acreage steadily expanded, especially after 1890, but, with a few exceptions, most of the agricultural expansion came into areas that were normally fairly dry. Much farm settlement came in periods of greater than usual rainfall, giving credence to a common belief that "rain followed the plow"—that railroads, cultivation, or tree planting modified the climate. And much of the farm growth before 1900 came on lands formerly dominated by cattlemen: in 1880, slightly more than one quarter of Montana farms were in the eastern two-thirds of the territory; by 1900, almost half.

The twentieth century would bring unprecedented expansion: Montana farm acreage jumped 2,325 percent between 1900 and 1920; wheat acreage in the same period went from 258,000 to 3,417,000. Homesteaders flocked in "like flies to sour milk," [6] attracted by the working of several interlocking forces.

6. John Leakey, *The West That Was: From Texas to Montana* (Dallas: Southern Methodist University Press, 1958), p. 183.

One factor was high grain prices, which climbed steadily from 1897 to 1920, with fantastic gains when World War came to Europe. If rustic poets could write of the "Joy of Dollar Wheat" when the war commenced, they could be doubly joyous before it was over. In general, wheat prices rose faster than farm costs, while at least from 1900 to 1913, cattle values fell off. If grain prices were high, land was easily available. The Newlands Act of 1902 put the government in the irrigation business and gave hope for reclamation, but dam construction moved slowly. Much more important for Montana's twentieth-century boom was the Enlarged Homestead Act of 1909, which allowed entry onto 320, rather than 160 acres of the public domain, with the stipulation that the settler cultivate half. A subsequent amendment reduced the residence requirement from five to three years and permitted the homesteader to be absent for five months of each year in order to bring in a cash income.

Add another ingredient: promotion by editors, chambers of commerce, agricultural experts, railroad spokesmen, politicians, and the state itself. Both the Northern Pacific and "Yim" Hill's Great Northern offered easy emigrant rates and boosted Montana as a land of incomparable flowery meadows, lush grasslands, and healthful climate, requiring only hard work to develop. The Northern Pacific had much land to sell; Hill had a dream of a family on every half-section, producing grain to be hauled by his eastbound trains. For only $12.50 the Great Northern would bring settlers one-way from St. Paul to eastern Montana, replete with visions of "little green fields and little white houses and big red barns, with lightning rods to deflect the shafts of the Northwest's primeval gods." [7] Railroad spokesmen and locals like Montana senator-promoter Paris Gibson challenged the idea that the land was arid or even semiarid. Given proper techniques, Montana farming was as certain "as in any of the states east of the Mississippi," they told their audiences. [8] The proper approach was dry-farming, which implied

7. Quoted in Carl Frederick Kraenzel, *The Great Plains in Transition* (Norman: University of Oklahoma Press, 1955), p. 127.

8. Quoted in Mary W. Hargreaves, *Dry Farming in the Northern Great Plains 1900–1925* (Cambridge: Harvard University Press, 1957), p. 55.

deep cultivation to keep down weeds and to pulverize the top-soil, it involved planting in season to catch what moisture was available, it meant allowing part of the land to lie fallow in the summer, a practice unfortunately not always followed. Montana Experiment Stations cited examples of dry-land successes, and Jim Hill offered prizes for the best grain displays and sent exhibition trains into the midwest to attract attention.

Thus the rush was on. "The old-timer dies hard and loathes to see these fertile prairies adorned with claim shacks," wrote one editor, "but the tide of immigration that has set in this direction cannot be stopped." [9] In 1909, the land office in Miles City was recording 1,200 claims a month; that year, over a million acres were homesteaded in the state; 4.75 million the next year. In 1914, there were 20,662 entries, as a tidal wave of farmers swept into northern and eastern Montana. In wet times, lured by free land and high grain prices, they came by the thousands in "emigrant cars" on the railroad, with a place for everybody and everything: babies, horses, chickens, household goods, and farm equipment. Or some chugged laboriously out in a Model T Ford, more optimistic forerunners of a desperate generation of migrants of the thirties.

Often disparagingly referred to as "honyockers" or "scissor-bills" and censored for their lack of farm experience, they reflected broadly diverse geographic, occupational, or social backgrounds. Some indeed did have adequate capital to enter upon a new life, a fact the State Department of Agriculture and Publicity sought to emphasize by quoting a "significant" remark of an old-timer who watched a group of forty or fifty men get off the train to look at homestead land in northern Montana. "Did you notice that practically every one of those men wore a watch chain?" [10] On the other hand, if Elliott C. Lincoln had a watch chain when he arrived to homestead near Lewistown, he had only fourteen dollars in his pocket. William Kilgour's father

9. Quoted in Vivian A. Paladin, comp. & ed., *From Buffalo Bones to Sonic Boom* (Glasgow Jubilee Committee, 1962), p. 45.

10. *The Resources and Opportunities of Montana* (Helena: Montana Department of Agriculture and Publicity, 1914), pp. 18–19.

was a Sioux Falls salesman, and whatever he knew about farming he gleaned from railroad literature and Department of Agriculture bulletins before he settled near Wolf Springs in 1913. But Chris Spence who brought his bride from Bourbon County, Kansas, to homestead near his sister and her husband out of Chester in 1910, came with plenty of back-breaking farming experience.

Perhaps slightly over one-quarter of the twentieth-century homesteaders were foreign-born, although twenty-one-year-old Lillie Klein, who moved from Nebraska to file on land north of Chinook, was impressed by those around her location. "P.S.," she wrote, "We have a Norwegian west of us; English, south; Irish, east; German, here; French, near; with Scotch and Mexican all around." [11] But these were among more than fifty families; and undoubtedly many of the rest came out of the midwestern farm belt.

Wherever they were from and whatever the state of their bankroll or their knowledge of farming, these were a determined, optimistic lot, united in their individual dreams of land ownership and prosperity. Along with their household gear, piled high on their wagons as they left the railroad stations, they carried with them midwestern values which they planted in the new towns with romantic names like Fairview or Gardenland or Pleasantdale—towns with unpaved streets which in damp weather became "bottomless wallows, slick as a pit of soap and sticky as molasses." [12]

Frequently the newcomers knew little of land and land values and might be exploited by sharp local operators—"the lowest class of vermin that ever infested a good country" [13]—who met them, drove them to see possible half-sections, and coached them in filing upon it, all at a profit of from $20 to $50 a head for a dozen or so a day. The standard joke had such an agent

11. Marie Snedecor, ed., "The Homesteaders: Their Dreams Held No Shadows," *Montana*, 19 (Spring 1969): 15.

12. Chet Huntley, *The Generous Years: Remembrances of a Frontier Boyhood* (New York: Random House, 1968), pp. 112–113.

13. Leakey, *The West That Was*, p. 183.

bragging of a deal just completed with a green but eager sod-
buster: "And d'you know, when we wrote the deed to that land,
I slipped two sections off on him and the dum fool didn't know
the difference! " [14]

Government land by homestead was not charity. A man
earned all he got; it took hard work, sacrifice, and sometimes
heartbreak.

> Buried up to his ears in debt,
> Fighting the heat, the cold, and wet,
> His chances worse than an even bet—
> You'll find the homesteader.[15]

As the newcomers arrived, housing was makeshift. When Robert Eunson and his family came from Wisconsin to settle near
Acton, they slept the first night off the train midst the smell of
horses, harness, timothy, and manure in a Billings livery stable.
The Kilgours spent their first night in the little town of Mel-
stone, where, because the hotel had burned, they took overnight
accommodations in a more-or-less private dwelling, which
turned out to be the local whorehouse. Some homesteaders built
sod houses, but most, like Chris and Lela Spence and their in-
laws, Will and Matilda Smith next door, put up two-room tar-
paper shacks. With almost no assets beyond determination, Will
put in his first crop of potatoes, cutting out the eyes to plant and
eating the rest, which, with jackrabbits, made up the main
source of food that first summer. The Kilgours lived mainly on
bread and navy beans, with an occasional rabbit or sage-hen.
Usually water had to be hauled some distance and the well-
ventilated tar-paper shanties were impossible to warm with cast-
iron cookstoves when winter temperatures plunged to subzero
depths.

Land had to be cleared of rocks, sagebrush, or cacti; it took
back-breaking work to turn the soil and put in the crops, which
usually consisted of hard wheat, perhaps a little oats, barley, or

14. Quoted in Eric Thane [Ralph C. Henry], *High Border Country* (New York:
Duell, Sloan & Pearce, 1942), p. 257.

15. Elliott C. Lincoln, *Rhymes of a Homesteader* (Boston & New York: Houghton
Mifflin Co., 1920), p. 27.

flax. A big vegetable garden and several acres of potatoes were "musts": these were cash commodities to trade at the Green Store in Chester. Often, to make ends meet, the sod-buster worked for wages in the winter, leaving the women on the land. Smith and Spence both had jobs on A. K. Prescott's sheep ranch in the winter and after the spring crop was in.

As it was everywhere on the Great Plains, farming was a gamble. Even in wet years, with prices good, a man never knew for sure. A sudden invasion of insects might leave a wasteland of stalks and stems. Rust could quickly ruin the season's work, and years passed before it was discovered that the Japanese barberry bush was the key to the life cycle of rust spore. A savage hailstorm might destroy a flax crop in a minute or two, wheat in a little longer. Will Smith usually bought hail insurance, but one time, driving the ten miles to Chester to pay the premium, he decided to save money and gamble. That evening he arrived home in his buggy just in time to see a hailstorm completely flatten his uninsured grain fields. Fortunately for the Smiths, this was an exceptional year: the grain came back from its still-living roots and made one of the best crops ever.

If the war pushed prices to peak levels, lean years were not far away. Wartime labor shortages posed problems. One homesteader was unable to get his grain threshed in 1917; it remained in the stack all winter and he got out enough for seed only by the primitive method of driving horses over it. Then came drought, along the High Line in 1917, spreading over much of the eastern two-thirds of the state the following year. But the summer of 1919 was the worst: the withering dryness touched even the western part of the state, with the threat of forest fire added to that of crop failure. There were brief wet interludes, but only six of the thirteen years from 1917 to 1930 would have average or above-average rainfall. The more timid sold out while wheat prices and land values were still up; but others expanded and borrowed to add to their holdings and equipment.

Locusts, cut worms, and wire worms all took their toll, and in the days before "miracle" pesticides, grasshoppers were particularly hard to control, especially when they moved in vast, obscene clouds. Farmers tried burning their fields, drowning them out by water in irrigated areas, or importing turkeys by the thousands. But nothing seemed to work; the poultry waxed fat but the course of the hoppers continued. Some relief came in 1917, when the state entomologist devised a poison-bran solution laced with arsenic provided by Anaconda, and home and county extension agents held "mixing bees" like the one in Flathead County, where ninety farmers mixed and spread twelve tons. Even so, two years later Flathead Valley farmers had total failure: drought struck, and grasshoppers ate everything but the mortgage. Only by borrowing on land and livestock were they able to buy hay at $45 a ton to get through the winter. Still, as one farmer put it, with the eternal optimism of the West, "Well, I have had three good crops: twelve years ago, five years ago, and *next* year!" [16]

Next came the removal of government price controls and skidding wheat prices. In two months in the autumn of 1920, wheat went from $2.40 to $1.25 a bushel and would steadily decline to 92 cents by 1922, although machinery costs remained high. Thus at the very moment natural difficulties were lowering the per-acre yields, falling prices compounded matters. In the first fifteen years of the century, plowed-up Montana grasslands averaged 25 bushels of wheat per acre; in drought-stricken 1919, a year which cost Montanans an estimated loss of 50 million, the land yielded only 4.6 bushels an acre.

Frequent, deep cultivation and an unwillingness on the part of many to rotate crops or to summer-fallow helped destroy the land. In dry years devastating winds blew the topsoil away. Ominous "black blizzards" of eastern Montana in the dry twenties would be suggestive of the more extreme Dust Bowl of other regions in the thirties. "Big movement in real estate today," Montanans would say. "Our land's going down into Dakota." [17]

Farmers' dreams turned to nightmares. Crop failures piled up, debts mounted, incomes dwindled. Little federal or state aid was available for victims. The Federal Land Bank, which went back to President Wilson's administration, gave limited support; the

16. Quoted in Vestal, *The Missouri*, p. 173.
17. Quoted in Thane, *High Border Country*, p. 258.

state even less. When the governor called a special legislative
session to consider the crisis in 1919, the assembly did little except to wring its hands and authorize counties to issue road construction bonds in the hope that new jobs might be created. But
counties already had their own problems. One of the by-
products of the great homestead boom had been county-
splitting, an expensive business, to say the least. In 1913, the
state and its 33 counties had owed some $16 million, or $39.68
per capita; by 1921, the state and its then 54 counties were in
debt more than $60 million, or $110 per capita. The Montana
tax levy, already the highest in the country, rose from $26.83
in 1912 to $50 in 1921; in the same period, while population
was up 23 percent, the cost of county government rose 108 percent. By 1921 with a score of counties bankrupt, the rate of tax
foreclosure was the highest in the nation, apart from Mississippi. For any hope of relief, drought-ridden farmers turned by
the thousands to private agencies like the Red Cross and the Salvation Army, who lacked the resources even to provide basic
food, clothing, and fuel.

Yet, with occasional good years, optimism died slowly. So
confident of the future was Scobey, the major wheat-shipping
point on the Great Northern, that it established a baseball team
which included two former big-leaguers barred from the profession after the 1919 Black Sox scandal in which Chicago threw
the World Series to Cincinnati. Rival Plentywood brought in its
own professional, a black pitcher "with more curves than the
Poplar River," and the game flourished, even though it was admitted that most players on both teams had permanent rings
over their noses "from drinking moonshine from quart fruit
jars." [18] But when the wheat boom died, so did big-time baseball. Up on the High Line, Shelby, another wheat center with
4,000 inhabitants, showed its faith in tomorrow by staging the
Dempsey-Gibbons fight in 1923, a fiasco at which only 7,000
spectators showed up to occupy the 45,000 seats built for the
occasion.

Despite such boosterism, the farmers simply moved on. An

---

18. Gary Lucht, "Scobey's Touring Pros: Wheat Baseball and Illicit Booze," *Montana,* 20 (Summer 1970): 91–92.

estimated 60,000 of the 80,000 who came between 1900 and 1917 packed up their meager belongings and left. As Robert Fletcher put it, they "just spit on the fire and whistled for the dog." [19] The ones who stayed, like old Marcus Howell, who at 101 was still on his Snake Creek homestead 24 years after he had settled there, tightened their belts, diversified, and adapted; scores of obituary notices in newspapers of the 1970s attest the hardiness of these never-say-die settlers who stuck it out. But most scattered. Across the state after World War I and into the twenties, the ugly utilitarian towns thrown up around grain elevators and one-horse banks began to dry up. Fields went to waste, captured by Russian thistles, the seeds brought in with imported grains. Empty shacks dotted the land, their doors swinging drunkenly, torn tar-paper flapping mournfully in the wind—the never-ending wind. A lonely land became even more lonely. Near the new post office of Korn, high in the state's midsection, Lillie Klein could see no lighted houses from her home, where fifty-five had been visible a few years earlier. With the great exodus, 11,000 farms were vacated (20 percent of Montana's total), between 1919 and 1925, and 2 million acres went out of cultivation. One of every two farm mortgages was foreclosed, as a weak banking structure made the crisis more acute. Despite Joseph Kinsey Howard casting the blame on the Federal Reserve managers, the fact is that Montana simply had too many banks, too many inexperienced and even incompetent bankers, and too many marginal homesteaders who could not pay their interest when the bad years came. The combination brought the system tumbling down: between 1920 and 1926, the peak of the banking crisis, 214 of the commercial banks—one half of Montana's total—failed.

In the decade of the twenties, when population increased nationally by over sixteen percent, Montana was the only state to register a decline. When the boomers left, most of them stayed in the West. Elliott Lincoln moved to California to teach and write poetry about the Montana homestead days he knew first-

19. Robert H. Fletcher, *Free Grass to Fences* (New York: University Publishers, Inc., 1960), pp. 149–150.

hand. After ten years of struggling with nature in Liberty County, Will Smith had to borrow money to get his family to Spokane, where he commenced a new career as a city fireman. His brother-in-law Chris Spence hung on for a few years longer, then went to work managing a ranch in Idaho for A. K. Prescott, but he kept the old homestead at Chester for another fifty years. It was his; he had earned it, by God, and through the rest of his life, his emotions about it were a mixture of pride and disappointment. Like most of the others, he probably expected more of his 320 acres than they could give. "Land is patient stuff," said an old Montanan, "but God help the man that provokes it." [20] Thus as the plains region changed from an open range grazing area to one of intensive dry farming, land that hung in a delicate balance failed when its sod was broken and relentlessly mined and when the natural hazards of drought and insects were added. From the experience commenced a slight move in the opposite direction: as sod-busters went "belly up," it was easy for stockmen to acquire their holdings for next to nothing, thus benefitting indirectly from the Enlarged Homestead Act.

In the wake of the homestead boom would come two decades of intermittent dryness, poverty, and out-migration. The frontier that historian Frederick Jackson Turner had said was closed by about 1890, was now truly ending. And with it went some of the self-confidence and unbridled optimism of a generation of Montanans.

20. Quoted in Russell McKee, *The Last West* (New York: Thomas Y. Crowell, Co., 1974), 264. The author wishes to thank William Smith of Houston, Texas, for his reminiscences of family homesteading experiences in Liberty County.

10

The Lean Thirties

"We Have No Credit and No Work."

ⓞN the surface they were good years. The Roaring Twenties, they were called; the Jazz Age; the era of the flapper, the flivver, and bathtub gin. Thanks to mass production, advertising, and liberal consumer credit, the American economy was gearing up for the even better days everybody knew lay just ahead. If a few economists raised their eyebrows at some obvious soft spots or at the antics of the Great Bull Market or if Bernard Baruch quietly sold his stocks and bought government bonds, these were but manifestations of the timid and the fainthearted.

Even in Montana, despite the grimness of farming and banking, there was optimism and what President Warren G. Harding called "normalcy." Harding himself had received a tremendous ovation when he stopped off in Butte briefly in June of 1923; less than two months later, the city ceased all activity for five minutes when he was buried on August 10. Even so, Montanans were thrilled when one of their own, Burt Wheeler, helped investigate the scandals of the Harding administration, and when the imperturbable Tom Walsh led the probe of the Teapot Dome

Quoted in MHS, *Precious Metals*, p. 182.

142

and Elk Hills oil deception. They were excited when Wheeler ran for the vice-presidency on the Progressive ticket with Bob La Follette of Wisconsin in 1924; and when Walsh, a bone-dry Catholic, received 123 votes for the presidential nomination on the 102nd ballot at the Democratic national convention that same year and when he made a second bid for the presidency in 1928, only to be turned back by "thirsty Republicans and misguided Drys." [1] And over 100,000 inspired citizens had turned out at Butte when Charles A. Lindbergh flew in the year before to inaugurate airmail service with Salt Lake City.

As politics indicated, conservatism spilled over into the twenties. The Ku Klux Klan had an estimated strength of 6,000 in the state. Watchers saw 1,000 Klansmen parade down Higgins Avenue in Missoula in 1925, but the group seems to have faded quickly away. A controversy bubbled when a professor at the university permitted the use of the good old western term "son of a bitch" in the student literary magazine. A law-school professor came under under attack as a pacifist and radical by student members of the American Legion and was put on leave without pay for the final year of his three-year contract, in spite of condemnation of state officials by the American Association of University Professors.

If the twenties saw some ailing economic areas, the decade also brought new industries. As the age of the automobile expanded, so did petroleum production. Although the geologist for a major oil company once said he would drink all the oil ever produced in Montana, wells in the Elk Basin field were pumping as early as 1915 and in the 1920s three more major fields were opened in central and eastern Montana. It was the Tin Lizzie, too, that gave a new boost to tourism throughout the West and made it a million-dollar business for Montanans.

Out of the depressed days of the cattle industry of the late twenties came new emphasis on the "paying guest," as Montana became dude-ranch country. A judicious blend of comfort and the rugged life, the dude ranch was extolled by Arthur

---

1. Quoted in Paul Carter, "The Other Catholic Candidate," *Pacific Northwest Quarterly,* 55 (January 1964): 2.

Chapman as "the West's soothing gift to a headachy world." [2]
There, easterners could

> . . . enjoy the thrills of a lifetime, the panoramic beauty of the real
> wild west, feel the old romantic spirit in the very air you breathe,
> and enjoy the wilderness of nature's own in a comfortable, secure
> environment midst the smiling faces of the very pioneers who have
> made this country one of the richest, most enchanting, most
> beautiful and interesting sections in the Union. [3]

If the pioneers were smiling, perhaps it was to conceal their am-
bivalent feelings. Income was income, to be sure; but greenhorns were greenhorns, and the best that could be said of dude-
wrangling was that it "beats sheepherding," as one Blackfoot
Valley veteran put it. [4] The old-timers passed along stories like
the one about the English nobleman hunting in Montana: a cowboy rode up to the ranch house and said to the boss, "One of
them kings has fell off his horse." Or they told about the eastern professor who was offered his choice of a McClellan saddle
or a stock saddle with a horn and who allowed he'd take the
stock saddle, but doubted that "the density of the traffic would
necessitate the use of a horn." [5]

Although dude ranching was not geared to the automobile,
another booming new industry of the twenties was—bootlegging. Officially the state went dry in 1918, but as Chet Huntley
said of the little hamlet of Saco, "The town drunks never so-
bered up, and whiskey remained an easy item to come by." [6]
Evangelist Billy Sunday came through Butte and calculated that
the bottles emptied there every weekend "would build a stair-
way from the top of its highest peak to the utmost depths of

2. Quoted in *Minutes of the Fifth Annual Dude Ranchers' Meeting Held at Billings,
Montana, November 17, 18, 19, 1930* (Cheyenne, Wyo.: Pioneer Printing, 1931).

3. *The Dude Rancher* (Billings), 6 (October-November 1938): 23.

4. Quoted in Virginia Weisel Johnson, *The Long, Long Trail* (Boston: Houghton
Mifflin, 1966), p. 120.

5. Both quoted in *Minutes of the Fourth Annual Dude Ranchers' Meeting Held at
Billings, Montana in the Northern Hotel Tea Room November 18, 19, 20, 1929* (Casper,
Wyo.: S. E. Boyer & Co., 1930), pp. 98, 103.

6. Huntley, *Generous Years*, p. 114.

hell." [7] Butte indeed was reputed to lead the nation in per-capita consumption of illicit liquor, but every town had its soft-drink parlors, soda laced with booze, or its shoe store or pool hall with liquid assets stored in the back room. High-speed automobiles and proximity to the Canadian border gave rise to a risky, if exciting, and usually profitable business of channeling smuggled hooch into Montana's major cities, although a federal crackdown cut the number of runners from 300 in 1921 to a mere 30 in 1924 and pushed prices sky-high. But Montana's isolation was ideal for local stills, which despite sporadic raids continued to produce for home markets. That Montanans realized the "noble experiment" did not work was indicated in 1928, when they repealed the state prohibition law, even though federal repeal was another five years away.

All in all, with harvests improved, metal prices rising, a number of new industries going, and fewer people unemployed, Governor John Erickson was sanguine when he addressed the legislature early in 1929 in words reminiscent of President Hoover. "There is every evidence that our State has entered upon an era of prosperity more general and permanent than it has ever before experienced," he said, "and we are justified in regarding the present with satisfaction and the future with optimism." [8] Then came more drought and, in the autumn, national disaster. The stock market plunged, and Burt Wheeler lost heavily, as the country began to reap the whirlwinds sown in the twenties. International disruptions, overextended credit, a maldistribution of income, and a number of "sick" industries, of which agriculture was certainly one, combined to bring an ever-widening spiral of depression which enveloped the entire economy. In the three years following 1929, national income was cut in half, 85,000 businesses and 5,000 banks failed; the physical output of manufacturing dropped fifty percent, steel furnaces ran at one-eighth of capacity, and one out of every four workers was out of a job.

7. Quoted in Montana Writers' Project, *Copper Camp,* p. 2.

8. *Message of Governor J. E. Erickson to the Twenty-First Legislative Assembly of the State of Montana, 1929* (Helena: State Publishing Co., 1929), p. 3.

As production cut back across the country, declining demands for raw materials hit Montana sharply. Copper prices fell from 18 cents to 5 cents a pound by 1933, and fierce competition from abroad forced the industry in the state to cut back to a quarter of its 1929 production and to close plants in Butte, Anaconda, East Helena, and Great Falls. Zinc and silver prices were at rock bottom with no takers, and lumbering, the live green gold industry was at a standstill. The Northern Pacific Railroad abandoned a number of projects, laid off men, and cut wages 20 percent. By 1933, manufacturing industries in the state had thrown more than half their workers into the unemployment lines.

Farmers were selling wheat at a quarter a bushel; beef went at a nickel a pound; and when the wool growers met in Butte in 1932 to consider how to prevent bankruptcy, wool was also down to five cents a pound. Dude ranchers found themselves swamped with cancellations. Farm communities around the state went "to the bottom of the economic valley," [9] as thousands of acres went under the sheriff's hammer at from 50 cents to 2 dollars an acre. Even with hamburger selling at 14 cents a pound and eggs at 12 cents a dozen, there was real suffering, especially in the rural areas. In the summer of 1931 an old man of 70 years wrote Governor Erickson of the hopeless situation in eastern Montana, urging the state to finance road construction to create jobs at a time "when so many of us poor farmers are in such desperate need.

> I and my old wife at the present time have one baking of flour left and one pound of coffee. We have no credit and no work. Our 400 acres of crop is utterly destroyed. We had no crop last year and only a very poor yield in 1929. In 1928 hail destroyed our crop with no insurance. In a short time the Bank will take our stock and other creditors our Machinery. We have lived here 20 years and I have paid $3500 in taxes since I have been in Montana and this is the end. What can you or anyone do about it? [10]

The governor's answer to this specific letter is not clear, but his general philosophy was summed up to the legislature earlier in

9. *The Montana Study* (Helena: University of Montana, 1947), 2:3.
10. Quoted in MHS, *Precious Metals*, p. 182.

the year. He was certain, he said, ". . . that the great heart of the people of Montana will see to it that destitution and suffering are relieved." As for the assembly: "Create no new activities and assume as few new obligations as possible." [11]

The state followed his advice, and municipalities which sought to assume some responsibilities simply lacked the wherewithal. The city of Glasgow, for example, trimmed the school budget by $12,000 and eliminated night police. Glendive reduced wages, setting a minimum of 30 cents an hour and a maximum of 50. The local newspaper editor agreed to accept three bushels of wheat for a year's subscription; doctors and dentists took coal and farm produce in exchange for their services. To meet food demands, deer and elk hunting increased so greatly that in some parts of the state "Save the Deer" campaigns were inaugurated. Where towns endeavored to create their own work relief programs, with park or playground improvements to provide jobs, a dwindling tax revenue soon subverted their efforts. Nor could private agencies like the Red Cross or the Salvation Army meet the rapidly multiplying needs of the destitute. Thus, whether they wanted to or not, Montanans turned their eyes toward Washington.

There, President Hoover only slowly modified his original position that a dole was demeaning and morally stultifying. Eventually he would subscribe to the "percolator theory"—that private, local, or state agencies should provide individual relief, and that the federal government should help destitute institutions such as banks, railroads, or savings and loan companies in order that the benefits percolate on down to needy persons at the bottom. One way or another, vital relief support was forthcoming. In 1930, almost 23 percent of all Montana households were receiving some aid; in the following year half of the state's counties obtained emergency relief from the Red Cross. This was mainly in the form of flour and stock feed and was federal drought aid filtered down through the private agency. Early in 1933, even while admonishing the legislature to reduce cost, Governor Erickson could report that up to the end of 1932,

11. *Message of Governor J. E. Erickson to the Twenty-Second Legislative Assembly of the State of Montana, 1931* (Helena: State Publishing Co., 1931), pp. 3, 16.

Montana had received a total of $507,738 in relief funds from Washington and that an additional $529,700 had been committed for the first two months of 1933.

Many Americans the country over viewed the coming of the depression simplistically and put the blame unfairly upon the shoulders of one man—Herbert Hoover. No doubt some Montanans shared these sentiments, although one mine manager attributed the disaster to Prohibition and automobiles. "When people mortgage their homes and Life Insurance Policies to buy cars to run about and drink Moonshine in, it can only lead to nothing else," he insisted.[12] But Hoover was for most people the sacrificial lamb. When he ran for re-election in 1932, he was swamped by the Democrat Franklin Roosevelt; the vote was about five to three in Montana, where Wheeler had been early on the bandwagon and Walsh had given substantial support during the convention and later. In reward, Walsh was nominated as the U.S. Attorney General, an appointment greeted with favor generally. As one editor noted, he was dignified and unbiased; to ask special favors of him "would be like asking the statue of Civic Virtue for a chew of tobacco." [13] Unfortunately, Walsh suffered a massive heart attack and died while on the train enroute to Washington.

Under the new President, Congress embarked on the New Deal program, that vast mass of federal legislation between 1933 and 1939 designed to provide relief, promote economic recovery, and hopefully to institute reforms to prevent recurrence of the disaster in the future. Taking first things first, Roosevelt moved quickly to combat the bank crisis, then to permit the sale of 3.2 beer. Bank failures were not new to Montanans in 1929, but now the pace increased, and depositors, like those who threatened to lynch the proprietors of Philipsburg banks that went defunct in 1930, grew more militant. Most of the banks that went under, left little behind; typical was the Reed Point State Bank whose assets late in 1933 consisted of "a safe, 120

12. Quoted in MHS, *Precious Metals*, p. 185.
13. *New York Sun*, March 1, 1933, quoted in *Dictionary of American Biography*, 20 vols. (New York: Charles Scribner's Sons, 1936), 19:394.

acres of dry land, a small bank balance, and some very small notes of doubtful value.'' [14] As soon as he took office, Roosevelt declared a bank holiday, closing the banks until March 15, while federal guidelines were worked out to strengthen and bolster them. A month later, beer flowed legally for the first time in 13 years, much to the distress of ''Pussyfoot'' Johnson, Butte prohibition leader. With the Eighteenth Amendment repealed, hard liquor became available in December, and all pending federal prohibition charges, of which Montana had plenty, were ordered wiped from the docket.

The flow of federal relief funds, obviously one of the New Deal priority items, was stepped up, at first through temporary programs like the Federal Emergency Relief Administration and the Civil Works Administration and with at least token consideration for the matching principle. Of the $1,007,435 paid out for relief in Montana through the FERA in February 1935, for example, $919,428 was federal, $39,347 state, and $56,659 county. Studies made early that same year showed that roughly one-fourth of the state's population was on relief, less in rural areas and more in urban. During the entire 1933–1939 era, Montana was second in the nation where the input of federal monies was concerned: $381,582,693 came in outright or matching grants and another $141,835,952 in loans, averaging about $170 per capita for grants and $264 for loans.

After the initial phase, much emphasis was put on work relief programs which provided jobs—and a stake in society—to the unemployed and at the same time left tangible public improvements. Most important in the long run were the Civilian Conservation Corps, the Public Works Administration, and the Works Progress Administration, all of which benefited Montanans and Montana in countless ways.

The colorful CCC, ''Roosevelt's Tree Army,'' proved popular and successful. Designed to provide employment under semi-military conditions for young men from 17 to 23, it put them to work in conjunction with the Forest Service, the National Park Service, the Montana State Forest Department, the

14. Quoted in MHS, *Precious Metals,* p. 185.

Montana State Parks Authority, or some other agency doing outdoor work. Ultimately there would be more than 2,100 camps in the country, with the first organized in May 1933 at Fort Missoula, a tent city, which would become the hub of a camp network within the state numbering as high as 32 and housing as many as 8,000 of the so-called "peavies," as the rookies were called. Most recruits were eastern, but by the time the program began to taper off in 1938, some 14,000 Montana boys had been employed; by the time it was abolished in 1942, the CCC would have provided training and jobs for nearly 3 million young men. Fire prevention and fire fighting took part of their time; they planted trees, dug water holes, built trails and campgrounds, fought insects—especially the pine bark beetle— and did the laborious handwork necessary to combat blister rust among the white pines—the removal of currants, goose-berry bushes, and other alternate hosts. The CCC performed a thousand-and-one tasks, and, in the words of one historian of the New Deal period, it "left its monuments in the preservation and purification of the land, the water, the forests, and the young men of America." [15] A young recruit from Brooklyn spoke for many when he commented:

> It took a little time to become accustomed to trees, instead of people. The sighing of the wind in the great trees was a sound of mystery and at first terrifying after the roar of the densely populated cities we came from. . . . Coming out here was a great break for me.[16]

Commencing its program in 1935, the Works Progress Administration by the middle of 1942 would have spent $70,246,610 for its own or other federal projects administered through it in Montana. It had been preceded by political maneuvering, when Governor Erickson was accused of packing the State Relief Commission with conservatives with unhealthy business and company ties. When Erickson bowed out to go to

15. Arthur M. Schlesinger, Jr., *The Age of Roosevelt*, 3 vols. (Boston: Houghton Mifflin, 1965 Sentry ed.), 2:340.

16. Quoted in Michael J. Ober, "The CCC Experience in Glacier National Park," *Montana*, 26 (Summer 1976): 39.

the Senate after Walsh's death, his successor, the more progressive Frank Cooney, with the help of federal investigations, forced a housecleaning, although the political in-fighting continued until 1935, when the legislature revamped the relief structure and the WPA brought more direct federal control.

The basic philosophy of the WPA was to put people to work. In its lifespan, it directed some 3,891 projects in Montana, employing at peak as many as 20,000 directly and supporting perhaps twice that number indirectly. Tangible results for the state included more than 10,200 miles of new and improved streets, roads, and highways; 2,990 new or improved bridges and viaducts; 41 new school buildings or additions and reconstruction or modification of 354 more, among them the rebuilding of Helena High School, which had been so severely damaged by earthquake in 1935 that classes were being held in 18 railroad coaches drawn up on the Northern Pacific sidings. The WPA was responsible for 440 other buildings, either new or additional construction: it built 5 new airports, put in 132 miles of new water mains or lines, 148 miles of storm and sanitary sewers, and it built 17,121 new sanitary privies. When a freak three-day snowstorm paralyzed Butte in mid-May 1938, 1,500 WPA laborers turned out to clear the streets, their work directed from the central WPA office in the old Silver Bow Club, where businessmen once ate thick steaks and played poker.

Under the agency, well over 4 million school lunches were served, and roughly 8 percent of all its expenditures went into programs designed to provide white-collar jobs. To that end, there were surveys of historical records, library cataloguing, the renovation of books, musical performances, and a Writers' Project that produced *Montana: A State Guide Book;* the delightfully irreverent story of Butte, *Copper Camp;* and the whimsical *Montanans' Golden Anniversary Humorous History, Handbook and 1940 Almanac.*

A kindred agency, the Public Works Administration was concerned more with large projects, not only with providing employment, but also with stimulating the market for steel, cement, lumber, or other materials. In Montana, the PWA was responsible for building at least 4 sewage-disposal plants, 24 waterworks, and 4 hospital facilities, but its great symbol, and indeed the great symbol of the entire New Deal in the state, was the Fort Peck Dam across the Missouri, just above the juncture with the Milk. Located on the site of old Colonel Campbell Peck's trading post, the dam was approved in 1933 as a PWA project in conjunction with the Army Engineers, although it had been opposed by the Montana Power Company and no doubt by the old Assiniboins, who shook their heads sadly in the valley below. As Franklin Roosevelt paid his political debts to Burton Wheeler, construction got swiftly under way, the giant undertaking at peak employing some 10,000 workers drawn from all corners and hunkered down in hell-roaring little towns with appropriate names like Wheeler, New Deal, or Delano Heights.

> From West Virginia, Georgia, Maine,
> From filthy tenement and country lane
> The families trek
> To North Montana . . . and Fort Peck.[17]

In the fall of 1938 about a tenth of the dam slipped into the water, taking with it railroad tracks, trestle, dredge, and eight workers, but the basic project—the greatest man-made adjustment of nature in Montana—was completed by 1939, although Wheeler had earlier fought and won the battle to install generating equipment at Fort Peck, and this work continued. The first power was generated in 1943, but expansion and refinements went on long after that. Until 1973 the largest earth-filled dam in the world, its 250-foot-high main section stretched 10,578 feet, and the dike section on the west bank added nearly two more miles; behind it backed up a lake 16 miles wide and 189 miles long. Not only did it provide electrical power, it and kindred dams meant that the river no longer fluctuated wildly; waters were stored and released as needed; in two state parks extensive recreation facilities were included. "Our Dam" was of great pride to Montanans. President Roosevelt visited it twice while it was under construction, and when Wheeler's opponent

---

17. Quoted from Sammy Sampson, *The Saga of Fort Peck* (Portland: Tumbleweed Magazine, 1941), p. 12.

for the Senate in 1934 referred to it as "nothing more than a duck pond," [18] that was a black mark against him. Fort Peck was a symbol of hope and of progress.

Fort Peck kilowatts were also symbolic. One of the by-products of the New Deal throughout the West was rural electrification. Beginning in the mid-thirties under the Rural Electrification Act, loans were made available to rural co-operatives to finance central power systems; the first to commence service in Montana was the Lower Yellowstone Rural Electrification Association in late 1937. But where in 1934 only 5.5 percent of Montana's farms and ranches were electrified, the number steadily increased to 85 percent by mid-1953.

Since agriculture was a primary industry and since both farming and ranching were already in distress before the debacle of 1929, the New Deal farm and land-use programs were of special significance to Montanans. Low farm prices were but one problem. Weather as dry as a government report in the middle-thirties brought more "black blizzards" across the northern plains and an influx of refugees from the Dakotas, dubbed Dakies, migrating westward with their belongings piled atop their rattle-trap autos like their blood brothers the Okies farther south. If that were not enough, 1937 brought a grasshopper invasion that left a wasteland fifty miles wide and over a hundred miles long across the state's midriff. A familiar story was repeated: farmers began to leave the land as its value declined. By 1940 the number of farms had dropped from 47,492 in 1930 to 41,823.

Under the Agricultural Adjustment Acts, the government would seek to raise prices of farm goods and at the same time reduce crop surpluses. By paying farmers to reduce acreage and under a complicated system of subsidization through contracts with individual growers, these programs had a major impact on wheat growing: each year between 1933 and 1937 somewhere between $4.5 million and close to $10 million was poured into Montana agriculture via 140,000 agreements with farmers, who came to rely heavily upon the arrangement. Chester Davis, state commissioner of agriculture, would later become director of the

18. Thane, *High Border Country*, p. 283.

AAA; and M. L. Wilson, a Montana homesteader, first county agent in the state, and long associated with Montana State College, would be one of the major architects of the national farm program.

Beginning in 1932, through an arm of the Reconstruction Finance Corporation—the Regional Agricultural Credit Corporation—cattlemen received modest loans on livestock. But in 1934 a much more fully developed federal drought purchase program bought 350,000 cattle and 492,000 sheep in Montana to save the herds from starvation and their owners from bankruptcy. At the same time, federal agencies provided low-interest loans to enable farmers and ranchers to refinance; nearly $78 million went into such loans in the state by mid-1938. But as the experience of a Melville rancher indicated, there was a limit to loans available to hold a herd together. William H. Donald fought drought and grasshoppers and in 1937 owed both the federal land bank and the Regional Agricultural Credit Corporation, and then, he recorded, ". . . this God Damned RACC is going to have me foreclosed because I borrowed too much money to buy feed & pasture." At the end of the year, Donald wrote a memorandum detailing his troubles:

> . . . 1937: Was a tough one & a year of great disappointments to me. First place, was just beginning to get around pretty well on my broken leg. Had flu & a bad relapse again. Nearly cut a finger off & rendered it useless in a buzz saw. Another bad infestation of grasshoppers cut down my summer pasture badly. We had a fair number of Dudes, but strung out very erratically & when I came to figure out how I have done, found I was in the hole. Didn't charge enough. In late August the RACC nearly put me out of business entirely & tried to force me to sell out. Had a mean automobile wreck where a fellow ran into me. Bill came down with appendicities [sic] & had to be operated on. Cattle market was good up to Oct. 1st, but I overstaid [sic] my market & did not get in on the good market. Calves still unsold [because] the RACC, the Fed. Land Bank started an action to foreclose my lands. . . . One Hell Of A Year Says I.[19]

19. Quoted in MHS, *Precious Metals,* p. 228.

From several directions, the New Deal came at the question of usage of the semiarid lands, often building on precedents developed by Montanans themselves. In earlier times, Theodore Roosevelt had sought to leave summer range available by withdrawing from entry homestead lands in areas where irrigation districts had been organized. In the mid-thirties, Franklin Roosevelt by executive order halted dry-land homesteading. In the 1920s, with approaches like the Fairway Farms project, imaginative Montanans from the State Extension Service had experimented with regional land use, consolidating small tracts that were submarginal for family farms into larger units, which, with better methods, gave higher per-worker output and could be amortized at annual rates varying with income to permit tenants to survive crop failure. Teton County was one of a select number in the country in which the U.S. Department of Agriculture, the agricultural colleges, and the experiment stations tried new multisided approaches to land-use questions, working with spokesmen from farm organizations and elected community committees on such questions as soil conservation, erosion control, water utilization, and range management. As early as 1930, Montanans had been experimenting with farm resettlement. Under the "Malta plan," irrigable lands in the Milk River Valley would be sold to dry-land farmers, who in turn would lease their arid holdings to stockmen, an idea that was still unfinanced when Roosevelt took office in 1933.

But it was the New Deal which made possible the practical application and extension of these earlier local proposals. First, water conservation itself received high priority. Dozens of water-storage projects were built with WPA or CCC help, jointly financed by state and federal government and operated by local user's associations through agreements with the State Water Conservation Board, which could borrow federal funds without the state's being liable for their repayment. Many small irrigation projects were developed, along with major ones like the Dead Man's Basin Canal along the Musselshell Valley or the Buffalo Rapids enterprise on the Yellowstone. Federal money also supported the movement of farmers from dry, marginal lands to irrigated soil, sometimes by leasing or sometimes by purchase on a matching basis. Under the AAA, some borderline farms were retired to grass by individual contracts; the Farm Security Administration also provided funds for resettlement, just as it underwrote those unable to get loans for already existing farm operations; at the same time, the CCC was actively engaged in a re-grassing program, and the net result was the restoration to usable range of much damaged and even abandoned cropland.

Earlier, with the Mizpah-Pumpkin Creek experiment, Montana ranchers had created the first co-operative grazing district in the country. Congress in 1928 had approved and withdrawn the area in Custer and Rosebud counties from homesteading. Under a ten-year lease agreement, stockmen there organized the Mizpah-Pumpkin Creek Grazing Association, which laid out ground rules, built reservoirs and fences, limited and controlled their grazing, and found that even in drought times the grass came back. By 1933 the legislature had passed a grazing-districts law to encourage other such joint efforts, and a year later, as part of the New Deal program, the Taylor Grazing Act authorized federal agreements with such associations, with land to be withdrawn from the public domain for low-cost grazing leases.

Countless other New Deal measures touched the lives of every Montanan, be it through Social Security, federal bank deposit insurance, regulation of public utilities, or the new Wheeler-Howard legislation that drastically altered policies toward American Indian tribes. Most Montanans benefited and were grateful, although there was much criticism of parts or of the entire philosophy of the New Deal—or as the bitterest of detractors called it, the "Raw Deal." As elsewhere, some damned "That Man" in the White House or belittled the work relief programs. ("Driver, what are those statues along the road?" Driver: "Those are not statues, they are WPA workers." [20]) Participants bemoaned the interminable red tape, or complained, as did Acting Governor Holt, of the influence of actual Reds in Washington. Others worried lest the relocation of marginal

20. Quoted in *The Dude Rancher*, 6 (April 1937): 26.

farmers imply that Montana was not fit for agriculture, while Democratic stalwarts grumbled over Republicans in state New Deal administrative posts and Republicans on their part accused Democrat field men of operating on the principle of giving "the good guys the jobs, the bad guys the gate." [21] But even critics were willing to share the benefits. If the president of the Dude Ranchers' Association in 1937 hoped the " 'powers that be' would have the good sense to let business and labor alone and not try to solve economic matters purely by legislation," [22] like his associates, he also hoped that the dude-ranching business would be eligible for loans under the Reconstruction Finance Corporation.

Be that as it may, by the late thirties Montana's economy was on the upswing, as was that of the nation in general. Governor Roy Ayers was optimistic in 1937, but even more so two years later, when he reported "a notable increase in employment . . . fairly satisfactory business and financial conditions" in many sections of the state, and a break in the drought, which enabled "a majority of our farmers to produce one of the largest cereal crops ever. . . ." [23] Undoubtedly the coming of World War II, the greatest pump-primer of them all, was a major factor in pulling the country out of the doldrums, but clearly the New Deal tided the state over, kept thousands alive, and at the same time imparted some sense of dignity and contribution to society. One point is clear: more than ever before, Montanans looked toward Washington. The role of the federal government had greatly expanded, but so, too, had that of the state. If many Montanans complained, there was no turning back.

Montana politics were in transition. From 1925 down to 1941, Democrats held the governorship, and also had the edge in control of the legislature, especially after 1934. At the same time, the state delegation to Congress was also Democratic.

21. Quoted in James T. Patterson, *The New Deal and the States: Federalism in Transition* (Princeton: Princeton University Press, 1969), p. 168.

22. Quoted in *The Dude Rancher*, 6 (January-February 1937): 15.

23. *Message of Governor Roy E. Ayers to the Twenty-sixth Legislative Assembly of the State of Montana 1939* (Helena: State Publishing Co., 1939), p. 3.

Gone from the scene was the titan Tom Walsh, dead on his honeymoon while traveling by train to Washington to become FDR's new Attorney General. Burton Wheeler, the rough-and-ready alley fighter, remained in the Senate and was quick to use his influence to block Bruce Kremer, Democratic National Committeeman and regarded as a company man, as Walsh's successor. Twice Wheeler came close to getting bills through Congress to remonetize silver and he had been Roosevelt's wheelhorse in pushing through restrictions on holding companies. But he split with the President in 1937 over FDR's attempt to "pack" the Supreme Court. When Wheeler won the fight, some called him the "President-Tamer"; [24] others were more critical, and students at the university in Missoula formed a "Wheeler for Ex-Senator Club."

Even so, Wheeler gradually mended his fences with the administration and retained his political clout at home, as chubby, progressive Jerry O'Connell learned in 1938, when "bouncing Bertie" and the company both used their influence to help defeat his re-election bid to Congress. Admitting that "nobody could be elected dog catcher in Montana" without Anaconda support,[25] Wheeler argued that the company had opposed him until 1934, when it considered him unbeatable. Anaconda and Montana Power, the Montana Twins—"a pair of fat boys like Tweedledum and Tweedledee, an arm of each flung chummily across the other's shoulders" [26] were still in command of the state, but they had modified their images in politics. No longer did the company attack candidates with bold, thundering headlines; now, as had been typical in O'Connell's case, its newspapers ignored their speeches and sought to smother them with a "copper curtain of silence." [27] Using purportedly paid advertisements, sharp public-relations men, and effective lobbyists in the legislative halls, the company used its power more obliquely but remained one of the strongest political forces in the state.

24. Wheeler, *Yankee*, p. 340.
25. Quoted in Gunther, *Inside U.S.A.*, p. 177.
26. Joseph Kinsey Howard, "The Montana Twins in Trouble?" *Harper's Monthly*, 189 (September 1944): 335.
27. *Denver Post*, May 11, 1952.

11

World War II and
After: the Political World.

"The War Cleaned the Dudes Out."

$\mathcal{W}$ITH a rich ethnic mix from all parts of the Old World, Montanans knew where Europe was, and they knew royalty when they saw it. Late in the spring of 1939, about the time Senator William Borah of Idaho was pooh-poohing the idea of a European war to Secretary of State Cordell Hull, Norwegian Crown Prince Olav and Princess Martha visited the state. Olav was outfitted in full cowboy gear, including chaps with "Montana" written on them; Martha was presented with a "beautiful doeskin habit." [1] With the governor proclaiming *Velkommen* Day, 15,000 people lined Helena's main street to greet the regal tourists, who were feted at a dinner and a reception and were properly adopted into the Blackfoot tribe as Rising Wolf and Flying Eagle.

But this was a pleasant interlude. Borah was dead wrong. War swept across Europe in the autumn of 1939, and in spite of distance and natural inclination for isolationism, Montanans

Quoted in *The Dude Rancher,* 8 (October 1939): 6.
1. *The Dude Rancher,* 8 (July 1939): 33.

quickly felt the impact. Wheat prices fell temporarily as grain exports declined 30 percent in the year following the German blitzkrieg into Poland. The uncertainty that hung over Europe was contagious and adversely affected tourism, even in the Rockies. "The war cleaned the dudes out of this country and many of us have had our hunters cancelled," wrote the proprietor of the Lazy 6-V Ranch in October.[2]

Montanans watched with great interest, too, President Roosevelt's efforts to modify the nation's strict neutrality laws to permit friends to buy arms or war materiel on a come-and-get-it, cash-on-the-barrelhead basis. Montana's senior senator, Burton Wheeler, violently opposed such a policy, calling it a prelude to American entry into the war and vowing never to support sending "an American boy across the water to fight on foreign soil, though I am hanged in effigy. . . ."[3]

But Wheeler lost on the neutrality issue. As German armies smashed across the Continent and poised for an all-out assault on Britain, Roosevelt's "nonpartisanship" eroded even more. In 1940, the President requested, and got, the first peacetime draft in history—with Wheeler protesting all the way. In September, of the same year, Roosevelt sanctioned the trade of over-age destroyers for bases on British possessions strung from Trinidad as far north as Newfoundland. Early in 1941 he advocated lending, leasing, or giving armaments to England and France, a proposal Wheeler fought bitterly. While Congress debated Lend-Lease, Wheeler allowed the use of his franking privileges on literature to oppose it, and he spoke out against it at numerous meetings sponsored by the America First Committee. In mid-January, he attacked Lend-Lease as the "New Deal's triple-A foreign policy; it will plow under every fourth American boy," a statement Roosevelt called ". . . the most untruthful, the most dastardly, unpatriotic thing that has been said."[4] Again Wheeler lost and became more than ever the

2. Quoted in *The Dude Rancher,* 8 (October 1939): 6.

3. Quoted in Richard L. Neuberger, "Wheeler of Montana," *Harper's Monthly,* 180 (May 1940): 617.

4. Samuel I. Roseman, comp., *The Public Papers and Addresses of Franklin D. Roosevelt,* 13 vols. (New York: Macmillan Company, 1941), 9: 711–712.

subject of controversy. Where a national magazine in 1940 had seen him as "a Washington landmark, not just another cow country Senator," [5] he was now accused by the Secretary of War of "near treason" and would be castigated by journalists as a negative, destructive, "political Fuzzy-Wuzzy." [6]

The Japanese attack on Pearl Harbor came as a shock and a surprise. When he heard the news, Wheeler gave the press a statement: "Let's lick hell out of them." [7] There was supreme irony in the fact that Jeannette Rankin, who had voted against World War I, was now serving a second term in the House of Representatives and in 1941 cast the only ballot against entry into World War II. At home, as history seemed to repeat itself, she was again denounced and referred to as "Japanette," although at least one supporter lauded her stance in a wonderfully mixed expression, "The only man in Congress with guts is a woman." [8]

Quickly Montana plunged into the war effort. Already the peacetime draft was in operation; now recruiting offices were jammed momentarily and again the state poured large numbers of its young men and women into the armed forces. The Adolph Schwartz family near Glasgow had seven sons in the service, and most Montanans had a personal interest when they listened on their radios to such catchy hit songs as "Coming in on a Wing and a Prayer" or "Praise the Lord and Pass the Ammunition." They followed the comic-strip career of Joe Palooka, who was drafted into the army, and Barney Google, who joined the navy (even old Dick Tracy took a commission—in plain clothes—in Naval Intelligence), and they tingled through a long series of war movies—some good, some bad—ranging from *Mrs. Miniver* to *Thirty Seconds over Tokyo*. But the real drama and anguish was wrapped up in the wartime destiny of their

5. Quoted in Joseph Kinsey Howard, "The Decline and Fall of Burton K. Wheeler," *Harper's Monthly*, 191 (March 1947): 233.

6. Gerald W. Johnson, "Wheeler Rides the Storm," *Colliers*, 114 (July 8, 1944): 11.

7. Wheeler, *Yankee*, p. 36.

8. Quoted in Eric Thane [Ralph C. Henry], *The Majestic Land* (New York and Indianapolis: Bobbs-Merrill Co., 1950), p. 136.

own—of men like Hubert Zemke, former University of Montana football player, who became consecutively a P-47 ace with 155 missions over Europe, prisoner of war in Germany, and Montana Jaycees Man of the Year even while still in Luft I; or of the 1,553 Montanans listed by the War Department as dead or missing in action.

New military installations opened in the state, including Army Air Force bases at Glasgow and Great Falls, the latter both a training field for bomber crews and a point of departure for ferrying aircraft over the Pole to our Russian allies. Nearly a third of the Canadian-American special services force training in Helena married local girls before going off to Italy, France, or the Aleutian Islands. Thousands of young men were part of the Army Specialty Training Program at the University of Montana and Montana State College, or as Aviation Students ("Junior Birdmen") they moved into campus dormitories or even sorority houses to begin the early phases of their preparation as aircrewmen.

Governor Sam (Model T) Ford promised a "blackout on partisanship," [9] pledging the state's resources to the war effort. Butte experimented with real blackouts, Glasgow put a curfew on bars and, along with other towns, pushed a "Scrap the Jap" campaign to gather metal. A statewide "Fats for Freedom" drive saved grease, and Montanans were exposed to a flurry of advertising that ran the gamut from "Lucky Strike Green has Gone to War" to "Back the Attack with War Bonds" and "Fertilizer Will Win the War." They liberally oversubscribed their war-bond quotas, cheerfully perjured themselves to get more gas than the three gallons a week authorized by A-ration cards, suffered through the rationing of such other commodities as sugar, meat, tires, and shoes, and acquiesced without grumbling when the Montana Education Association eliminated state championship playoffs in major sports. While they viewed Japanese aliens dismally and reacted vociferously and negatively at the idea of Japanese-American students being accepted by the university at Missoula, Montanans did not repeat the hysteria

9. Quoted in Paladin, *From Buffalo Bones to Sonic Boom*, p. 84.

of the World War I period. They went coolly about their business, sometimes emotional but not frenetic in their views, able to mix an occasional bit of humor with their distaste for the enemy.

> Laughter rings the loudest in Montana
> Poverty turns proudest in Montana
> We can't pay half our taxes
> We love the Waves and Wacks-es
> But how we hate the Axis! in Montana.[10]

Economically, the state boomed, although some types of activities were sidetracked for the duration, and there was a shift of workers. Montana's war supply contracts through April 1945 totaled about $25.3 million; those for Oregon, $1.78 billion; and for Washington, $4.5 billion. Thus, when special adult courses in welding or sheet-metal work prepared Montanan's for jobs, it was not for home industry, but for the shipyards or aircraft plants on the Coast. Civilian population flowed westward; in April 1940 Montana's population of 558,270 was slightly more than Seattle's; by November 1943 the state had lost 88,237 people—about 15.8 percent—while Seattle had gained about the same percentage and number of civilians. Only North Dakota would exceed Montana in wartime migration, and this was a trend which would continue to plague the area in later years.

Dude ranching remained in the economic doldrums, while owners complained of rationing, travel difficulties, and a scarcity of labor, and argued that their operations were at least indirectly essential to the war effort. With gasoline and tires rationed and travel by train also discouraged, the entire tourist industry suffered. By federal order of 1942, gold mining was restricted, and the dredges belched to a halt. The one exception was a bucket dredge in Granite County, south of Drummond, which ran through the war years, mining scheelite, a source of tungsten, as its prime objective, and gold as a by-product.

---

10. Washington J. McCormick, "In Montana: A Land of Contrasts," in *The Dude Rancher*, 14 (January 1945): 18. Reprinted by permission of the Dude Ranchers' Association.

But other types of mining flourished, especially copper, zinc, lead, manganese, chrome, and coal. With thousands drawn off for the armed services or for Pacific Coast war industries, labor was in short supply. Some deferments for miners were given and some early discharges; and wages, though controlled, rose much more rapidly than the cost-of-living index. It was at the No. 3 Smith Mine at Washoe, in the Red Lodge fields that the worst coal mine disaster in Montana occurred in 1943, when an open flame touched off a blast that instantly killed thirty men and trapped forty-seven more. In the end, only three survived, some of the victims leaving poignant notes chalked on scraps of boards:

We 5 men pass 11 oclock
dear Agnus & children
I'm sorry we had to go this
God bless you all Emile with lots kiss.[11]

Production of lumber, crude oil, and electric power expanded greatly to meet wartime needs. Beginning with Lend-Lease in 1941, farmers and ranchers stepped up the output of foodstuffs and would enjoy unprecedented prosperity. The years 1941 through 1943 were exceptionally moist; 1943 was the best year in Montana history for wheat growers. Around the country, the federal government became the chief buyer of food; and American farmers, with 10 percent fewer workers, raised 50 percent more food annually than during World War I. But machinery, fertilizer, and insecticides were scarce. To meet the labor shortage, Montana teen-agers were recruited for a farm corps; Japanese-American internees and imported Mexican *braceros* were also utilized. Cattlemen, too, enjoyed halcyon days for the first time in years, despite a paucity of cowhands, a complex system of meat rationing, federal quotas for packers, and a brief upswing in cattle-rustling. Amidst grumbling about high taxes and controls by the Office of Price Administration, farmers and ranchers alike paid off debts and expanded their holdings during

11. Quoted in G. O. Arnold, et. al., *Final Report of Mine Explosion, Smith Mine, Montana Coal & Iron Company, Washoe, Carbon County, Montana, February 27, 1943*, p. 104.

the fat years. Like their counterparts in the mines, the smelters, or the oil fields, they provided both bread and butter for themselves and sinews of war for the Allies.

After Hiroshima and Nagasaki, while bartenders at Helena's Placer Hotel concocted atomic cocktails and smiled politely at soon tired jokes about Japan suffering from atomic ache, thoughtful Montanans, like a Glasgow editor, saw the dawn of a new era, and the need of humans to adjust their thinking "to a new conception of battle almost total in its death-dealing efficiency and frightfulness." [12] A few weeks later, on September 2, 1945, the war came to a close on the deck of the battleship *Missouri* in Tokyo Bay. Montanans whooped it up, heaved sighs of relief, and settled back to what they hoped was normal living.

Normal by this time was a curious political schizophrenia, which went back to the twenties and which would continue down to the present. By and large, Montana voters have sent liberal Democrats to Washington and conservatives to Helena. In keeping with the populist-progressive tradition, the state has sent but one Republican senator to the nation's capital since it began electing U.S. senators in 1912. Far more important than he were the moderate liberals with devoted following and national reputations: Burton Wheeler, James Murray, Mike Mansfield, and Lee Metcalf. U.S. representatives would be more evenly split between the two parties; Republicans would control the governorship during most of the years from World War II to the late sixties, and domination of the legislature was often divided, with Republicans more in the ascendancy than not. And throughout the twentieth century, perhaps because it lacks a disciplined political system or because it is a middle ground, drawing from both the Pacific Northwest and the Midwest for emigrants, the state has been an excellent weathervane in presidential elections, failing only to line up behind William McKinley in 1900, John F. Kennedy in 1960, and Jimmy Carter in 1976.

No doubt part of Montana's split political personality is the product of the ability of leaders to develop personal followings

12. Quoted in Paladin, *From Buffalo Bones to Sonic Boom,* p. 88.

in a lightly populated state where grass-roots contacts were relatively easy for real vote-getters like Wheeler or Mansfield to maintain. Clearly, too, rural voters and corporate groups alike could make themselves more readily felt at the local scene; and voters concerned with lower tax levies and expenditures at home might understandably send men to Washington effectively to channel federal dollars into Montana. Basic issues often focused upon how revenues should be raised and how they should be utilized; on efficiency of state government; or on Washington-connected questions that touched Montanans directly and tangibly: farm price supports, the closing of air bases, construction of dams or missile sites, disposition of water or mineral rights, environmental pollution. And over-arching were the broader national controversies like the Cold War, Vietnam, inflation, or welfare legislation.

During World War II, party lines blurred a bit, but Burton Wheeler had been returned to the Senate by a bipartisan landslide and his liberal colleague, James E. Murray, squeaked through by a mere 1,200 votes in 1942. It was Murray who introduced legislation in Congress to create a Missouri Valley Authority, patterned after TVA, to unify development of the huge Missouri River basin into one comprehensive system to provide power, irrigation, flood control, soil conservation, and improved navigation. The Missouri, said supporters of the proposal, was like an errant husband: "It is frequently guilty of desertion, nonsupport, and misconduct; it pulls out, leaving wife and kiddies to starve, and goes around smashing things in other people's houses." It was simply "not good sense to let such a river wander around at will in a civilized country." [13] But the MVA idea divided Montanans sharply. Murray stood solidly behind the plan, most independent newspapers supported it, and Joseph Kinsey Howard defended it in *Harper's Monthly* and before a Senate committee. Wheeler, who had once voted for and praised TVA, joined Governor Sam Ford in opposing it. Ford, who also testified before a Senate committee, saw MVA

13. Quoted in Joseph Kinsey Howard, "Golden River," *Harper's Monthly* 190 (May 1945): 511.

and a comparable proposal to develop the Columbia River as "the most insidious and sinister threat to Montana's sovereignty today. . . ." [14] While supporters charged power monopolies and "plunderbunds" with spreading lies, critics cried "socialism, communism, superstate" and damned a Montana State University advocate as a "feather-footed, wild-eyed sociology professor." [15] In the end, despite additional bills, strong lobbying, and support of the Hoover Commission, no MVA was ever created. Instead, a less unified approach under the Pick-Sloan compromise would accomplish only a part of Murray's hopes, with multipurpose dams like Hungry Horse or Canyon Ferry being completed in the early fifties.

MVA was very much a hot issue when the election of 1946 was held. As usual, the garrulous Wheeler was expected to win re-election by a solid margin. Butte gamblers gave odds of three to one on him and were as stunned as the senator's partisans when "old B.K." was beaten in the primary by Leif Erickson, a young liberal Sidney lawyer and former justice of the state supreme court who had been defeated for governor two years before. Wheeler's demise no doubt was the product of a number of factors brooding in people's minds for some time. The old New Deal split over Roosevelt's court-packing plan had never completely healed. Montana veterans could not forgive his extreme isolationism of the pre-war period, and he was accused of having joined with the company to keep out war industry that might have competed for the labor supply. His union support had been sorely undercut. "All the Butte chaws and cousin-jacks voted for Erickson," explained one attorney.[16] Wheeler's position on MVA was at best controversial. He was accused of anti-Semitism and of trying to undercut the United Nations, though he had grudgingly voted for its charter. Certainly by 1946 he had moved far to the right; certainly, too, he was out

---

14. *Message of Governor Sam C. Ford to the Twenty-ninth Legislative Assembly of the State of Montana, 1945* (Helena: State Publishing Co., 1945), p. 4.

15. Quoted in Richard Waverly Poston, *Small Town Renaissance* (New York: Harper & Bros., 1950), p. 68.

16. MHS, *Precious Metals*, p. 234.

of touch with his constituents; as a maverick attempting to play both Democrats and Republicans he came a cropper. As Joseph Kinsey Howard put it, Wheeler

> . . . fell between two stools which were yanked out from under him just when he thought he had them securely anchored and while he was busily attempting to convert them into a bench. He was convinced that he was bigger than any one party—big enough for two.[17]

Ironically, Erickson did not succeed Wheeler. Instead, Montanans elected Zales Ecton, an ultra-conservative rancher and veteran legislator from near Manhattan, the only Republican ever elected to the Senate so far from Montana. There is additional irony in the fact that in later years, important state Republican leaders would urge Wheeler to run for the Senate on the GOP ticket. How Wheeler—the last of the old-time progressives—had changed!

But James Murray, although not Wheeler's choice, continued the liberal tradition. Elected to fill Walsh's unexpired term back in 1934, Murray was himself a bundle of contradictions. A man of inherited wealth (a "Millionaire Moses"),[18] he owned William A. Clark's 22-room chateau, imported stone by stone from Brittany, and rebuilt in Butte. At the same time, this fervent New Dealer championed a long list of reforms for the underdog. The darling of labor, he fought for minimum-wage laws, proposed a national health insurance program, and was instrumental in passing the Employment Act of 1946, committing the federal government to a policy of action to maintain prosperity and a high level of jobs. He pushed hard for MVA, for reclamation in general, and he consistently criticized the power lobby in Congress, but managed to remain relatively disentangled from company matters at home. Not an effective campaigner, Murray narrowly survived one tough fight after another. In 1954 Vice-President Nixon attacked him on behalf of his opponent Wesley D'Ewart who ran as an Eisenhower Republican but whose con-

---

17. Howard, "Decline and Fall of Burton K. Wheeler," p. 228.
18. Quoted in *The Saturday Evening Post,* 218 (December 8, 1945): 9.

gressional record was strongly anti-Eisenhower and anti-labor. Murray was hit for his "softness" on Communism, but his Catholicism offset that. Finally, in 1960 at the age of 84, his health failing, he withdrew from the primary when it became clear that he would have a hard time winning.

In 1953 Murray had been joined in the Senate by Mike Mansfield, who in 1942 had won Jeannette Rankin's seat in the House. The son of Irish emigrant parents, Mansfield had served time in the army, navy, and marines, had worked for several years as a mucker in the Butte mines, and had studied first at the Montana School of Mines, then at the university in Missoula, where he taught history and political science. A specialist in foreign affairs, the low-key Mansfield spent ten years in the House before he beat the dull and uninspiring Ecton in a smear-ridden Senate race in 1952, with the then-fashionable charges of coddling Communists directed at him. Immensely popular at home, Mansfield gradually built a larger reputation as a progressive nationalist who looked beyond his own state. Harry Truman thought him ". . . the sort of man who could look at an acorn and see a giant oak tree with its great limbs spreading upward and outward in the years to come." [19]

In the Senate, Mansfield worked closely with Lyndon B. Johnson and, in 1961, became his successor as Majority Leader, a position he would hold longer than anyone else in history. But his quiet, pipe-puffing, nonpartisan approach was as different from LBJ's, Drew Pearson once said, "as ginger ale is from a martini." [20] Mansfield tended to Montana's needs, to be sure, but he looked beyond. He made strip-mining control a national issue, authored the voting-rights bill for 18-year-olds, opposed Nixon's ABM program (though Montana would have benefitted from it), early criticized Vietnam policy as "unnecessary, unwarranted and uncalled for," [21] and nudged the Senate toward an investigation of Watergate. For thirty-four years, Mansfield

19. Quoted in Margaret Truman, *Harry S. Truman* (New York: William Morrow & Co., 1973), pp. 434–435.

20. Quoted in Neal R. Peirce, *The Mountain States of America* (New York: W. W. Norton, 1972), p. 119.

21. Quoted in *Great Falls Tribune*, March 12, 1976.

sat in Congress—one-sixth of the nation's official 200-year
span. He served under seven presidents, and during his time the
entire membership of the Senate, except two, had changed.
When he announced his retirement early in 1976, he had
"earned a higher degree of national and worldwide prestige and
influence than any other Montanan ever achieved," in the eyes
of the *Great Falls Tribune*.[22]

Mansfield himself thought that Lee Metcalf, who replaced
Murray in 1961, was the "best legal mind in the Senate." [23]
Tough, quick-tempered, "built like a lumberjack," and looking
much like the football tackle he had been at Montana State University before he ruined a knee and transferred to Stanford, Metcalf was a liberal veteran of the legislative wars and had served
both on the state supreme court and in the U.S. House of Representatives. Though he was overshadowed by "good ol' Mike,
fair-play Mike, low-key Mike," he was much underrated, according to many,[24] and was both progressive and conservation-
minded. Much of his accomplishment had to do with protection
of forest and grazing lands, and he was clearly Congress's most
militant opponent of the multi-billion-dollar power industry.
Closely identified with Medicare and with mine-safety legislation, Metcalf had a voting record much like Mansfield's, but his
bluntness earned him the label "ultra-liberal." But he won re-
election in 1966 and 1972—the first time in a tight race against
Governor Tim Babcock, formerly a Billings trucking-company
owner, whose "Win with Tim" billboards covered the land. A
staunch conservative, Babcock hit the administration's "no-
win" policy in Vietnam and received open support from Barry
Goldwater of Arizona, who told a Great Falls audience that he
would "climb the highest mountain on my knees" to see him
elected.[25] Thousands of bumper stickers distributed by Babcock
men proclaimed "We Eat Montana Beef, Not L.B.J. Ba-
loney," [26] but the governor was hurt by his veto of the air-

22. *Great Falls Tribune,* March 7, 1976.
23. Quoted in *Great Falls Tribune,* March 12, 1976.
24. Robert Sherrill, "The Invisible Senator," *The Nation,* 212 (May 10, 1971): 584.
25. Quoted in *New Republic,* 155 (October 1, 1966): 10.
26. Quoted in *Time,* 88 (October 28, 1966): 29.

pollution bill and by his moratorium on state water development, and, with campaign help from Mansfield—"the mahatma of Montana politics"—". . . plain, progressive Lee Metcalf" won,[27] although outsiders tarred him with allegations of Red connections.

If Montana generally sent liberal Democrats to the United States Senate, the pattern in sending representatives to Washington was less consistent. Originally the state had but one representative; after 1912, two, who were elected at-large until 1918, when Montana was divided into two Congressional Districts. The first embraced roughly the western third of the state and until recently, because of the concentration of labor in cities and the attitudes of small farmers, could ordinarily be considered safely Democratic. Only three times between 1918 and 1970, did Republicans capture it; Jeannette Rankin was the last, in 1940. It was the First District that would be the door to distinguished careers for both Metcalf and Mansfield. On the other hand, Montana's Second Congressional District, including the eastern two-thirds of the state, tended to be dominated by oil men or large ranchers or wheat farmers, and often sent rock-ribbed Republicans to Washington. True, Democrats dominated through the New Deal and war years, but in 1946 Park County legislator Wesley A. D'Ewart, a staunch GOP conservative, began the first of four terms as representative for the district. A Democrat exception came in 1956 when D'Ewart's equally reactionary successor, Orvin B. Fjare, was defeated by LeRoy Anderson, in part because of an unpopular Eisenhower farm policy and the delay in beginning Yellowtail Dam attributed to Ike's administration. In more recent years, progressive Democrat John Melcher of Forsyth, an able, popular, and farm-oriented representative, would hold the Second District seat for more than three terms before replacing Mansfield in the Senate in 1976. But the older lines are becoming blurred: extremes are shrinking, labor's impact has lessened, and the middle-class voter has become more important.

Montana's governors since 1940 have, in general, been Re-

27. *New Republic,* 155 (October 1, 1966): 10.

publican and conservative. National issues crept into campaigns, but predominant have been questions of tax base, whether reliance should continue on property and income levies or be shifted partially to a sales tax. A central controversy has also been whether state government should expand or contract the services it offered. How to expand Montana's economic base, attract industry, and develop resources were also paramount concerns, which by the 1960s would be joined by a strong anxiety for the environment.

Elected governor in 1940 was Sam Ford, who had served as assistant U.S. attorney with Burton Wheeler during the hysteria of World War I. Considered by some "a company-bound disciple" [28] of Wheeler, even though of the opposite party, Ford, too, by this time was something of a tired radical who spoke positively of the need for good government. "In carving out her future," he said, "Montana wants sculptors, not chiselers." He gave loyal Wheeler Democrats places in his administration, and fought and won a patronage battle with Dan Whetstone, the Republican national committeeman. He was concerned with MVA, the sales tax question, reorganization of state offices, investment of public school funds, and the need to divorce both the state university and the enforcement of state liquor laws from political influence, for—as he put it, like the good Baptist he was—"Liquor and politics, fermented in the same vat, have always produced corruption and always will." [29]

Ford was beaten in 1948 by John Bonner, former attorney general and a veteran of the Normandy campaign, in an election characterized by smears and innuendoes. A moderate Democrat, Bonner, too, took a firm stand on development of power and water resources for the state, not downriver strangers. "Our duty to Montanans is to see to it that these waters are not taken away from us." [30] During his administration, the state pursued a large highway program, built new institutions for the handi-

28. Quoted in MHS, *Precious Metals*, p. 234.

29. *Message of Governor Sam C. Ford to the Twenty-seventh Legislative Assembly of the State of Montana,* 1941 (Helena: State Publishing Co., 1941), p. 11.

30. Quoted in MHS, *Precious Metals*, p. 262.

capped, increased workmen's compensation and aid for the aged and blind, but a split legislature limited achievements.

Montana shared the calm and consensus of the Eisenhower fifties. But because of falling grain and livestock prices—attributed to the Truman administration, because Bonner was timid on trucking taxation and the school land oil royalty question, and probably because of a negative bluenose reaction to a personal escapade of his in New Orleans' French Quarter a couple of years earlier, he was defeated in 1952 by J. Hugo Aronson—the "Galloping Swede"—who rode in on Ike's coattails. Bluff, "barrel-chested and ramrod-erect," [31] seemingly as rugged as the Rockies themselves, Aronson had come a long way since he dropped off a freight at the little town of Columbus in 1914. The story of his rise, Horatio Alger style, from poor immigrant to farmer, trucker, rancher, oil man, and long-term legislator had been dramatized by the Voice of America in six languages, including Russian, a fact which certainly helped at the polls. Aronson rocked few boats; even his own advisors said he didn't have a platform "twelve inches square." [32] He emphasized a business approach to government and struggled with the question of whether gasoline taxes should be used exclusively for highway construction, an issue settled positively by voters in 1956, when he was re-elected over smooth, handsome Arnold Olsen, 39-year old attorney general from Butte. Democrats harped on low farm prices, and Eisenhower "Peace, Prosperity, Progress" billboards dotted the state, but the major campaign issue was over the leasing of oil rights on school lands to private interests. Aronson favored a lenient policy; Olsen believed lease rates should be higher and accused his opponent of being a tool of the oil interests and of giving away valuable resources for a pittance.

After eight years of middle-of-the-road politics, Aronson retired to join Bonner in another role. "Old governors don't just

31. Quoted in Paul Healy, "Montana's Galloping Swede," *The Saturday Evening Post,* 230 (December 7, 1957): 49.

32. J. Hugo Aronson and L. O. Brockmann, *The Galloping Swede* (Missoula: Mountain Press Publishing Co., 1970), p. 103.

fade away," he said with a twinkle in his eye, "they just become lobbyists." [33] Conservative Republican Donald Nutter was elected on a slogan of "Put Montana in the March of Progress," and a platform calling for a better business climate, lower taxes, and reduced government costs and services. Under the diehard Nutter, who refused to proclaim United Nations Day in the state, the legislature slashed appropriations sharply. But early in 1962 Nutter perished in a plane crash, projecting Lieutenant-Governor Tim Babcock into the gubernatorial chair. Very much a stand-patter, Babcock ran on his own in 1964, but complained that his legislative program was stymied on a purely political basis by a Democrat-controlled house. When he came up against former supreme-court justice and attorney general Forrest Anderson in 1968, the pendulum would swing in the other direction. Babcock had alienated many by vetoing an air-pollution bill and in the campaign had urged a new sales tax at the time when his opponent was advocating thrift and the raising of old taxes.

Meanwhile, basic changes were coming in state government. Since World War II, Republicans had dominated the state senate three times as often as the Democrats, and control of the house had been about even. The press never ceased to ridicule the legislature, viewing it as a "gathering of crooks and fools" and poking fun at bills dropped in the hoppers (one in 1965 forcing owners to provide shelter for their pets was labeled the Cat House Bill).[34] But generally voters showed respect for the work done by their assembly: called upon between 1940 and 1968 to pass on 4 initiatives, 16 referenda, and 17 proposed constitutional amendments, the electorate accepted one initiative, sustained 12 laws by referenda, and adopted ten of the amendments.

Liberals gained in the legislature after 1967, when the U.S. Supreme Court's mandate for reapportionment under the "one man, one vote" concept was put into effect. Even so, beef,

33. Quoted in Margaret Scherf, "One Cow, One Vote," *Harper's Monthly*, 232 (April 1966): 109.
34. Quoted in Scherf, "One Cow, One Vote," p. 105.

wheat, and oil counties with small populations were opposed, preferring, it was said, "one cow, one vote." Soon the assembly would sanction extensive executive reorganization; independent lawmakers would pass the first minimum-wage law in Montana history, enact robust environmental statutes, and refer the annoying sales-tax question to the voters, who rejected it by a margin of two to one. The seventies would bring a more liberal governor yet, Thomas Judge; and the aftermath of Watergate in 1974 brought Democratic control of both houses.

Montana's new progressives in 1970 called for a revision of the outmoded 1889 constitution. Successful in their efforts, when they convened their convention, they deliberately precluded direct participation by elected officials or legislators in favor of a grass-roots body of 100, among them lawyers, ranchers, professors, ministers, even a beekeeper and a retired FBI agent. The new constitution was enlightened in tone, only half as long as the old, and called for single-member legislative districts, annual sessions (later modified), statewide assessment, and a definite strengthening of the legislative branch. Members worked hard to sell the document to the electorate in 1972; and the campaign of "Praise the Lord and pass the Constitution," [35] as a national magazine called it, brought acceptance by a narrow margin.

No change in recent Montana politics has been more noticeable than the role of Anaconda Copper. Beginning in the 1930s, when John D. Ryan no longer headed Anaconda and Montana Power, the company impact became less direct and more subtle. The potency was still there, as was indicated in 1952 when Anaconda and a few allies managed to keep off the ballot a measure giving industrial accident benefits to silicosis victims. But in keeping with its role as the world's largest producer, smelter, and fabricator of copper, with interests in Mexico and Chile as well, the firm would soften its image. When its underground block-caving approach to Butte's low-grade ores failed dismally, in 1955 it began the Berkeley open-pit operation on the east end of the town. About the same time it opened

35. *Time*, 99 (April 10, 1972): 18.

an aluminum plant at Columbia Falls, but automation in both instances meant fewer employees. Recession, falling copper prices, and a long strike in 1959–1960 bruised the entire Montana economy. By this time, the Montana Twins were pulling apart. Anaconda's more global interests and its willingness to exploit the cheap power available from Hungry Horse and other public dams would weaken its ties with Montana Power. In June 1959 Anaconda publicly divested itself of its chain of eight daily newspapers, which, taken together, represented four of the five largest cities and about 55 percent of the circulation in the state. After 1971, when the Chilean government nationalized Anaconda's Andean holdings (with no settlement of claims until 1977), there began for the company a new era of cut-backs, the closing of its zinc operations, the selling of its forest lands, and the laying off of more than a third of its Montana payroll by the end of 1975. Anaconda became more concerned with bankruptcy than with politics, and, indeed, became a subsidiary of Atlantic Richfield Company. True, the company still keeps a discreet eye on the copper-covered capitol dome, but it has abandoned the free booze of its legislative watering holes in favor of a more Madison Avenue approach, and its lobbying is more defensive than offensive.

As Anaconda declined, Montana Power remained probably the most influential interest, but with a more discerning and unobtrusive profile than before, and with other skillful and persuasive power brokers sharing the role previously played by the company. Among these conservative groups are big farmers and ranchers, trucking interests, liquor dealers, oil men, the Burlington Northern Railroad, and the First Bank System, with an interlocking chain of banks strung west from Minneapolis. Leaven the mix with strong liberal power groups, which would include the Farmers' Union, electric co-operatives (some of which ironically buy their energy from Montana Power), teachers' associations and the AFL-CIO and other labor organizations strong enough in 1958 to keep a right-to-work measure off the ballot.

In retrospect, it seems that Montana's politics have often been as rugged as her terrain and sometimes as unpredictable as her weather. Where population is sparse and mobile and the political system basically unstructured, personality—both individual and corporate—has been an important ingredient. If climate, distance, and resources have shaped economic development, this in turn has helped shape politics, and students of Montana government speak openly of "a politics of copper, a politics of wheat, a politics of cattle, and so on." [36]

36. Thomas Payne, "Montana: Politics Under the Copper Dome," in Frank H. Jonas, ed., *Politics in the American West* (Salt Lake City: University of Utah Press, 1969), p. 205.

12

Post-War Economic Bases

A Boiler Room for America?

WRITING in 1963, Californian Neil Morgan believed that the "compelling act of wilderness" had removed Montana from "the mood of urgency which grips its neighbors in the coastal states. . . ." [1] As it had through its history, Montana still looked inward, he said, its people forgetful or unaware that their extractive industries were tied to national and world conditions. When he wrote, Montana took its space for granted: it had but 4.7 people per square mile, less than one-tenth that of the nation in general, though by 1960, for the first time, it had more inhabitants living in urban than in rural settings. Located in an economic and geographic backwash, the state reminded Morgan in some ways of the Deep South. But what Morgan seems not to have caught was that isolation was breaking down, that after World War II, Montanans were becoming increasingly aware of the larger whole and of the limitations of their role as producers of raw materials. By the seventies, they refused to become "a boiler room for the nation," [2] and were approaching resource development with a new spirit of independence.

Great Falls Tribune, September 25, 1975.
1. Neil Morgan, *Westward Tilt* (New York: Random House, 1963), pp. 248, 249.
2. *Great Falls Tribune,* September 25, 1975.

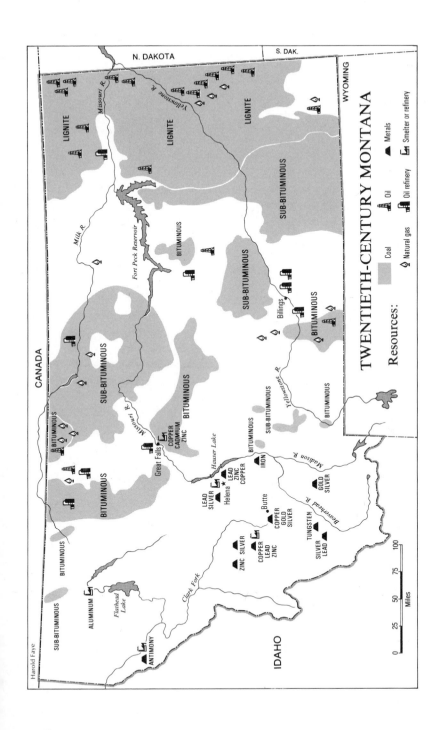

TWENTIETH-CENTURY MONTANA

Resources:

▨ Coal
▨ Oil
◇ Natural gas
▲ Metals
🏭 Oil refinery
⛴ Smelter or refinery

CANADA

N. DAKOTA

S. DAK.

WYOMING

IDAHO

LIGNITE

LIGNITE

LIGNITE

SUB-BITUMINOUS

SUB-BITUMINOUS

SUB-BITUMINOUS

SUB-BITUMINOUS

SUB-BITUMINOUS

BITUMINOUS

BITUMINOUS

BITUMINOUS

BITUMINOUS

BITUMINOUS

BITUMINOUS

Missouri R.

Yellowstone R.

Milk R.

Fort Peck Reservoir

Madison R.

Beaverhead R.

Yellowstone R.

Clark Fork

Flathead Lake

Hauser Lake

Billings

Great Falls

Helena

Butte

COPPER
CADMIUM
ZINC

LEAD
ZINC
COPPER

LEAD
SILVER

IRON

COPPER
GOLD
SILVER

COPPER
LEAD
ZINC

ZINC SILVER

TUNGSTEN

SILVER
LEAD

GOLD
SILVER

ALUMINUM

ANTIMONY

Harold Faye

0   25   50   75   100
Miles

Morgan was ignoring, too, the fact that Montana now fell into two separate orbits. Long ago the economic links with St. Louis had faded, and through the railroad, mail-order business, telephone network, New Deal agencies, banks, and the regional electric-power grid, Montana strengthened its bonds with the Pacific Northwest. At the same time, by land and by water and again through banking ties, it was joined as part of the Great Plains to Chicago and the Twin Cities, always important to the marketing of grain and beef. So the state still faces two directions, even as it struggles to expand its economic base and to gain what perhaps it never really had—control of its own resources.

At the end of the war there was no return to a bygone era. In the skittish beginnings of the nuclear age, Montanans soon found themselves direct participants in the Cold War, though Butte wags discounted the possibility of Soviet invasion from the north: ". . . Everybody knows the Company won't let them into Montana!" [3] In the fifties, along with other Americans, Montanans built bomb shelters, organized a Ground Defense Corps and a Civil Defense unit, conducted air-raid drills in their schools, and listened to farmers complain that atomic testing was changing the weather. When the Cold War became hot, at least 146 of Montana's sons would die in Korea and another 259 in the jungles of Vietnam. And when the Strategic Air Command beefed up Malmstrom Air Base at Great Falls, in the mid-fifties built a new base north of Glasgow, and subsequently brought in ICBM missile installations, defense became an important part of the state economy. A photograph in the Montana Directory of Public Affairs in 1960 brought together some of the symbols of state wealth when it showed the smokestack of the Anaconda smelter at Great Falls, alternating "golden and brown patterns of strip farming," [4] and overhead the vapor trails of Malmstrom planes.

But this was misleading. Actually, since World War II Mon-

---

3. Quoted by Payne, "Montana: Politics Under the Copper Dome," p. 213.

4. Ralph E. Owings, *Montana Directory of Public Affairs 1864–1960* (Ann Arbor: Edwards Brothers, 1960), p. 58.

tana's economy has been "relatively colorless," without dramatic ups and downs, but with a "steady erosion of the state's position relative to the national economy." [5] A sluggish overall growth rate has persisted since 1950, when per-capita income of $1,606 was about 8 percent above the national average; by 1970 Montanans lagged more than 12 percent behind. In terms of purchasing power, real per-capita income rose more than 60 percent nationally, but only 26 percent in Montana. A producer, not a processor of raw materials, Montana failed to attract new industry. Big steel did not develop, as it did in Utah, nor the thriving electronics industry that came to Colorado. Montana did not develop national or global companies comparable to Idaho's corporate giants J. R. Simplot, Morrison-Knudsen, and Boise Cascade. Remoteness from markets meant high freight rates; strong financial communities were lacking; the state did not fit into major corporate distribution networks; and the business climate was not good (a survey of 1975 ranked Montana thirty-first, with Texas first and New York forty-eighth). Although productive, fields like agriculture and mining declined as a source of jobs and income; with the unemployment rate consistently above the national average, the state saw a substantial out-migration of its educated young people—one of its most valuable resources. Noting early in 1976 that agriculture, the top employer, hired about 35,000, while 68,100 Montanans worked for local, state, or federal government (an increase of 65 percent over 10 years), a spokesman of the Montana Taxpayers' Association calling for a freeze on the 14,104 state workers, believed that the "only real growth industry in Montana is government." [6]

Citizens know that the federal government is the largest landholder in the state, owning about 30 percent, still a far cry from Nevada, where it holds title to more than 70 percent. Directly, in 1969, the national government spent $644 million in Montana and took back $343 million in taxes. Federal expenditures in

5. *Montana Economic Study* (Missoula: University of Montana School of Business Administration Bureau of Business and Economic Research, 1970), 1: 2.2.

6. Quoted in *Great Falls Tribune,* January 22, 1976.

descending order of magnitude came through the Department of Agriculture; Health, Education, and Welfare; Defense; Transportation; and Interior. The Forest Service, Bureau of Indian Affairs, the Bureau of Reclamation, and dam projects like Fort Peck, Canyon Ferry, or Hungry Horse provide considerable employment; and air bases and missile installations are important enough that Montanans complained bitterly when the Glasgow base was closed in 1968–1969 and the anti-ballistic missile program terminated in 1972. Indirectly Washington's attitude with respect to tariff, metals stockpiling, or farm price supports closely concerns Montana's copper, wool, sugar beet, and wheat industries, all of which want to be left alone—except when they need help.

Although agriculture would diversify somewhat with increased irrigation, the main thrusts after World War II would be on two products—grain and beef, which together made up about three-quarters of the state's annual output. With higher labor costs and slackening demands for wool and lambs, sheep-raising declined, as stockmen turned to cattle. Especially in the early fifties, beef prices were attractive: in 1951, they reached an all-time high of $29.69 per hundred, but had settled back to $16.92 by 1955. Many stockmen would mix farming and ranching; but in any event, cattle-raising became increasingly large-scale, scientific, and sophisticated, with a trend to marketing younger animals rather than finishing them up.

In 1975 Montana farmers harvested a record 217 million bushels of wheat, barley, and oats, worth $699 million; with more than two-thirds of her exports in wheat, modern Montana comes close to living by bread alone. Grain-farming, too, has become ever more mechanized, modernized, and "big business." Its productivity and profitability depend upon the magic of insecticides, herbicides, and fertilizers like anhydrous ammonia; upon massive sixty-thousand-dollar self-propelled combines; and upon the highly efficient modern tractor, which, according to Carl Kraenzel, incorporates the traits of animals native to the upper plains—"the power of the bison, the speed of the antelope, the mobility of the jackrabbit, and the adaptability of the coyote." [7] Drought was still an occasional visitor, as in the mid-fifties, but new techniques did much to reduce wind and water erosion. Farmers moved away from deep plowing to disking and cultivating operations designed to tear the subsoil but disturb the topsoil as little as possible. They used stubble as mulch, alternate fallowing, and contour stripping, which left patterns like "giant angle worms across the land." [8] As elsewhere, rising land costs, the expense of equipment, and the economy of scale meant ever-larger operating units and the demise of the family farm. Where in 1920 the average Montana farm was 608 acres, in 1974 it was 2,510. In the same period, the total number of farms and ranches in the state dropped from 57,677 to 26,400; and the number of people employed in agriculture went from 82,000 to 36,100 by 1970. Thus, while production was high, the job and income bases were narrow.

After World War II, demands for petroleum greatly expanded, and in 1949, for the first time, Montana production of oil was worth more than its output of copper. One discovery after another came in the fifties—the Williston Basin, East Poplar, Sidney, Cabin Creek, Wibaux, and others. Major new refineries were built, and Billings became the focal point as the state's oil yield doubled; by 1970 the Yellowstone pipeline from Billings to Spokane handled much of the processed product and was another tie to the Northwest. Yet the petroleum industry employed relatively few—only some 3,000 in the fields and the refineries as of 1970.

Tourism now ranks behind only agriculture and mining. Even with rising fuel costs, visitors to Glacier and Yellowstone national parks climbed to new heights in the seventies. With an emphasis on campers and outdoor recreation, tourists spent $274 million in Montana in 1974, a nearly 50-percent increase over the previous year. Directly and indirectly this creates some 20,000 jobs for Montanans and is a clean, renewable, and expanding industry, but rests on an unspoiled environment. On the

7. Kraenzel, *Great Plains in Transition*, p. 315.
8. Owings, *Montana Directory*, p. 57.

other hand, purists who would build a fence around the state and issue three-day passes to visitors argue that tourists merely cheapen the quality of life, jam good trout streams, and leave a trail of litter in their wake. Some economists contend that less than a quarter of each tourist dollar remains in the state as direct income, and that to equal the income generated by lumbering and the wood-products industry in western Montana would require 9.2 million out-of-state visitors, rather than the 3.8 million of 1971. But with modern equipment, even an expanding plywood, veneer, pulp, and paper industry employs relatively few people; and has been the target of environmentalists from the mid-fifties until antipollution devices cleared the foul-smelling and smoky air in the seventies.

Only in the past decade or two have Montanans become conscious of the importance of their prime resource, coal, although as early as the 1880s a spokesman for the Yellowstone Land and Colonization Company was aware of its presence under much of eastern Montana: "It is hardly an exaggeration to say that every man who owns an acre of ground may mine coal." [9] Historically there have been a number of shifts in Montana coal mining: from underground to surface operations, from bituminous to inclusion of lignite and sub-bituminous, from the western to the eastern part of the state, and from use as a smelter and locomotive fuel to a source of generating electric power.

Much of the eastern third of Montana was ignored for years, apart from a few areas like Coalridge in the extreme northeast corner. In the early twenties, labor trouble in the Red Lodge fields prompted the Northern Pacific to build the town of Colstrip and to open up a 25-foot-thick Rosebud seam by strip methods; soon these operations surpassed all others and, with vast World War II expansion, were producing more than half the coal in the state. But until the late sixties, most of the "black gold" mined in Montana was for domestic consumption; then, as power demands escalated elsewhere and nuclear energy

9. *The Yellowstone Valley and Town of Glendive* (St. Paul: Pioneer Press Co., 1882), p. 28.

production fell behind projections, the state faced new pressures. As early as 1959 a Montana Power Company subsidiary obtained a long-term lease on Northern Pacific deposits and surface rights at Colstrip and nine years later began shipping coal to its Billings power plant. At the same time, Peabody Coal (owned by Kennecott Copper) contracted to supply a Minnesota utility with coal from the same area. Montana Power and its Pacific Northwest partners built two 350-megawatt, coal-fired power plants at the Colstrip fields and proposed two additional 700-megawatt units—all of which would transmit electrical energy to the Pacific Coast. As other concerns, petroleum companies included, joined the scramble for leases, it became increasingly apparent, as Governor Thomas L. Judge indicated in 1975, that coal "will probably be the most dominating force shaping our state in the forseeable future." [10]

Estimates of Montana's coal resources range from 40 billion to 107 billion tons, much of it strippable, and more than any other state in the Union. Low in sulphur content, but also low in BTUs, the fuel is located close to the surface in relatively thick seams. With giant equipment, production jumped from a million tons in 1969 to 13 million in 1974, with more than 40 million tons projected by 1980. But no greatly expanded work force is involved: in 1972 at Colstrip only 150 men produced 5.5 million tons.

The national energy crisis and the rediscovery of Montana coal have injected new issues into everyday life and into state politics. Revived are the old arguments of colonial exploitation for the benefit of outsiders. With 80 percent of the power to be generated at the four Colstrip plants destined for Oregon and Washington, Montana became an area of self-sacrifice to benefit the western two-thirds of the country, according to K. Ross Toole, one of the most articulate of the critics. Environmentalists are concerned about devastation of the land and disagree violently with the dragline operator, originally from Illinois, who argued, "Mining is the best thing that could happen to

10. Quoted in *Great Falls Tribune,* October 16, 1975.

eastern Montana. It's just a desert, anyway. Hell, strip it." [11]
They contend that diversion of water from the Yellowstone to
cool the Colstrip plants violates federal water quality standards,
and they are worried about air pollution.

The issue is compounded because only about 15 percent of
the sub-surface rights of coal lands is in private hands: the federal government owns some 55 percent and the Crows and
Northern Cheyenne about 30 percent. Between 1966 and 1971,
the Northern Cheyenne sold leases on about half their lands to
six outside corporations, mainly oil companies, but subsequently would seek to void these contracts and renegotiate on
more advantageous terms. The Crows also have attempted to
rewrite earlier leases with Shell, Amex, Gulf Oil, and Peabody Coal, arguing that they do not comply with federal
environmental-protection regulations. Both tribes were represented at Denver meetings of western Indians in 1975 to co-
ordinate strategy on coal, water, and land questions. Referred to
by outsiders as a kind of Indian OPEC and calling themselves
"Native American Naders," [12] they claimed huge quantities of
water on the Colorado and the Upper Missouri under a 1908
decision awarding treaty tribes "prior and paramount" rights on
streams flowing through their reservations—an extremely important set of cases not yet determined by the courts. In Montana
this would offset the fact that thirteen companies, primarily petroleum firms, had U.S. Bureau of Reclamation options on
nearly half the water behind Yellowtail Dam, not too far from
the major coal deposits.

Some political alliances have been shattered over the coal
controversy. Montana Power and the Montana Stockgrowers'
Association, time-tested bedfellows, broke over Colstrip 3 and
4. Conservative ranchers joined in groups like the Bull Mountains Landowners' Association and the Northern Plains Resources Council to co-operate with assorted gun and rod clubs,
the Farmers' Union, and the Sierra Club in opposing the un-

---

11. James Conaway, "The Last of the West: Hell, Strip It!" *Atlantic Monthly,* 232
(September 1973): 98.

12. *Great Falls Tribune,* December 22, 1975; *New York Times,* December 21, 1975.

checked opening of the coal reserves, which they saw as a definite threat to their own life-style.

In practice, a kind of compromise has prevailed. Ignoring those who could clamp a moratorium on strip-mining, Montanans in general have accepted the idea that they have some responsibility to share their resources with the rest of the nation, but that the state should not "be raped to feed the rest of the country's appetite," as Governor Judge put it.[13] Nor should the commitment include the boom-and-bust cycle of earlier exploitation, be it fur, open-range cattle, or copper; nor should it include air and water pollution, destruction of land, nor way of life. Montana coal should be developed on Montana's own terms, not those of absentee exploiters.

The tangible result in the seventies was a series of tough laws governing the location of proposed mines, the regulation of mining activity itself, and the development of resources with a minimum of waste and disruption. Beginning July 1, 1975, the state began to tax strip-mined coal on the basis of value rather than quantity, with a 20 percent severance tax on low-grade lignite and 30 percent on other coal, the highest levy in the country. Expected to bring in roughly $67 million over the next biennium, by 1980 such laws earmark half the revenue for a state trust fund, which, it is anticipated, will provide a reserve of more than $20 billion by the end of the century—a powerful buffer against potential future pressure from the coal industry. The remainder goes into the so-called "coal pie," to be split a dozen different ways for purposes ranging from school and park improvements to county land planning and solar energy experimentation.

Midwest editors labeled such statutes "usurious" and "fuel blackmail." [14] In the eyes of the president of the Detroit Edison Company, with long-term contracts for delivery of Montana coal, Helena legislators became the "Arabs of the West," and Montana was "raping the rest of the country." [15] But clearly

13. Quoted in *Great Falls Tribune,* August 26, 1975.
14. Quoted in *Denver Post,* June 13, 1977.
15. Quoted in *Great Falls Tribune,* August 26, 1975.

the state had broken with the past; it had reached the conclusion that the ultimate consumer should share environmental and economic costs. No longer would it subsidize the plunder of the soil or allow unregulated mining without curbs. Cries of economic imperialism persisted, and Montanans urged tighter state controls lest Montana's future "be decided in the centers of commerce and government elsewhere." In the shadow of energy development lurked possible industrialization or urbanization and encroachment on "areas of singular environmental amenity." [16] In jeopardy was Montana's "unique quality of life"—a mode of living conditioned by nature and broad, unspoiled horizons. No longer apathetic, Montanans were becoming aware that their greatest long-term wealth was what had shaped the course of their history from the beginning. "It's air, it's sky, it's mountains, it's prairies, it's space," said Ross Toole; [17] above all, space, where, as Joseph K. Howard once put it, a man has room "to swing his elbows and his mind;" where, in the view of A. B. Guthrie, a man can still gallop a horse "unequipped with rear-view mirror" and "can look across the miles without being reminded that the continent is infested with his kind." [18]

16. Montana Environmental Quality Council, *Second Annual Report* (October 1973), pp. 7, 2.

17. Quoted in Peirce, *Mountain States of America*, p. 92.

18. Quoted in A. B. Guthrie, Jr., "The West Is Our Great Adventure of the Spirit," *Life*, 46 (April 13, 1959): 94.

13

The Most Western Part
of the West

N the 1890s, the perceptive Englishman James Bryce
called the West "the most American part of America." [1]
It was, he noted, a region of feverish activity, of vivid
contrasts, a wonderful "mixture of science and rudeness," and
of intensification of common traits and attitudes. A contemporary of Bryce, historian Frederick Jackson Turner, would set out
the most succinct statement of the role of the West in shaping
American thought and outlook, and since that time generations
of scholars have argued and re-argued the question. Was the
western experience responsible for molding into the American
character such traits as individualism, optimism, materialism,
initiative, or democracy? Or did it, as some have suggested,
select and draw westward those types already bent in these directions?

Historians, too, have long pondered the essential conditions
of "westernness," and, without closing the door on further con-
jecture, conclude that there is not one but a number of
"Wests," each different, but united by common qualities or
features: climate, open space in some form, dreams of future

1. James Bryce, *The American Commonwealth* 2 vols. (New York & London: Macmillan Co., 1905 ed.), 2: 830.

immigration and growth, perhaps. To Texan Walter P. Webb, who saw a continuity in aridity, it was the wild grandeur, the subtle mysteries and the contrasts in climate and in topography that set the West apart and gave it its fascination. For Wallace Stegner, one of the most observant interpreters, there is about the West "a pervasive atmosphere, a dryness, a spaciousness, a loneliness, a quality of light, and a special set of colorings." [2] All of this describes Montana, clearly a geographical and spiritual part of such a West. But to what extent has Montana's past been typical? Are Montanans merely westerners in sheepskin coats or do they have a separate outlook uniquely shaped by both history and environment?

Although some twentieth-century writers, John Gunther included, assert that Montanans lack tradition and a sense of historical continuity, a case can be made for them not only as "the most western of westerners," to paraphrase Lord Bryce, but also as the westerners most conscious of the nineteenth- and early-twentieth-century past. In their own minds, they feel a special kinship with and inheritance from the early settlers, whom they tend to deify as a breed apart and who themselves had a sense of history in the making. Montana residents today pay homage to Lewis and Clark, John Owen, and Granville Stuart, all of whom scribbled their diaries with some awareness that posterity was looking over their shoulders. As early as 1864, the Montana Historical Society was incorporated by the first legislature; twenty years later the Society of Montana Pioneers was formed to give due credit to "old-time Montanians" responsible for the territory's "panorama of human progress. . . ." [3] County societies followed, including the one at Philipsburg which once adopted a resolution reserving to those original settlers "the right to get decently drunk"; and in 1892 the founding of the Society of Sons and Daughters of Montana Pioneers bridged the generation gap. Through such groups, at sum-

2. Quoted, Editors of *Look, Look at America: Central Northwest* (Boston: Houghton Mifflin, 1947), p. 34.

3. Society of Montana Pioneers, *Constitution, Members, and Officers, With Portraits and Maps* (n.p.: Society of Montana Pioneers, 1899), p. xix.

mer picnics or around pot-bellied stoves in the winter, white-thatched

> Old timers in Montana for more than fifty years,
> Yarned the night away 'bout Injuns, gold and steers.[4]

By the 1920s, when "the pioneers" were as revered as the Pilgrim Fathers, according to one onlooker, Montanans had embraced "a form of ancestor worship of which hardly less is heard than in Massachusetts Bay itself." [5] Even the physiognomy of town and country seemed more remindful of the past than elsewhere: in the late 1930s novelist Thomas Wolfe thought Montana's blistered little hamlets had "more of a false-front, shack-like old West appearance" than any others he had seen.[6]

This consciousness of the struggles of earlier times was no doubt common throughout the West—and the entire nation; but it has been more pointed and more enduring in Montana than elsewhere, and more easily transmitted, even to newcomers who ingest some of the spirit when they purchase their first pair of spike-heeled boots. Part of this is the result of those who have interpreted the past, especially the sweeping influence of that salty, convivial cowboy artist, sculptor, and writer, Charles M. Russell, whose ability to capture a genuine feeling for nineteenth-century Montana had made him a favorite son and an important, if subtle, agent in keeping the pioneer spirit alive. The West in general, and Montana in particular, had claimed other distinguished artists, but none has been taken to a state's bosom as has been Charlie Russell. Montana's best-known writers are those who concern themselves with the historic past, among them Dan Cushman, Dorothy Johnson, Joseph K. Howard, and especially A. B. Guthrie, Jr., whose major theme is the encroachment of civilization onto the wilderness.

4. Federal Writers' Project, *Montanans' Golden Anniversary Humorous History, Handbook and 1940 Almanac* (Helena: State Publishing Co., c.1939), p. 6.

5. Arthur Fisher, "Montana: Land of the Copper Collar," in Ernest Gruening, ed., *These United States* (New York: Boni & Liveright, 1924), p. 40.

6. Thomas Wolfe, *A Western Journal* (Pittsburgh: University of Pittsburgh Press, 1951), p. 57.

   This concern for events and attitudes of bygone days is more
intense, virile, and personal in Montana than in sister states. It
is manifested not merely in the more perceptible ways—revival
of ghost towns like Virginia City, annual voyages down the
Missouri by would-be Boone Caudills, the popularity of Bob
Fletcher's puckish historical signs across the state, or the publication of day-by-day entries from Lewis and Clark's journals in
the *Great Falls Tribune*—but, more importantly, in people's attitudes. Recurring in today's discussions of resource use and environmental impact are many references to "our heritage, our
land and our people," [7] implicit allusions to a uniqueness of
spirit tied to a particular life-style that Montanans believed (and
still believe) set them apart. Opponents of strip-mining still
think in terms of a raw, vast, and empty land and the struggle of
their ancestors to conquer and bequeath both material and spiritual legacies. When Wally McRea of the Rocker R. Ranch hits
hard at development of nearby Colstrip, he makes much of continuity—of the fact that family ownership of at least some of his
27,000 acres goes back to 1882, when his grandfather bought a
quarter-section from a trapper. Bud Redding, another antago-
nist, harkens back to his father's homestead on Sarpy Creek in
1916; the rigors of life at thirty below zero in tent and cabin; the
struggles through drought and depression; and a gradual expansion of landholdings in the face of great adversity.
   As Guthrie points out, each wave of migrants—fur traders,
miners, ranchers, and farmers—looked back over their shoulders. "Today's aging homesteaders, destroyers of one West,
pine for their own good old days," he notes. [8] And like Guthrie,
many Montanans recognize that much of the waste, pollution,
and devastation in the state stemmed from "the lingering spirit
of the frontiersman," who simply could not conceive of resources being finite and exhaustible. [9] Be that as it may, Montanans, probably more than any other people in the West, are

   7. *Great Falls Tribune*, March 10, 1976.
   8. A. B. Guthrie, Jr., "The West Is Our Great Adventure of the Spirit," p. 97.
   9. Quoted in Marshall Sprague, *et al.*, *The Mountain States* (New York: Time-Life
Books, 1967), p. 7.

convinced that unspoiled space and those who survived the
tough process of conquering it handed down a special something
of abstract but inestimable value. The pioneer heritage lingers;
change is not always for the better. "You can't trust these new
people," said one Forsyth resident of the strangers there in the
coalfields. "You get in a fight with one of them, and he goes
off and presses charges." [10]

During much of the twentieth century at least, Montana,
along with neighbors Idaho and Wyoming, has been more isolated and less dynamic than the Pacific Coast states, politically
more conservative and culturally less creative. That mid-century
conscience of Montana, A. B. Guthrie, detects a "sort of anti-
intellectual vigilanteism, an inhospitability to deviation both in
and beyond politics and economics." [11] Montana's record with
minorities has not been without blemish. Witness her treatment
of the Indians and her early persecution of the Chinese—both
about par for the western course. Her World War I discrimi-
nation against foreign-born and radical elements was more intense than that of most of her kindred states, as was harassment
of the strange, communist Hutterites who moved in in the
1940s. But on the whole, probably ethnic and religious preju-
dices have been more isolated and less passionate here than in
most parts of the West, if only because there were few minority
groups of any size in Montana, apart from the Indians and the
"Mongolians," who in 1900 numbered some 4,100—more than
in other mountain states. Blacks were to be counted in the
hundreds, and not until 1974 did Montanans elect a black to the
legislature. The foreign-born element was always high: Montana's 27.6 percent in that category in 1900 was twice the national average and higher than any of the mountain or upper
plains states except North Dakota.

In Montana, the land and what comes from it has always been
the important thing. Past emphasis has been largely on non-
renewable resources like minerals, furs, or petroleum, or on
renewable resources—forestry, farming, or grazing—treated as

10. Quoted in James Conaway, "The Last of the West: Hell, Strip It!" p. 92.
11. Guthrie, *Blue Hen's Chick,* p. 225.

if they were inexhaustible. Homesteaders surging into eastern Montana early in the twentieth century ultimately demonstrated that grasslands and plowlands were not necessarily interchangeable, just as they once again proved the truth of an old adage: Dry-farming succeeds best in wet years. But this was not a unique experience. Settlers who fanned out across Kansas and Nebraska in the seventies verified the same points. So did thousands of others smitten with "Dakota fever" on the northern plains between 1878 and 1887, who came smack up against drought, low prices, and disaster in the nineties. In contrast to the dry-land experience was the great Southern California land boom, which peaked in 1887 also; but when the bubble burst, the newcomers—mainly men of means and business acumen—remained, invested further capital, and they and the region prospered. Montana was the main thrust of the 20th-century sodbuster impulse: the Dakotas boomed until about 1910, but Montana continued another decade. Idaho and Wyoming developed far less: Wyoming turned more to grazing, Idaho to irrigated farming. Thus, when the economic bottom fell out, Montana was hardest hit.

One major recent western characteristic not fully shared by Montana has been unchecked growth. In a West that Gerald Nash has called an "urban oasis," [12] two-thirds of the people cluster in towns and cities. Montana is an exception as is Wyoming and, to an increasingly lesser extent, Idaho. Most of her residents were rural until 1960; in 1970 Montana had but two metropolitan areas, *i.e.*, concentrations of 50,000 or more—Billings and Great Falls, which together comprised but 23 percent of the state's population. By contrast, 52 percent of Arizona's inhabitants were concentrated in Phoenix, 52.6 percent of Utah's in Salt Lake City, and 55.1 percent of Colorado's in Denver.

Although the urban component grows, space and distance still dominate the Montana scene, but elbow room has its price. It was in the cities that the Pacific Coast aircraft and shipbuilding

12. Gerald D. Nash, *The American West in the Twentieth Century: A Short History of An Urban Oasis* (Englewood Cliffs: Prentice-Hall, 1973).

industries boomed during World War II; it was the presence of metropolitan areas that drew big steel to Utah and defense-related firms to Denver. It was city amenities and services which helped pull both retirees and industry to the Southwest Sunbelt. And in Montana, the lack of urban centers has been seen as a negative economic factor. In the 1950s, sociologist Carl Kraenzel argued that Montana faced poverty "because of the high social cost of space." [13] Where people live farther apart, commodities and the ordinary amenities of civilization are more expensive. Schools are frequently poorer, church congregations less cohesive, effective community life often absent, and space-bound inhabitants drink in boredom or leave.

Historically, they left for other reasons as well: war, drought, depression, financial opportunity, for as one scholar phrased it, "An exploitive, colonial economy does not favor roots in the soil." [14] This touches a raw nerve among Montanans, who have long felt victimized by the East. In the eyes of interpreters like Joseph Dixon, K. Ross Toole, and Joseph Kinsey Howard, in the breakneck transition from frontier to machine age, Montana was a subject dominion, a pitilessly misused state. From the American Fur Company to Anaconda, the Federal Reserve System and the fossil-fuel giants of the 1970s, spokesmen deemed the region an economic, political, and cultural satrapy of other parts of the nation, a not uncommon western complaint. Such charges were sometimes true, sometimes not, and while Montanans often believed that they were being exploited, more than once they ignored the practicality of the situation. If tariff and pricing systems (Slightly higher west of the Rockies) were discriminatory, their bases were often deeply imbedded in federal legislation or in commission-set freight schedules, if not inherent in the social cost of space. If Montanans condemned eastern or overseas capitalists who profited at their expense, they also protested loudly when Washington sought to limit foreign in-

13. Carl F. Kraenzel, "The Small Town and Village in Montana," *Montana Opinion,* 1 (October 1956): 27.

14. Paul Meadows, *The People of Montana* (Mimeographed Report to the Montana Study, 1945), 1: 25.

vestments in 1887. If they bemoaned their colonial status in the nineties, they must have known full well that Montana bankers could not have financed the copper industry at that time. If they complained of federal controls, they nonetheless stepped up demands for government expenditures touching almost all walks of life. If they sometimes sneered at the snobbery of the effete East, they proceeded to copy eastern architecture and to send their children to eastern schools. And these influences were solicited, not imposed from above.

Moreover, Montanans from the beginning were material-minded—many there solely to exploit, to "git and git out," to make their pile, then head home or to more salubrious climes. This is what an old rancher alluded to in the 1920s when he noted, "Montana's real trouble is that her graveyards aren't big enough." [15] Too few people looked upon the state as their final residence.

Together with Idaho and Wyoming, Montana has been one of the last strongholds of resentment against "colonialism." With World War II, much of the rest of the West fractured this relationship and, indeed, became pacesetters, with a booming economic base and a life-style (the "barbecue culture," someone has called it), emphasizing mobility, outdoors, leisure, and informality, which would be warmly embraced by Americans in general. But in Montana, the idea of colonialism, both as fact and myth, has been brought into sharper focus and has lingered longer than in most other states, in part because of isolation, but primarily because of the reality of the aptly named Anaconda Company, which at the crest of its power did retain a constrictorlike grip on much of what went on there.

Montanans complained that after its 1899 reorganization, this Wall Street-directed "octopus of Butte" was used by Standard Oil to change "a land of enchantment into one of their banks." [16] The struggle with Anaconda was "Montana's epic."

> What the Harvard-Yale game is to intercollegiate football, what the
> Davis Cup matches are to international tennis, what the Grand

---

15. Quoted in Fisher, "Montana: Land of the Copper Collar," p. 45.

16. Benjamin Appel, *The People Talk* (New York: E. P. Dutton & Co., 1940), pp. 270, 282.

National is to the English racing world, the World Series to
baseball, the Mardi Gras to New Orleans, or the Rose Festival to
Portland, what a good county court-house trial used to be before the
days of the movie, all this and more the battles with the Company
are to Montana.[17]

In truth, the company did play an exceptional role. In neigh-
boring states, none of the major mining concerns—the Bunker
Hill & Sullivan in Idaho: Kennecott Copper, which came to
own "the richest hole in earth"—the Bingham pits in Utah;
even the fabulous Homestake of South Dakota, the most productive gold mine in the entire Western Hemisphere—exerted a
comparable influence in their own domains. To be sure, the
Mormon Church was a power in Utah, the Wyoming Stock
Growers' Association in Wyoming, the Great Northern Railroad
in Washington, and the Rockefeller interests in Colorado, but
none controlled newspapers to the extent of Anaconda, and
other influence groups tended to act as effective counterweights
upon them. Perhaps only in Delaware, where DuPont was supreme, and in California, where the Southern Pacific maintained
a stranglehold on railroading and politics from the 1880s until
progressive reformers broke its grip in 1911, did corporate
power compare with Anaconda at its prime in Montana. And
even then, despite its unprecedented control of the press, the
company was not able to blunt the progressive movement in the
Treasure State. But, building on a legacy left by little William
Clark, Anaconda set the tone. Thus in 1947, when a Missoula
lawyer wrote of Ohioan Robert A. Taft's chances as a presidential candidate in the state, he alluded cynically to the historic
past:

> If he must have Montana, my advice to Senator Taft is to buy it:
> from B. K. Wheeler, Sam Ford, Wellington D. Rankin and J.
> Burke Clements, and from the Monopoly. In Montana politics, that
> approach is most direct, least expensive and best understood.[18]

Apart from corporate dominance, which was more pronounced than in most states, Montana's political patterns were

17. Fisher, "Montana: Land of the Copper Collar," p. 36.
18. MHS, *Precious Metals*, p. 234.

in some ways unusual. Territorial government brought the standard complaints of "carpetbag" officers, federal interference, inadequate funds, lack of representation in Washington, and determination of statehood by party politics. What was exceptional in Montana was the bitterness and the duration of Civil War antipathies reflected both on the local scene and in relations with Congress. Worthy of note, but not unique, was the no-party alliance, the coalition of Sam Hauser, Martin Maginnis, and Governor Potts, which, backed by voters, controlled the territory for nearly half the era. Elsewhere, other interest groups also cut across party lines successfully: the Mormons in Utah, and business alignments in both Wyoming and New Mexico. By contrast, Idaho evolved a more mixed and complex arrangement; Dakota a single-party pattern; and Colorado a more conventional two-party structure.

Montana's neighbors had their politicans of national prominence—Idaho its William E. Borah, Colorado its Edward Costigan, Wyoming its Joseph O'Mahoney, Utah its Reed Smoot—but few can match the list of able, influential, and distinguished spokesmen sent to Washington by Montanans: Joseph Dixon, Thomas Walsh, Burt Wheeler, Jeannette Rankin, James Murray, Lee Metcalf, and Mike Mansfield. Especially in the twentieth century, when magnolias were "losing out to sagebrush," [19] when the West was gaining power in the Congress at the expense of the South, Montana's voice was exceptionally strong for a state so small in population and so large in corporate interference.

To vote conservatively on the local scene and to endorse more liberal politicians in the nation's capital was not unusual in the West, but like her climate and her terrain, the extremes were more pronounced in Montana than in most states. In keeping with those from the mountain states in general, Montana voters often showed an independence and a willingness to split tickets and turned out for presidential elections in higher percentages than the national average. And in the 1970s they show sparks of

19. Neal A. Maxwell, *Regionalism in the United States Senate: the West* (Salt Lake City: University of Utah, 1961), p. 5.

political leadership of more than passing importance. At a time when the average age of state constitutions was 80.96 years and when Idaho, Washington, Colorado, Utah, Wyoming, Nevada, and the Dakotas all retained their original documents, Montana was one of a handful of states to adopt a new and forward-looking constitution in 1972. Whether this is "100-proof populism," as journalists called it,[20] is debatable, but it was an unusual action for a western commonwealth. At the same time, the new charter reiterates the charge given in the Environmental Policy Act of 1971 to create and maintain "conditions under which man and nature can coexist in productive harmony . . . for present and future generations." [21] The more recent legislation regulating strip-mining and taxing coal output heavily has been bold and provides models for neighbors east and south. Aware that energy and land use are intertwined and that intelligent use must be based on discussion, long-term planning, and restraints, Montanans also serve notice that the progressive vein in their thinking has not been submerged. Experience proves that Montana "is a gentle and generous mistress," as promoters in 1914 said; [22] but Montanans have learned that she can also be harsh and fickle and, in maturity, requires love and care.

This is part of the legacy handed down to children yet unborn—and an awareness that an era is closed. If part of the inheritance is ugly cutover stumplands, Butte's grotesque Berkeley Pit, and raw wind-whipped soil where once grass grew lush, another part is still wild, unspoiled scenery, horizons without end, the immensity of land and sky. Montanans of tomorrow may retain much of the dynamism, optimism, and mobility of their forebears, but with less of the emotionalism of earlier days—of the excitement of Indian dangers, the intoxication of the mineral rushes or the exuberance of the land booms—and

20. *Time,* 99 (April 10, 1972), 18.

21. Montana Environmental Quality Council, Fourth Annual Report (December 1975), p. 3.

22. *The Resources and Opportunities of Montana* (Helena: Independent Publishing Co., 1914), p. 229.

Suggestions For Further Reading

For a well-written, comprehensive history incorporating the most recent research and bringing Montana's story up to date, see Michael P. Malone and Richard B. Roeder, *Montana: A History of Two Centuries* (Seattle: University of Washington Press, 1976). Still readable, but dated, are Joseph Kinsey Howard, *Montana: High, Wide, and Handsome* (New Haven: Yale University Press, 1943) and K. Ross Toole, *Montana: An Uncommon Land* (Norman: University of Oklahoma Press, 1959). Readers can get the feel of Montana's past through a number of collections compiled in single volumes. Malone and Roeder's *Montana's Past: Selected Essays* (Missoula: University of Montana Publications in History, 1973) brings together a series of scholarly articles. Joseph Kinsey Howard, *Montana Margins: A State Anthology* (New Haven: Yale University Press, 1946) blends both history and literature; so, too, does H. G. Merriam, ed., *Way Out West* (Norman: University of Oklahoma Press, 1969), which draws from the Montana publication, *Frontier* and *Frontier and Midland* of the 1920–1939 era. A most enjoyable smorgasbord for those with an appetite for Big Sky history is the Montana Historical Society's recent *Not In Precious Metals Alone* (Helena: Montana Historical Society, 1976), a compilation of previously unpublished manuscripts—the stuff of which history is written.

For Lewis and Clark, Bernard De Voto's *The Journals of Lewis and Clark* (Boston: Houghton Mifflin, 1953) is a superb abridgment of the standard eight-volume, *Original Journals of the Lewis and Clark Expedition, 1804–1806,* edited by Reuben Gold Thwaites (New York: Dodd, Mead, 1904–1905). Popular and sound is John Bakeless, *Lewis and Clark: Partners in Discovery* (New York: William Morrow, 1947). David Thompson, *Narrative of His Explorations in Western America, 1784–1812,* edited by J. B. Tyrrell (Toronto: Champlain Society, 1916) includes the very early Montana fur trade. The classic treatment of the fur men by a novelist is A. B. Guthrie, Jr., *The Big Sky* (New York: William Sloan Associates, 1947).

Also a classic in its own right is Seymour Dunbar and Paul C. Phillips, eds., *The Journals and Letters of Major John Owen* (New York: Edward Eberstadt, 1927), 2 vols., which bridges the gap between the declining fur trade and the coming of the gold seekers. Helen McCann White, ed., *Ho! For the Gold Fields: Northern Overland Wagon Trains of the 1860s* (St. Paul: Minnesota Historical Society, 1966) includes narrative travel accounts and some detailing of life in the diggings as well. Muriel Sibell Wolle, *Montana Pay Dirt* (Denver: Sage Books, 1963) gives much information on early mining camps and some fine artistic sketches. Larry Barsness, *Gold Camp: Alder Gulch and Virginia City, Montana* (New York: Hastings House, 1962) is lively; one of the best day-by-day accounts of life in Virginia City is Andrew F. Rolle, ed., *The Road to Virginia City: The Diary of James Knox Polk Miller* (Norman: University of Oklahoma Press, 1960). A rich, thoroughly enjoyable social history is *Copper Camp: Stories of the World's Greatest Mining Town, Butte, Montana* (New York: Hastings House, 1943), compiled by the WPA-sponsored Montana Writers' Project. In fiction, *The Glittering Hill,* by Clyde F. Murphy (New York: E. P. Dutton, 1944), is a boisterous and rowdy treatment of the Butte Irish of the 1890s; and Dan Cushman, *The Silver Mountain* (New York: Appleton-Century-Crofts, 1957) is authentic for the same period.

Another of the basic accounts for nineteenth-century Montana history is Paul C. Phillips, ed., *Forty Years on the Frontier as seen in the Journals and Reminiscences of Granville Stuart* (Glendale: Arthur H. Clark Company, 1957, reprinted from the 1925 edition), 2 vols., an admirable personal account that runs from the late 1850s through the mineral booms and the era of the range-cattle industry of the 1880s. The broad story of Montana cattlemen is sketched out in Robert H. Fletcher, *Free Grass to Fences* (New York: University Publications, Inc., 1960). An excellent cowboy memoir is E. C. Abbott and Helena Huntington Smith, *We Pointed Them North* (New York & Toronto: Farrar & Rinehart, 1939). A. B. Guthrie, Jr.'s *These Thousand Hills* (Boston: Houghton Mifflin Company, 1956), although one of his least successful novels, does justice to cattle ranching in the 1880s.

Two broader works cover the treatment of Montana Indians well:

Merrill G. Burlingame, *The Montana Frontier* (Helena: State Publishing Company, 1942) and James M. Hamilton, *From Wilderness to Statehood* (Portland, Ore.: Binfords & Mort, 1957). On the Little Big Horn episode, Edgar I. Stewart, *Custer's Luck* (Norman: University of Oklahoma Press, 1955) is still the best, but Stephen E. Ambrose, *Crazy Horse and Custer* (Garden City: Doubleday, 1975) is provocative. H. G. Merriam, ed., *Frontier Woman: the Story of Mary Ronan as told to Margaret Ronan* (Missoula: University of Montana Publications in History, 1973), includes much reminiscence about the Flatheads, to whom her husband was agent for a number of years. A funny, yet bittersweet treatment of Montana Indians in the mid-twentieth century is the novel by Dan Cushman, *Stay Away, Joe* (New York: Viking Press, 1953).

For early politics, augment both Burlingame and Hamilton with Clark C. Spence, *Montana Territorial Politics and Government, 1864–89* (Urbana: University of Illinois Press, 1975). On the politics of copper, two books are pungent and rewarding: C. B. Glasscock, *The War of the Copper Kings* (New York: Bobbs-Merrill, 1935) and C. P. Connolly, *The Devil Learns to Vote* (New York: Covici Friede, 1938). A delightful piece of fiction dealing with the high spirits and low politics of Montana at the turn of the century is Dan Cushman, *The Old Copper Collar* (New York: Ballantine Books, 1957). The People's party is covered in detail in Thomas A. Clinch, *Urban Populism and Free Silver in Montana* (Missoula: University of Montana Press, 1970). For the Progressive movement, see Jules A. Karlin, *Joseph M. Dixon of Montana* (Missoula: University of Montana Publications in History, 1974), 2 vols., and K. Ross Toole, *Twentieth-Century Montana: A State of Extremes* (Norman: University of Oklahoma Press, 1972), the latter a badly mistitled book that simply gives up in the 1920s. Burton K. Wheeler (with Paul F. Healy), *Yankee from the West* (Garden City: Doubleday, 1962) is autobiographical; the standard biography by Hanna Josephson, *Jeannette Rankin: First Lady in Congress* (New York & Indianapolis: Bobbs-Merrill, 1974) is interesting but uncritical. Although not a political novel, A. B. Guthrie, Jr.'s *Arfive* (Boston: Houghton Mifflin, 1970) is set in the progressive era and gives an excellent impression of life in a small, changing Montana town, perhaps patterned after Choteau, where the author grew up.

General books which put Montana into perspective as part of the upper plains agriculture include Mary Wilma M. Hargreaves. *Dry Farming in the Northern Great Plains, 1900–1925* (Cambridge: Harvard University Press, 1957) and Carl F. Kraenzel, *The Great Plains in Transition* (Norman: University of Oklahoma Press, 1955). Elliott C. Lincoln, in *Rhymes of a Homesteader* (Boston: Houghton Mifflin, 1920) catches the spirit of the sod-buster in the World War I era.

Good writings on mid-twentieth-century Montana history are scarce. The novel by Mildred Walker, *Winter Wheat* (New York: Harcourt, Brace & Co., 1944) is excellent for farm life at the time of the Second World War; A. B. Guthrie's sequel to *Arfive, The Last Valley* (Boston: Houghton Mifflin, 1975) incisively reflects the changes between the period a bit before and after that same war, with a nice glance at dude ranching included. J. Hugo Aronson and L. O. Brockmann, *The Galloping Swede* (Missoula: Mountain Press Publishing Company, 1970) is worth reading but disappointing for the light it casts on politics. K. Ross Toole, *The Rape of the Great Plains* (Boston: Atlantic-Little, Brown & Co., 1976), an exposition on the current struggle between environmentalists and those who would develop resources without restraint, loses some of its wallop because of its polemical tone, .but should not be ignored.

And finally, no suggested reading list on the Montana past would be complete without mention of the fine illustrated quarterly published by the Montana Historical Society, *Montana: the Magazine of Western History*.

Index

Agricultural Adjustment Acts (AAA), 153–154, 156

Agriculture: importance of rivers to, 5; growth of, 38, 130–132; and politics, 98, 115, 171; and pollution, 114; in early 1920s, 126, 132–133; and taxation, 129; and railroads, 131–133; and prices, 131, 133, 138, 166; methods, 133–134, 138, 154, 194; and World War I, 137; and government support, 138–139; and exodus of farmers, 139–141, 153; and 1929 crash, 146; and New Deal, 153; and World War II, 164–165; and conservatism of farmers, 176; decline of, 180; post-World War II, 182–183; mentioned, 163–164

Alder Gulch, 26, 31, 35, 42

Alderson, Mary Long, 116–118

Amalgamated Copper Company, 95, 104–105, 112, 115

American Fur Company, 17–18, 21, 56–57, 195

Anaconda (city): and copper, 6, 19, 36, 106; as state capital, 100; and 1929 crash, 146

Anaconda Copper Mining Company: formed, 105; role in politics, 109, 111, 115, 125–129 passim, 158, 167–176 passim; and pollution, 113–114; and farming, 138; during World War I, 125; and exploitation of resources, 195; influence of in Montana, 196–198; mentioned, 180

Anaconda Gold and Silver Mining Company, 96, 97, 104

Anaconda Standard, 101, 126–127

Anderson, Forrest, 174

Anderson, LeRoy, 171

Anti-Semitism, 89, 167

Apex, law of the, 103–105

Argenta, 24, 32

Arkira Indians, 17

Ashley, James, 60, 67, 78–79, 88

Assiniboin Indians, 54, 57, 68, 71, 152

Atwater, Dr. Mary, 108

Automobiles, 143–148 passim

Babcock, Tim (governor), 170–171, 174

Banks and banking: and 1893 depression, 99; and 1929 crash, 147–149; and farming crisis, 138, 140; and copper industry, 196

Bannack, 26–34 passim, 39, 41, 71, 75

Beaver, 6, 15–18. See also Fur trade

Big Horn Mountains, 27, 58, 62, 70

Big Horn River, 15–16, 58

Billings: and Indians, 63; and farmers, 132, 136; and oil industry, 183; mentioned, 7, 100, 108

Bitterroot Valley, 11, 20, 22, 66–70 passim, 124

Blackfoot Indians, 11–21 passim, 54–60 passim, 68, 71, 159

Blacks, 74, 76, 78, 89

Blood Indians, 71

Bootlegging, 144–145

Borah, William, 159, 198

Bozeman, John, 27, 59

Bozeman (town), 61, 100, 132

Bozeman Road, 27, 42, 58–62 passim

Bridger, Jim, 17, 18

British Northwest Company, 10, 16

Bryan, William Jennings, 101

Buffalo, 13, 18, 21, 64–65, 70

Butte: and copper, 34–38 passim, 95–96, 104, 106, 111, 113, 175, 196, 199; as industrial city, 39; and railroads, 81; and depressions, 99, 146; and politics, 112–113, 167; and unionism, 114–115; and prostitution, 120–121; and World War I, 124; visitors to, 142–144; and Prohibition, 144–145, 149; and WPA,